LORD'S FIRSTS

200 YEARS OF MAKING HISTORY AT LORD'S CRICKET GROUND

PHILIP BARKER

AMBERLEY

First published 2014

Amberley Publishing
The Hill, Stroud
Gloucestershire, GL5 4EP

www.amberley-books.com

British Library Cataloguing in Publication Data.
A catalogue record for this book is available from the British Library.

ISBN 978 1 4456 3315 2 (print)
ISBN 978 4456 3329 9 (ebook)

Typesetting and Origination by Amberley Publishing.
Printed in the UK.

CONTENTS

FOREWORD

Across the world, there are many great cricketing arenas, but Lord's Cricket Ground remains supreme as the home of the game.

Every time you walk through the pavilion onto the field, you are acutely aware of the history of the place. Every cricketer of note in the last 200 years has taken the same pathway.

The appearance of the ground has altered radically, even since the mid-seventies when I came to play for Oxford in the university matches. Back then, spectators were still allowed to sit on the grass. Nowadays, there is a gleaming white grandstand, and the turrets of the Mound Stand, rebuilt for the MCC Bicentenary in 1987, add an exotic touch. The media centre, a monument to the modern game at the Nursery End, is a striking contrast with the unchanging pavilion, famous wherever the game is played.

There have been international cricketing visitors since 1858, when the Gentlemen of Ireland became the first team from overseas to come to the ground. Since then, players from all over the world have dreamed of performing beneath the unchanging gaze of Father Time. Their adventures are to be found in these pages, right up to the most recent newcomers, the Japanese team of 2013.

Australia contested the first Lord's Test in 1884 and, since then, the test match family has grown. Each time, a Test at Lord's has set the seal on their status as part of world cricket's elite. Pakistan first came sixty summers ago, although after their experience, they might well have doubted the use of the term 'summer'. Rain forced the abandonment of the first three days in 1954. Play did not get underway until late afternoon on the fourth and a draw was inevitable.

The weather was much better in 1982 as Pakistan recorded their first Test win at Lord's. We were inspired by a wonderful double century from Mohsin Khan, and Mudassar Nazar bowled the spell of his life to set up the victory. I was proud to lead the team and the memories will last a lifetime.

The rains returned in 1987 to wash out three days of our Test match with England. The weather also put paid to the MCC Bicentenary match, just as it was building towards a fascinating climax.

Now Lord's celebrates another anniversary. The game itself has changed much since the pioneering days of Thomas Lord, who established his ground in Marylebone, then twice rolled up the turf before installing it on the present site in 1814. Back in his day, he promoted all manner of events, which even included a flight by hot-air balloon. So what would he have thought of cricket in 2014? He might just have been in the front row, leading the cheers and enjoying the spectacle of coloured clothing, floodlights and yes, even T20!

Imran Khan

THE FIRST SEASON

An aristocrat, a soldier and a wine merchant made the bargain that started it all. All three were devotees of the fast developing sport of cricket, and all were connected with the recently founded and fashionable White Conduit Club in Islington – except that it was not quite as exclusive as its members wished it to be.

The Daily Universal Register, a newly founded newspaper, reported on 22 June 1785:

> It is recommended to the Lordling cricketers who amuse themselves in White Conduit fields, to procure an act of parliament for inclosing (sic) their playground which will not only prevent their being incommoded, but protect themselves from a repetition of severe rebuke which they justly merit and received on Saturday evening from some spirited citizens whom they insulted and attempted to drive *vi et armis* from their footpath pretending it was within their bounds.

Soon, the newspaper changed its name to *The Times*, and the club it had described would soon also have a new identity.

The Earl of Winchilsea, the ninth of his line, was a 'great supporter of the noble game'. The soldier, the Hon. Col. Charles Lennox, was an enthusiastic wicketkeeper and a fine athlete: 'His agility and great speed were very conspicuous.'

They gave Thomas Lord, a bowler at the club, the task of establishing a new ground that would offer greater exclusivity to members. Islington was also felt to be too far from Oxford Street and the West End of London.

Winchilsea and Lennox had certainly found the right man for the job. Thomas Lord was an entrepreneurial spirit. The parish records in the Yorkshire town of Thirsk attest to his birth on 23 November 1755 as the 'Son of William Lord, Labourer'. He made his way to London by way of Diss in Norfolk. Shortly after his arrival, he began to play cricket and was noted as a slow underhand bowler. He used to bowl to the gentlemen of the White Conduit Club and later also became a member of the St Marylebone Vestry, which afforded him further status.

Lord set about negotiating a lease for some land on the Portman family estate. The ground was set out on Dorset Fields, a few paces from what is now a main line railway station. The new club took its name, Marylebone Cricket Club, from the parish of St Marylebone. In time, it would be known simply by its initials, MCC.

Lord was not an outstanding cricketer, but his fame would be assured as the new cricket field became known simply as 'Lord's'.

In the late eighteenth century, matches were publicised in the advertising columns of newspapers. On 19 May 1787, the *Morning Herald* carried the announcement that a grand match will be played on Monday May 21 in the new cricket ground Marylebone between 11 noblemen of the White Conduit Club and 11 gentlemen of Middlesex with two given men for 500 a side, the wickets to be pitched at ten o'clock and the match to be played out.

The reporting of matches in those days was notoriously sporadic, so this may well have been the first match played on the ground, but no record of the score survives. It is even possible that bad weather prevented it from taking place.

Middlesex did play in a match on the last day of May 1787. The opponents were Essex. The contest was to be for 100 guineas a side. Lord himself played for Middlesex, an eleven that included two men from Berkshire and one from Kent. He was bowled by Butcher for a single in the first innings. His teammates did not do much better as Middlesex were dismissed for 58.

Butcher returned the first five-wicket haul on the new ground, and may even have been short-changed at that. In those days, the bowler was not given the credit if a batsman was caught out. Nor were bowling figures recorded. Overs in those days were of four balls.

When Essex batted, Richard Newman carved a niche for himself with the first half-century made on the ground. Even so, Essex only totalled 130, but this still gave them a first innings' lead of 72. When Middlesex batted a second time, Lord scored 36, and his teammates rallied to post 203. John Boorman top scored with 37 and then took four wickets, as Essex crumbled to 38 all out in their second innings.

31 May 1787
Middlesex (with two of Berkshire and one of Kent) beat Essex (with two given men) by 93 runs.

MIDDLESEX First Innings
Stanhope run out 3, T. Lord b Butcher 1, J. Boorman b Butcher 23, W. White b Butcher 5, Z. Boult st Clark 0, W. Bedster b Martin 13, G. Louch b Martin 0, G. T. Boult b Butcher 3, A. Boult b Martin 3, C. Slater b Butcher 0, Oliver not out 0
Byes 7
Total 58

ESSEX First Innings
R. N. Newman Esq c Louch 51, M. Remington run out 28, N. Graham b Bedster 4, T. Clark c Louch 13, R. B. Wyatt b Boorman 5, Butcher c Z. Boult 3, Jones b White 16, Davies b Boorman 1, Dent not out 4, J. Martin b White 0, Barker b Boorman 2
Byes 3
Total 130

MIDDLESEX Second Innings
Stanhope Esq b Butcher 1, T. Lord c Newman 36, J. Boorman b Butcher 37, W. White run out 12, Z. Boult b Butcher 18, W. Bedster st by Clark 14, G. Louch b Butcher 14, G. T. Boult b Martin 36, A. Boult b Butcher 0, C. Slater b Martin 23, Oliver not out 1
Byes 11
Total 203

ESSEX Second Innings

Newman b Boorman 5, Rimmington c G. Boult 0, Graham run out 0, Clark c Boorman 1, Wyatt c Louch 14, Butcher c Slater 0, Jones c Boult 1, Dent b White 1, Martin not out 4, Barker b Boorman 9

Byes 1

Total 38

Later that month, the White Conduit Club met a team styled 'England'. It was the first match to receive an extensive report in *The Daily Universal Register* (*The Times*): 'The utility of the batten fence was evident as it kept out all improper spectators.'

The match was made at 1,000 guineas a side. The White Conduit Club had six given men in their team. 'Several capital bets were laid but they were all great odds and in favour of All England.'

James Aylward opened with Billy Beldham for England. Both had made their reputations as members of the famous Hambledon Club.

Aylward reached the nineties before he was run out, just short of what would have been the first hundred on the ground. England totalled 247.

The story was picked up in *The World,* a popular newspaperof the time. It was said of the Earl of Winchilsea that 'though he hit as finely as was possible, made but one stroke of three and was bowled third ball'. The newspaper was scathing of the contribution of the 'given' men. 'The picked men were like the men who had picked them, unable to bring up the Game.'

By 3.30 p.m., the White Conduit Club were all out. Some of the difficulties in recording those early matches become clear, as the totals did not tally from one account to another.

The England second innings began at quarter past four. Beldham and John Small junior consolidated their advantage. By the time rain brought proceedings to a premature end at 6.30 p.m., Beldham had reached 52 not out, Small 30, and England were 87 for 0.

This was Beldham's first time at Lord's, but his reputation as a fine batsman was enhanced by this effort. His one-time Hambledon Clubmate John Nyren described him as 'a most venomous hitter' in his famous series of reminiscences entitled *The Cricketers of My Time*.

The fall of the first wicket is not recorded, but the opening pair probably posted more than 100. John Small senior was unbeaten on 32 when England were dismissed for 197. Again, reports of the time are a little shaky on the fine detail. Some show White Conduit as all out for 67 the second time round. Another source gave the total as 93.

The match was reported in positive fashion by the press. In all it had attracted a crowd of some 2,000 'who conducted themselves with the utmost decorum', according to the correspondent of *The Daily Universal Register*. In addition, the Lord's catering was mentioned for the first time: 'A very good cold collation was spread out under a covered recess for the accommodation of the cricketers and subscribers. Two tents were also prepared with refreshments for the spectators.' said a report dated 22 June.

Scoring was generally modest. It was recognised that the state of the pitch was not good: 'The ground, though somewhat rough at present will be laid out next year like a bowling green.'

Although he had made only 3 runs in the first innings and 9 in the second, the Earl of Winchilsea was evidently delighted with proceedings. He gave Thomas Lord £100 for the admission money, 'In much good nature and liberality, wishing to ascertain to Lord the ground keeper, a nett profit of fair account.'

20–22 June 1787
England beat White Conduit Club by 239 (265) runs

ENGLAND First Innings

J. Aylward run out 93, Wm Beldham b Clifford 17, R. Hosmer c H. Walker 41, R. Stanford c H. Walker 0, S. Amherst not out 20, N. Mann b Harris 11, J. Small junior c Clifford 3, R. Purchase b Harris 0, W. Bullen b Harris 14, J. Small senior b Taylor 30, John Wells b Harris 8
Byes 8
Total 247

WHITE CONDUIT First Innings

Sir Peter Burrell c Stanford 0, J. Dampier senior b Bullen 26, E. Hussey b Beldham 21, T. Walker c Bullen 11, J. Ring c Bullen 18, H. Walker run out 0, T. Taylor c Bullen 12, R. Clifford run out 6, Earl of Winchilsea b Beldham 3, G. Drummond c Hosmer 1, D. Harris not out 5
Byes 9
Total 112

ENGLAND Second Innings

J. Small junior c Clifford 42, Wm Beldham run out 63, R. Purchase c Taylor 3, J. Aylward c Taylor 16, N. Mann c Hussey 6, J. Small senior not out 32, John Wells c Clifford 12, R. Stanford c H. Walker 0, S. Amherst c H. Walker 18, R. Hosmer c H. Walker 2, W. Bullen b Clifford 0
Byes 4
Total 197

WHITE CONDUIT Second Innings

T. Walker b Beldham 12, H. Walker c Amherst 5, T. Taylor c Mann 25 (12), J. Ring b Beldham 2, R. Clifford b Purchase 0, Sir Peter Burrell b Mann 10, E. Hussey Esq b Mann 12 (9), Dampier b Bullen 13, Earl of Winchilsea run out 9, Drummond c Beldham 1, D. Harris not out 2
Byes 3
Total 93 (67)

Umpires: Lawrence and Hawkins

Although only a village team, Hambledon's exploits at Broadhalfpenny Down were already the talk of cricketers everywhere. By 1787, their star players were already appearing for other teams. Some even played in the White Conduit Club v England match. Their first appearance as a club at Lord's was in a six-a-side match against a team from Kent who batted first.

John Ring top scored with 24. He came from Darenth near Dartford, but his greatest claim to fame was hastening the introduction of the lbw law. 'The law was not passed or much wanted till Ring was shabby enough to get his leg in the way and take advantage of the bowlers,' Billy Beldham told James Pycroft in an interview for *The Cricket Field* many years later.

David Harris was the star bowler. He took all but one of the Kent wickets. Although he batted left-handed, he bowled with his right.

'Unless a batter was of the very first class and accustomed to the best style of stopping, he could do little or nothing with Harris,' wrote Nyren.

At Lord's, 2/3 August 1787
Kent beat Hambledon by 23 runs in a single-wicket match

SIX OF KENT First Innings
W. Bullen b Harris 5, W. Bowra b Harris 1, J. Ring b Harris 24, J. Aylward b Harris 0, R. Clifford b Harris 14, W. Brazier b Mann 9
Total 53

SIX OF HAMBLEDON CLUB First Innings
J. Small senior b Clifford 9, D. Harris b Clifford 0, T. Walker b Bullen 4, H. Walker b Clifford 7, N. Mann b Clifford 6, T. Taylor b Clifford 1
Total 27

SIX OF KENT Second Innings
W. Bullen b Harris 0, W. Bowra b Harris 0, J. Ring b Harris 1, J. Aylward b Harris 2, R. Clifford b Harris 1, W. Brazier b Harris 9
Total 13

SIX OF HAMBLEDON CLUB Second Innings
J. Small senior b Brazier 0, D. Harris b Bullen 1, T. Walker b Brazier 5, H. Walker b Brazier 0, N. Mann b Bullen 4, T. Taylor c Booker (in for Bowra absent Hurt) 6
Total 16

As Lord's reached the end of its first season, it had become national news and was also used for more than cricket. 'The ground was attended by many people of fashion', noted *The Daily Universal Register*.

Reporters were not coy about mentioning the odds on a particular outcome, for at the time, betting on sport was everywhere. On 12 September 1787, an unusual challenge came to light.

'In the course of this month, a most extraordinary pedestrian attempt will be made on this cricket ground. A gentleman has made a bet of 100 guineas that he shall produce a man who will run 21 miles in two hours and thirty five minutes.' This would have been the first athletic contest at Lord's, but only a few days later, the same paper reported a change of heart from the anonymous backer, although no reason was given for his decision. Over the next few years, foot races became a regular attraction at the ground.

Although the members of the new club now had greater exclusivity, the patrons were still not immune from the more unpleasant aspects of life. A report on the grand match between elevens raised by the Earl of Winchilsea and Sir Horace Mann included this disturbing incident.

'A gentleman of the name of Cole had his pocket picked of his purse, and upwards of twenty guineas coming off the cricket ground on Tuesday evening.' It was the first reported crime to affect a spectator attending a match at Lord's.

THE FIRST MCC MATCH

In 1788, the name of Marylebone Cricket Club was recorded in a match at Lord's for the first time. They had already put their name to a revision of the laws of cricket. This was recorded by Samuel Britcher: 'The wickets must be opposite to each other at the distance of twenty two yards.' The document also gave dimensions of the creases and stipulated that 'the bat must not exceed four inches and a half at its widest point'. It also restated the principle that 'the umpires are the sole judges of fair and unfair play and all disputes shall be determined by them.'

Members of the White Conduit Club (WCC) had been responsible for the establishment of Lord's, so it was appropriate that they should be the first recorded opponents for MCC on 27 June 1788.

The first MCC innings was not a success. In fact, only three men reached double figures and they were dismissed for 62, which was still sufficient for a first innings' lead, after White Conduit were bowled out for 42. Sir Peter Burrell top scored for MCC in their second innings and WCC were asked to score 145 to win, which was beyond them. Gilbert East from Berkshire took four wickets in the innings. He was later to become a baronet. His performance was in marked contrast to his first appearance that season. He had raised his own team to play but was out for a duck in both innings.

27 June 1788
MCC beat the White Conduit Club by 83 runs

MCC First Innings
Earl of Winchilsea c Price 2, Lord Strathavon c W. Le Gros 4, Sir Peter Burrell run out 14, Hon. H. W. Fitzroy b Weston 0, G. East b Nicoll 0, G. Drummond b Le Gros 1, G. Louch b Weston 0, G. Talbot not out 20, E. Hussey b W Le Gros 16, Tyson b Weston 1, Warren b Weston 0
Byes 4
Total 62

WHITE CONDUIT First Innings
Everitt b Drummond 3, W. Le Gros b East 3, Ogle b Drummond 0, Sellers b East 0, Z. Button b East 0, J. Weston b East 3, T. V. R. Nicoll b Hussey 16, Chippendale c Tyson 0, C. Anguish run out 11, J. Le Gros b Drummond 0, Price not out 0
Byes 6
Total 42

MCC Second Innings
Earl of Winchilsea b W. Le Gros 8, Lord Strathavon b Nicoll 1, Sir Peter Burrell c
Button 33, H. W. Fitzroy c Sellers 0, G. East c Button 16, G. Drummond b W. Le
Gros 4, G. Louch c Button 12, G. Talbot b Nicoll 31, E. Hussey b Nicoll 7, Tyson b
Nicoll 5, Warren not out 5
Byes 2
Total 124

WHITE CONDUIT Second Innings
Everitt run out 2, W. Le Gros b East 2, Ogle b East 2, Sellers b East 0, Z. Button c Earl
of Winchilsea 17, J. Weston b Drummond 0, T. V. R Nicoll c Hussey 2, Chippendale
b Fitzroy 13, C. Anguish b East 4, J. Le Gros not out 10
Byes 9
Total 61

Very soon, the name White Conduit Club would disappear from the picture, absorbed
into MCC. The new club endured and, within two years, *The World* newspaper carried a
notice for another important aspect of club life.

The anniversary dinner of the Marylebone Club is fixed for the 30th April at Mr Lord's
on the cricket ground at half past five o'clock. Those members who intend to dine are
desired to send their names to Mr Lord that dinner may be provided accordingly.

Lord had become a wine merchant, so he probably had a vested interest in encouraging
attendance at these functions. At some stage, a wine store stood at the entrance to the
ground, a spiritual forerunner of the famous Tavern.

A First Hundred at Lord's

To this day, it remains the ambition of every cricketer to score a hundred at Lord's, but it was not until the ground had been open for five years that a batsman reached three figures for the first time. That man was Tom Walker. His innings came in a two-day match for MCC against Middlesex. A right-hander, he made 107 in a first innings' total of 193. Although he is listed at number eight in the contemporary scorecards, these often recorded the scores of the gentlemen first. It seems more likely that he would have batted higher up the order, or even opened.

'I have frequently known Tom to go in first and remain to be the last man. He was the coolest, the most unperturbable fellow in existence, it used to be said of him that he had no nerves at all. He was the 'Washington of cricketers,' said Nyren when he tried to explain the secrets of Walker's success.

When Middlesex batted, Walker took three wickets. Billy Beldham was the other successful bowler recorded as Middlesex were bowled out in their first innings for 111. Among his victims was Thomas Lord, out for a single.

Walker was out for a duck in the second MCC innings, and the Lord's batting record he had set was immediately eclipsed by Beldham, who struck 144. It was the highest innings yet scored at Lord's and a career best for Beldham, later known as 'Silver Billy' for the colour of his hair.

They bowled Middlesex out for 114 to complete victory.

Both centurions are recognised as among the greatest of the early players. Tom Walker was one of a band of cricketing brothers. They came from Hide Farm in the village of Charte, near Hindhead in Surrey.

Walker had already forged a reputation as a legendary occupier of the crease, and was nicknamed 'Old Everlasting'.

Beldham's career at the top level spanned thirty-four years and he lived to ninety-six.

7 May 1792
Nine Gentlemen of the Marylebone Club with Beldham and T. Walker beat Middlesex by 274 runs.

MCC First Innings
T. Walker c Bedworth 107, Hon. E. Bligh b Fennex 0, W. Beldham c Goldham 13, Earl of Winchilsea b Cantrell 11, T. Ingram b Turner 3, G. Louch b Fennex 11, J. L. Kaye Esq b Turner 1, T. A. Smith b Lord 15, R. Brudenell b Fennex 0, Dehany Esq b Fennex 0
Byes 12
Total 193

MIDDLESEX First Innings
N. Graham b Walker 6, Butler b Walker 6, W. Bedster b Walker 3, W. Fennex not out 60, T. Lord b Beldham 1, G. T. Boult Esq c Louch 14, S. Amherst b Beldham 0, Dale c Kaye 4, J. Goldham run out 1, Cantrell c Bligh 5, R. Turner c Kaye 10
Byes 1
Total 111

MCC Second Innings
T. Walker b Bedster 0, Hon. E. Bligh st Amherst 40, W. Beldham b Bedster 144, Earl of Winchilsea b Lord 28, T. Ingram b Bedster 4, G. Louch c Turner 40, J. L. Kaye b Turner 1, A. Pitcairn c Amherst 0, T. A. Smith c Boult 0, R. Brudenell (Earl Darnley) not out 0, G. Dehany c Lord 30
Byes 10
Total 297

MIDDLESEX Second Innings
N. Graham st Bligh 5, Butler c Darnley 8, W. Bedster c Beldham 3, W. Fennex c Bligh 6, T. Lord b Beldham 12, G. T. Boult st Bligh 13, S. Amherst Esq hit wicket 16, Dale not out 8, J. Goldham c Bligh 13, Cantrell b Walker 10, Turner c Kaye 16
Byes 4
Total 114

KING GEORGE COMMANDS AND
A PRINCE AT LORD'S

In the last decade of the eighteenth century, the threat of war and a French invasion loomed large. Many volunteer regiments were founded. Thomas Lord did his patriotic duty by making the ground available for military parades for the first time.

On 28 July 1797, the *Morning Chronicle* reported, 'Yesterday, noon the second regiment of East India Volunteers were reviewed in Lord's Cricket ground under the command of Captain English to receive their colours from the fair hand of Lady Jane Dundas.'

The ceremony included a blessing from the military chaplain. Afterwards, the officers went to the London Tavern for 'an elegant entertainment' provided by their colonel.

From the paintings that now hang in the Bank of England, it is clear that these parades at Lord's were imposing affairs, with rows of redcoats and huge military ensigns. On one occasion, Thomas Lord was present and even joined the party on the reviewing stand.

Cricket had been played at the Royal Artillery Ground since the mid-eighteenth century, so it was little surprise that a fixture with MCC was soon established. In 1800, the Army team proved far too good; MCC batted first and were skittled out for 40. Only William Barton reached double figures but the match serves as a good indication of the problems in recording early matches. The chief wicket taker for Woolwich is recorded in some sources as Tanner while others show him as Turner. John Ward of Kent also got among the wickets and when Woolwich batted, he struck 111. With customary caution, Haygarth noted, 'It must be observed in justice to other cricketers that Ward's long score was not obtained against the best bowling and fielding.'

Tanner or Turner got among the wickets once again, and MCC were all out for 60.

28/29 May 1800
Woolwich beat MCC by an innings and 94 runs

MCC First Innings
T. A. Smith b Turner (Tanner) 5, G. Leycester b Turner (Tanner) 8, C. Douglas lbw 0, R. Whitehead c Stillman 2, W. Barton b J. Ward 14, G. Cooper b J. Ward 0, J. Weller run out 0, J. Gibbons b Turner (Tanner) 6, T. Lord b Turner (Tanner) 1, H. J. Tufton not out 2, T. Ray b Turner (Tanner) 0
Byes 2
Total 40

WOOLWICH First Innings
Bassett run out 1, C. Reed c Weller 7, J. Ward not out 111, Bennett b Douglas 4, Crowhurst c Douglas 31, W. Wells c Smith 5, W. Turner (Tanner) b Lord 8, J. Burgess b Lord 11, A. Ward run out 0, Talmege st Leycester 9, Stillman b Lord 0

Byes 9
Total 196

MCC Second Innings
T. A. Smith b J. Ward 4, G. Leycester b Turner (Tanner)9, C. Douglas b Turner (Tanner),
9 R. Whitehead b Turner (Tanner) 25, W. Barton b Turner (Tanner) 0, G. Cooper b
J Ward 3, J. Weller c J. Ward 0, J. Gibbons b J. Ward 4, T. Lord not out 2, H. J. Tufton b
J. Ward 5, T. Ray b J. Ward 0
Byes 1
Total 62

To date, no French cricket team has played at Lord's. In the late eighteenth century, the
Duke of Dorset did his best to promote the game in France. Unsurprisingly, the French
Revolution brought an end to any such missionary work.

In the summer of 1802, however, a Frenchman was the star attraction at the ground. He
was a balloonist named André-Jacques Garnerin.

A monthly publication called *The Sporting Magazine* caught the mood in its July
edition, which promised,

> A full and interesting account of the ascents of M. Garnerin, Sowden, Locker etc
> in balloons ... The late spirit of ballooning which has been so unprecendentedly
> predominant for nearly two months past...

Such was the excitement generated by this and other matters that they had no space for
reports on cricket: 'We are very much in arrears with our cricket correspondents, but hope
to pay it off with a copious insertion of their favours in our next.'

Garnerin was the man of the moment. He was already a great celebrity in France, where
they called him 'the Aeronaut', and his fame had spread across the Channel. He announced
that his next ascent would be made from Lord's Cricket Ground.

Handbills proclaimed that Garnerin also planned to demonstrate his 'parachute'.
The date set for the flight at Lord's was 3 July 1802. 'The general expectation of seeing
Monsieur Garnerin descend from his balloon in the forenoon had such an effect, that
by eleven in the forenoon people were flocking to Marylebone from all quarters,' said a
report of the day.

Trouble was brewing. By the time he arrived at Lord's, strong winds were blowing. The
Aeronaut was said to be 'expressing some alarm at the state of the weather'. His friends
pressed him to make a decision before the gates were open 'assuring him it was very
material to the preservation of order'.

Reluctantly, Garnerin decided to postpone the attempt. Sir Richard Ford, the chief police
magistrate, stood down the captain of the guards, but sensibly kept the police officers
in attendance.

A notice had already gone up in central London announcing the postponement of the
attempt because of bad weather, but many in the crowd who made their way to Dorset
Fields had not seen this.

The balloon was to be stored for safekeeping in central London. It was transported
away from Lord's by cart after the abortive attempt, but its progress was accompanied
by an angry mob, described at the time as 'an immense concourse of people hissing and
groaning all the way'.

Some even threatened to destroy the balloon. As a precaution, it was taken to a strong room in the Public Office in Marlborough Street.

Back at Lord's, the atmosphere was still volatile: A party of the Horse Guards attended in consequence of a request from Thomas Lord. Garnerin was crestfallen and resolved to try again as soon as possible.

It is with the utmost concern that M. Garnerin found himself compelled to disappoint the public in the ascension he had announced ... The high winds having rendered his experiments completely impracticable ... He trusts his apology will be acceptable to a liberal and discerning public at the shrine of which he pledges himself that nothing will prevent his ascension taking place.

So on the new date, the crowds once again flocked to Lord's.

Seats to watch the ascent were available at 10s 6d and 5s. The opportunity to become Garnerin's passenger for this second ascent caused a further clamour of excitement. Amid the general hubbub, two men came forward to claim the seat. They were a man called Charles Broderip, who tossed a coin for the privilege of joining the adventure, and a mysterious gentleman who, according to *The Times*, wished to be known only as 'Brown'. It was the stranger who called correctly and enthusiastically took his place in the balloon.

Later, his identity was revealed as one Edward Locker, who wrote of his experience in the *European Magazine*.

The strong assurance of my companion, added to what I had read on the science of aerostation had so fully persuaded me of my perfect security that I enjoyed the wonderful and enchanting prospect which now presented itself with unmixed pleasure.

The balloon was fastened close to the long room. Inside, sheltered from the weather, members of the 'Picnic Society' watched the preparations with great interest.

Guns were fired to announce the imminent departure. Then came the grand entry of the Prince of Wales, who had arrived to watch the attempt.

As a Frenchman, Garnerin had been challenged aggressively by concerned local residents as he landed his craft after his previous flight. When he saw the Prince, he asked him to sign a letter of authentication.

We the undersigned having been present at the ascension of Mr Garnerin with his balloon and witnessed the entire satisfaction of the public, beg to recommend him to the attention of any gentleman in whose neighbourhood he may descend.
Signed George PW, Cathcart G. Devonshire, Bessborough, R. Ford

Eventually, at around ten to five in the evening, Garnerin announced that all was ready and let loose the final safety rope. The balloon was buffeted in the wind but disappeared into the clouds within 3 minutes.

Within fifteen minutes, the intrepid travellers had reached Essex. They came down in Chingford Green and touched ground in a field owned by a Mr Owens. They celebrated their achievement in time-honoured fashion, making straight for the Kings Head pub in the village before returning to London.

Back at Lord's, away from the dignitaries, the atmosphere had already grown ugly: 'the most flagrant acts of plunder and robbery were committed by gangs of thieves and pickpockets.'

THE FIRST BIG HIT

In 1808, Thomas Lord promised he would forfeit twenty guineas if anyone could hit the ball out of the ground and 'thus prove his ground too small'.

Today, the site of the first Lord's Cricket Ground in Dorset Square is lined with elegant town houses. All that remains of the original field is a private garden, but in the early nineteenth century, it was a wide open space.

At this time, Edward Hayward Budd was rapidly forging a reputation as a clean striker of the ball. He had been born in the Buckinghamshire village of Great Missenden. His rural background gave him the nickname 'Squire' Budd. According to James Pycroft 'he hit well from the wrist'.

In July 1808, he took part in a match between 'England' and Surrey on the ground. England batted first but, although Lord Frederick Beauclerk scored 24 and Budd made 14, they could only muster 77 all out.

Surrey replied with 130, but England made a much better showing in their second innings.

Budd stood only 5 foot 9 but was 12 stone in weight. His weapon of choice was a bat that weighed 3 pounds. When he connected with his big hit, the ball flew over a 12-foot wall and 'into a greenhouse shattering many panes of glass'. He top scored with 45 but was clearly unaware of the bounty on offer.

'So we all crowded around Mr Budd and told him what he might claim', said Billy Beldham as he recalled the moment for *The Cricket Field*, James Pycroft's early history of the game.

'Well then,' he said, 'I'll claim it and give it among the players.' Budd duly presented himself to Lord to ask for the money: 'Lord was shabby and would not pay.' To add to his woes, his team lost by three wickets.

Budd's hit was not an isolated incident.

'Lord Frederick said Budd always wanted to win the game off a single ball,' recalled Beldham. 'If Mr Budd would not hit so eagerly, he would be the finest player in all England.'

6/7 July 1808
Surrey beat England by three wickets
ENGLAND 77 and 179 (Budd 45)
SURREY 130 and 127 for seven

SOME UNUSUAL ELEVENS
MAKE THEIR FIRST APPEARANCE

In May 1790, the *British Gazette* and *Sunday Monitor* reported 'A great cricket match'.

The criteria for team selection was very simple. Left-handers against right-handers. These 'were picked from all England' and a prize of 1,000 guineas was at stake. The match was an excellent excuse for a wager as odds were laid. In this instance, it was 6 to 4 on the right-handers.

Even then, matters were not quite so straight forward. When William Epps published his volume of *Scores of Grand Matches* in 1799, he noted that that John Crawte 'only threw with his left hand'. He did not mean throwing in the modern cricketing sense but rather bowling. Crawte was thought to have bat right-handed.

Tom Sueter from Hambledon top scored in the match with 39. 'He is said to have been the first or one of the first who departed from the custom of the old players who deemed it heresy to leave the crease for the ball,' said Nyren. 'He was evidently a very clean hitter. Egad it went as if it had been fired.'

10 May 1790
Left-handers beat Right-handers by 39 runs

LEFT-HANDED First Innings
D. Harris c Ring 4, R. Clifford c Beldham 4, J. Aylward b Beldham 30, W. Brazier c John Wells 5, J. Crawte run out 1, T. Sueter b Purchase 39, H. Walker c Bullen 15, Freemantle not out 23, T. Ingram b Purchase 4, F. Booker c Taylor 3, N. Graham run out 1
Byes 2
Total 131

RIGHT-HANDED First Innings
G. Louch b Brazier 8, W. Bullen not out 1, R. Purchase b Harris 3, T. Taylor b Brazier 1, John Wells c H. Walker 4, W. Beldham c Ingram 4, T. Walker b Clifford 14, J. Small senior c Ingram 0, J. Small junior b Harris 9, J. Ring run out 21, W. Fennex c H. Walker 3
Byes 1
Total 69

LEFT-HANDED Second Innings
D. Harris b Beldham 0, R. Clifford b T Walker 0, J. Aylward b Beldham 7, W. Brazier c Louch 0, J. Crawte c Ring 8, T. Sueter c Louch 0, H. Walker b Beldham 15, A. Freemantle c Fennex 0, T. Ingram b Beldham 4, F. Booker c Purchase 10, N. Graham not out 2

Byes 1
Total 47

RIGHT-HANDED Second Innings
G. Louch c Clifford 1, W. Bullen run out 0, R. Purchase b Clifford 2, T. Taylor run out 8, John Wells b Brazier 13, W. Beldham b Harris 18, T. Walker run out 1, J. Small senior b Harris 4, J. Small junior not out 19, J. Ring b Harris 4, W. Fennex b Harris 0
Byes 0
Total 70

Only rarely did this match take place. This was because not enough players batted or bowled left-handed, so it often proved impossible to raise a complete team.

Travelling cross-country was still time-consuming, uncomfortable, tiring and dangerous. Country roads were mosty dirt tracks and there was no railway to take the strain. The organisers of cricket matches therefore tried to arrange ingenious combinations to vary the fare on offer and, of course, to provide more interesting betting opportunities for their patrons.

There was nothing second-rate about the personalities in a team known as 'the Bs' during their first Lord's meeting with All England in 1805.

Their top scorer was Lord Frederick Beauclerk. He was fourth son of the fifth Duke of St Albans, and a great grandson of King Charles II. A leading member of MCC, he had been introduced to the game by none other than the Earl of Winchilsea. He was a controversial figure, and later became a vicar. However, he also had a fiery temper and many considered his cricketing career, bound-up as it was with wagers, to be incompatible with a man of the cloth.

The opposition included Tom Walker, but John Hammond and John Small proved the bedrock of the innings as they took a first innings' lead. Lord Frederick was out for a duck second time around, but when England batted again, he made a decisive impact with the ball and took three wickets. England were all out for 107.

8–10 July 1805
The Bs beat England by 21 runs

THE Bs First Innings
W. Barton b Hampton 3, J. Wells c Small 11, James Bennett b Hammond 19, R. Beckett b Hampton 0, Lord Frederick Beauclerk run out 40, W. Beldham st Lambert 1, John Bennett c Freemantle 2, H. Bentley st Hammond 12, S. Bridger not out 9, G. Beldham b Lambert 1, T. Burgoyne b Lambert 2
Total 100

ENGLAND First Innings
T. Walker b Wells 14, A. Freemantle lbw 10, R. Robinson b Beauclerk 5, W. Lambert b Wells 1, J. Hammond st W. Beldham 41, J. Small c W. Beldham 42, G. Leycester b Wells 3, J. Pointer b Beauclerk 2, A. P. Upton b Wells 5, J. Sparks c Beauclerk 0, J. Hampton not out 1
Byes 2
Total 126

THE Bs Second Innings
W. Barton lbw 16, J. Wells run out 1, James Bennett b Hampton 9, R. Beckett run out 24, Lord Frederick Beauclerk c Freemantle 0, W. Beldham c Hampton 34, John Bennett c Upton 38, H. Bentley not out 16, S. Bridger b Pointer 13, G. Beldham c Hammond 0, T. Burgoyne b Lambert 0
Byes 3
Total 154

ENGLAND Second Innings
T. Walker c W. Beldham 3, A. Freemantle b Beauclerk 36, R. Robinson b Bennett 17, W. Lambert b Beauclerk 0, J. Hammond run out 8, J. Small b Beauclerk 13, G. Leycester c W. Beldham 1, J. Pointer c W. Beldham 0, A. P. Upton b Wells 2, J. Sparks not out 27, J. Hampton c Beauclerk 0
Total 107

The Bs were not always as successful. In one match in 1810, they were all out for 6.

At the turn of the nineteenth century, cricketers were able to play for much longer at the top level than they do today. In 1810, the first match based on age was organised at Lord's. The cut-off point was thirty-eight years, beneath which players were considered to be young.

In this first contest, the Old batted first. The top scorer in their first innings was Robert Robinson, a left-handed farmer who had played in the first Gentlemen v Players in 1806. He was now forty-five years of age but still renowned for his cutting and made 52. He was supported by forty-year-old John Hammond, a left-hander who lived at Storrington in Sussex. He added 27 as the Old reached 156.

When the Under-38s went in, William Lambert top scored with 69. Lambert was one of the outstanding players of the day, despite a fighting weight of 15 stones.

Thomas Howard added a useful 38 for the Young. A wicketkeeper, he was at one stage Lord Calthorpe's gamekeeper.

Thomas Assheton Smith made 37. Sent to Eton when he was only seven years of age, he had learnt cricket at the college and later played for the Eton eleven. He had first played at Lord's some fourteen years before as part of the Bullingdon Club side. He was also said to be brilliant at shooting and was nicknamed 'The British nimrod'.

Lord Frederick Beauclerk made only five runs but had a hand in the cheap dismissal of Billy Beldham in both innings. Only two men reached double figures for the Over-38s as they were dismissed for 55 in their second innings. The Young only needed six to win and Beauclerk and Assheton Smith saw them home without losing a wicket.

The Old had their revenge with a 90-run victory in a match three weeks later. It began in July but because of interruptions by rain, it was not finished until 17 August, the last match to be completed on the Dorset Square ground before the cricketers moved out.

Haygarth later noted,

About fifty years hence, scarcely a single cricketer of note will be found engaged in the great matches of the day that had reached the age of 38 years. Cricketers were then so numerous that the older ones were pushed out before their time by the rising celebrities.

2–4 July 1810
UNDER-38s beat Over-38s by ten wickets

OVER-38s First Innings
J. Wells run out 3, T. Walker c Howard 1, R. Robinson c Bridger 52, J. Hammond st Howard 27, W. Beldham c Beauclerk 4, A. Freemantle c Bridger 17, E. Bligh b Lambert 0, J. Small junior c Beauclerk 32, W. Ayling c Budd 5, T. Ray b Lambert 12, Collins not out 0
Byes 3
Total 156

UNDER-38s First Innings
H. Bentley b Collins 4, S. Bridger b Collins 3, E. H. Budd b Wells 21, W. Lambert c Beldham 69, Lord Frederick Beauclerk b Lambert 5, T. A. Smith b Collins 37, John Bennett b Robinson 3, T. C. Howard b Wells 38, James Harding c Wells 16, J. Tanner not out 8, E. Carter b Hammond 0
Byes 2
Total 206

OVER-38s Second Innings
J. Wells c Harding 6, T. Walker c Bennett 4, R. Robinson st Howard 7, J. Hammond run out 0, W. Beldham c Beauclerk 5, A. Freemantle b Lambert 10, E. Bligh c Smith 0, J. Small junior b Budd 14, W. Ayling b Budd 0, T. Ray b Lambert 5, Collins not out 3
Byes 1
Total 55

UNDER-38s Second Innings
Lord Frederick Beauclerk not out 1, T. A. Smith not out 5
Total 6 for 0

THE LONGEST RIVALRY

In 1805, Lord Byron was still at school and that summer, his fellow cricketers at Harrow School sent a letter to their counterparts at Eton.

> The Gentlemen of Harrow school request the honour of trying their skill at cricket with the gentlemen of Eton on Wednesday July 31 at Lord's Cricket ground. A speedy answer declaring whether the time and place be convenient will oblige.

With these words, written and sealed on 20 June, the longest-standing rivalry in cricket was established. The match that happened a few weeks later is now regarded as the first meeting between the two schools, yet some believe that the fixture may even have originated before then.

Etonians past and present had been used to visiting London in order to play cricket. In 1787, a newspaper called the *World Fashionable Advertiser* announced a match at White Conduit Field in Islington. It would feature 'eleven gentlemen educated at Eton and members of the Star and Garter against eleven other gentlemen of the same club'. The match was to be for 1,000 guineas. The following year, the Etonians played at Lord's for the first time. On 31 May 1788, *The World* gave notice that 'on Monday, a match between the gentlemen educated at Eton against the rest of the schools will be played at the New Ground Marylebone'.

The old boys were free to play as they chose, but the schoolboys often encountered official disapproval. This problem was revealed in an account of a match between Eton and Westminster, which took place at Hounslow in 1796: 'the masters know nothing of it, nor are they intended to do so until it is over.' Westminster won by 66 runs. Edward Harbord, later to become Lord Suffield, suggested that those participating in the match might be subject to school discipline.

One match that does seem to have received official approval came in 1799, when the Etonians played Westminster at Lord's. The Etonians were dismissed for 47 and Westminster were struggling at 13 for 5 when the match was abandoned. There remains the tantalising prospect that some other matches may have passed undetected.

In 1796, the eleven-year-old Lord Palmerston wrote to his mother in some excitement: 'I wish you would send me two pairs of stumps for cricket and a good bat. Some of the boys say we have accepted the challenge sent us by the Eton boys.'

The match was to be eighteen-a-side, yet there is no record of the result or a trace of the scores. At the time, many challenges were laid down, and not all of them were fulfilled.

Even an Upper Club scorebook that contained the details from 1805 went missing for many years. When it eventually came to light in the 1950s, it was discovered that the book had been used as the account ledger for a farm, so the details of cricket matches fought for prominence with agricultural incomings and outgoings.

The book includes a postscript, obviously written by an Etonian hand. 'The Harrow were beat in one innings by twelve notches easy, Hurra.' It adds, '*Exeunt omnes*' – though happily not pursued by a bear.

The Etonians were jubilant at their success and sent a taunting note to their opponents: 'Adventurous boys of Harrow school of cricket you've no knowledge, ye played not cricket but the fool with men of Eton College.'

Lord Byron was a member of the Harrow eleven and is thought to have composed the Harrovian reply: 'So Eton wits to play the fools not the boast of Harrow school, No wonder then at our defeat, folly like yours could ne'er be beat.'

Two days after the match, he wrote to his friend Charles Gordon:

> We have played the Eton (sic) and were most confoundedly beat, however it was some comfort to me that I got 11 notches in the first innings and seven the second which was more than anyone of our side except Brockman and Ipswich could contrive to hit.

He seems to have exaggerated his own contribution, for according to the scorebook he was out for seven and two. Byron may have overstated his score but he spared no detail on the celebrations that followed.

> After the match we dined together and were extremely friendly, not a single discordant word was uttered by either party. To be sure we were most of us rather drunk and went together to the Haymarket theatre and kicked up a row as you may suppose when as many Harrovians and Etonians met at one place. The result was such a deal of noise that none of our neighbours could hear a word of the drama, at which not being highly delighted, they began to quarrel with us and we nearly came to a battle royal. My mind was so confused by the heat of the wine I drank, I could not remember in the morning how I found my way to bed.

2 August 1805
Eton beat Harrow by an innings and two runs

HARROW First Innings
Lord Ipswich b Carter 10, T. Farrer b Carter 7, T. Dury b Carter 0, Boulton run out 2, J. A. Lloyd b Carter 0, A. Shakespear st Heaton 8, Lord Byron c Barnard 7, T. Erskine b Carter 4, W. D. Brockman b Heaton 9, E. Stanley not out 3, W. Assheton b Carter 3
Byes 2
Total 55

ETON First Innings
J. Heaton b Lloyd 0, J. Slingsby b Shakespear 29, W. Carter b Shakespear 3, G. C. Farhill c Lloyd 6, S. Canning c Farrer 12, G. Camplin b Ipswich 42, F. Bradley-Dyne b Lloyd 16, C. T. Barnard b Shakespear 2, H. W. Barnard not out 3, J. H. Kaye b Byron 7, H. Dover c Boulton 4
Total 122

HARROW Second Innings
Lord Ipswich b Heaton 21, T. Farrer c Bradley-Dyne 3, T. Dury st Heaton 6, Boulton b Heaton 0, J. A. Lloyd b Carter 0, A. Shakespear run out 5, Lord Byron b Carter 2, T. Erskine b Heaton 8, W. D. Brockman b Heaton 10, E. Stanley c Canning 7, W. Assheton not out 0
Byes 3
Total 65

The match seems not to have taken place the following year. Not until 1818 did it become a regular fixture, and if the post-match behaviour described by Byron was repeated, it goes some way to explaining why Eton headmaster Dr Charles Goodford threatened to bring the fixture to an end by the 1850s.

An Old Etonian cricketer who signed himself 'Fielding Ball' went to the trouble of printing a pamphlet on 'A Protest Against the Abolition of the Annual Public School Matches', in which he outlined a 'humble but earnest protest'.

The cricketers carried the day, and the match survived to become the longest regular fixture staged at Lord's. It celebrated its 200th anniversary in 2005.

GENTLEMEN *v.* PLAYERS

This was a match that defined the status quo in cricket for almost 150 years. Above all others, it emphasised the divide between amateurs and professionals.

A notice in the *Morning Post* of 7 July 1806 announced the first match 'between nine gentlemen with Wells and Lambert and against eleven of England'. The 'eleven of England' would in time be styled 'Players'.

In the early years of cricket, gentlemen played for leisure. Considerable sums were staked on the outcome of a match and these wagers were an integral part of the pleasure principle. The result was a matter of prestige, and it became customary for the gentry to pay for better players to bolster the teams. Hambledon's early accounts include 'payments made to players'.

Lord Tankerville, an early MCC member and member of the Privy Council, advertised for a footman in the *Morning Herald* in 1792. His specifications were precise: 'He must neither drink gin nor brandy nor keep any company which smoaked (sic) tobacco, and that he must play at cricket decently.' His Lordship had already employed Lumpy and Bedster, both noted early players.

In 1798, two matches between Gentlemen and Commoners were advertised, but it is not thought that these actually took place and the first for which a score survives is the encounter of 1806.

Entrance to the ground was sixpence, and the bills gave the stern warning 'no dogs admitted'. The match stake was 1,500 guineas. The publicity for the match also announced 'a marquee to let – will hold 100 persons'.

William Beldham was listed in the England eleven published in the *Morning Post* shortly before the match, so it may well have been a late decision to give him to the Gentlemen alongside Lambert. Beldham and John Nyren had both played for Hambledon, and the famous old Hampshire village club provided five participants in all. In the England team, later known as 'Players', there were some noted names of the day. Tom Walker, John Small, and Robert Robinson, a left-handed batsman. A farmer, he stood six foot tall and was known as 'Long Bob' or 'Three-Fingered Jack'. The latter nickname came about because he had lost a finger in a fire. Robinson had his cricket bat specially modified to enable him to hold it. He had, it was said, 'introduced spikes of monstrous length for one shoe and had also made for himself "pads" of two thin boards off which the ball went with great noise. Being laughed at he discontinued them.'

The Gentlemen included John Willes, one of the very early exponents of round arm bowling, and Lord Frederick Beauclerk. Neither had their best day.

It had been decided that 'the wickets will be pitched at eleven o'clock'.

Beldham's bowling made a big impact in the Players' first innings. They were bowled out for only 69.

Lambert top scored in the Gentlemen's reply. His was the first half-century recorded in the series of matches as they totalled 195. They bowled the players out second time for 112 to win the match by an innings.

7–9 July 1806
Gentlemen beat England (Players) by an innings and 114 runs

ENGLAND (Players) First Innings
T. Walker c Upton 14, J. Hampton st Lambert 18, R. Robinson c Bligh 13, John Bennett c Beldham 1, J. Hammond c Lambert 0, T. C. Howard c Smith 2, J. Small junior c Beldham 0, W. Ayling b Willes 1, A. Freemantle not out 14, W. Fennex b Beldham 5, H. Bentley c Bligh 0
Byes 1
Total 69

GENTLEMEN (with Beldham and Lambert) First Innings
The Hon. E. Bligh c Hammond 22, Pontifex b Howard 14, W. Lambert st Hammond 57, T. A. Smith run out 48, W. Beldham c Howard 16, Lord Frederick Beauclerk c Bennett 1, John Willes c Hampton 1, G. Leicester c Walker 14, The Hon. A. Upton run out 11, J. Nyren c Ayling 4, C. Warren not out 2
Byes 5
Total 195

ENGLAND (Players) Second Innings
T. Walker c Upton 24, J. Hampton c Upton 4, R. Robinson b Beauclerk 15, John Bennett c Upton 13, J. Hammond c Beldham 2, T. C. Howard c Upton 13, J. Small junior not out 21, W. Ayling c Bligh 8, A. Freemantle st Lambert 1, W. Fennex c Upton 0, H. Bentley lbw 8
Byes 3
Total 112

Eleven days later, the players reconvened at Lord's for a second match. Beldham became the first man to play for both Gentlemen and the Players in the same season, although this time he finished on the losing side. The Gentlemen won this match by 82 runs. After two matches in the space of a fortnight, it seems somewhat strange that the next was not held for another thirteen years.

The match itself was often on uncertain footing in the early years, but it later became an integral part of Victorian life, to the extent that R. H. Lyttelton wrote in 1904, 'in conclusion let us hope that the Gentleman and Players match will never fall through, it ought to be the summit of ambition in every cricketer.'

In fact, the series lasted until 1962, when the authorities finally decided to abolish the distinction between amateur and professional, a decade before football made the same far-reaching decision.

The last fixture was left drawn when the rains came, which was perhaps an appropriate way to draw the curtain down.

TAKING THE MIDDLE GROUND

In 1811, Thomas Lord opened his second ground near North Bank. It was known as the New Middle Ground.

By 1808, it had become clear that cricket at the first Lord's Cricket Ground was under threat. Lord was told that there would be a rise in the rent and he set about finding an alternative ground.

In October, an agreement was signed whereby Henry Samuel Eyre agreed to let Lord have part of his estate. Two fields, known as the Brick Field and the Great Field, were to be leased for a term of eighty years at a rent of £54 per annum. By 1809, Lord was able to place the following announcement in the *Morning Post*:

> Lord begs to inform the gentlemen lovers of cricket, that he has inclosed (sic) and levelled a large piece of ground which for size and beauty of situation cannot be excelled.

Lord said the ground 'would be ready by the beginning of May and would be known by the name of Lord's Saint John's Wood Cricket Ground.'

In the first years of its existence, the ground was leased to the St John's Wood Cricket Club, though details of the matches they played do not survive.

The first match on the new ground for which records survive was played on 8 and 9 July 1811. It was between elevens raised by Benjamin Aislabie, the future MCC secretary, and Squire George Osbaldeston, an MP. Both men had helped Lord identify the site as the second ground.

As at Dorset Fields, the bowlers held sway. Thomas Howard and Budd dismissed Aislabie's team for 80. William Lambert scored more than half his side's runs and apart from him, only Silver Billy Beldham reached double figures. Andrew Schabner made his debut at the new ground. It was not the happiest of baptisms, for he was bowled for a duck by Thomas Howard. Aislabie himself was left high and dry on 8 at the end of his team's first innings of 80.

Henry Bentley got the top score for Osbaldeston's team with 38, and recorded the fact in his *Matches from 1786 to 1822*. The Squire himself hit 31 as his side took a first innings, lead of 95. When Aislabie's side batted again, they did better. Beldham made 28 before he was out hit wicket, but Budd and Howard restricted them to 122. The Squire's side won easily by eight wickets.

8/9 July 1811
Osbaldeston beat Aislabie by eight wickets

AISLABIE'S First Innings

J. Rice c Howard 1, N. Mann b Howard 0, W. Beldham c Budd 12, W. Lambert c Hoare 42, John Bennett b Budd 0, W. Barton b Budd 0, J. Tanner b Howard 7, A. W. Schabner b Howard 0, T. Ray b Howard 0, B. Aislabie not out 8, H. Hampton b Howard 4

Byes 6

Total 80

OSBALDESTON'S First Innings

H. Bentley b Beldham 38, T. Vigne b Lambert 32, T. C. Howard b Beldham 8, J. Hammond c Rice 28, E. H. Budd hit wicket 6, G. Osbaldeston st Lambert 31, J. Jenner st Lambert 7, Frances c Lambert 0, G. M. Hoare c Bennett 4, G. Cole run out 5, J. Poulet not out 16

Byes 0

Total 175

AISLABIE'S Second Innings

J. Rice c Budd 9, N. Mann c Hammond 0, W. Beldham hit wicket 28, W. Lambert c Howard 9, John Bennett b Bentley 20, W. Barton b Budd 24, J. Tanner c Jenner 1, A. W. Schabner b Howard 10, T. Ray b Howard 16, B. Aislabie b Howard 0, H. Hampton not out 2

Byes 3

Total 122

OSBALDESTON'S XI Second Innings

H. Bentley not out 2, G. Osbaldeston not out 16, G. M. Hoare st Beldham 7, J. Poulet b Lambert 3

Total 28 for two

The new ground did not prove popular with members. Records of matches at the second ground are scarce and it lasted for only three seasons. No centuries are recorded but in 1812 Lord Frederick Beauclerk led his own side against George Osbaldeston's eleven. He made 86 before he was bowled by Osbaldeston. His runs came out of a total of 132 and only one other man reached double figures.

The development of the Regent's Canal, first signalled a decade before, finally began. The route, originally intended to go south of the ground, was now altered to bisect it. On 13 July 1813, Lord signed over his interest in the ground to Messrs Munro, Delafield and Nash, directors of the Regent's Park Company.

THE THIRD AND PRESENT GROUND

On 7 May 1814, an advertisement appeared in the *Morning Post*:

> T. Lord respectfully informs the noblemen, Gentlemen and members of the Marylebone and St John's Wood Cricket Club that the new ground is completely ready for playing on. The new road leading to it is commodiously finished.

This was the third ground and proved to be the final one. As he had done when the club relocated from Dorset Square, Lord dutifully supervised the removal of the turf from the ground at North Bank. This was relayed on the present field.

Four days before the new ground was due to open, there was a large explosion at the tavern that adjoined it. However, this appears to have caused minimal damage and the present Lord's was soon in use for the first time.

Henry Bentley records that on 4 June 1814, a single-wicket match was played between 'Four of the Marylebone Club against Four of Hampshire'. The club was represented by the Hon. Gen., George Osbaldeston, the big hitter E. H. Budd and Lord Beauclerk. They totalled 41 runs in their innings. When Hampshire's four batted, they could muster only eight in their first innings and seven in the second, so MCC's quartet won 'in one innings by 26 runs.' This must have been for a sum of money, but on this occasion details of the wager did not appear.

Bentley actually played in the first recorded 'grand match'. It was set for 22 June 1814, and was to be between MCC and Hertfordshire.

Bentley was a given man to the Hertfordshire team. They batted first but were undone by the bowling of Lord Frederick Beauclerk and Budd. It was by no means the first time that these two had made such an impact on a match at Lord's and between them, they ripped through the Hertfordshire batting. The decision to give Bentley to the visiting team was vindicated by his performance in the first innings. He was top scorer in the Hertfordshire innings and finished unbeaten on 33. When he produced his monumental volume on scores of early matches, this accomplishment must have given him considerable pleasure.

When MCC batted, Andrew Schabner scored the first-ever half-century on the current ground, but MCC totalled only 161. This was more than enough.

Bentley was out for a duck in the second Hertfordshire innings, and was one of three men run out as they were dismissed for 55. MCC had begun life on their third and final ground with an emphatic victory.

22 June 1814
MCC beat Hertfordshire by an innings and 27 runs

HERTFORDSHIRE First Innings
Mowbray c Ward b Beauclerk 4, Bentley not out 33, Bruton b Budd 7, S. Carter b
Budd 0, Sibley b Beauclerk 6, Taylor b Beauclerk 6, Denham b Budd 10, Carter b
Budd 1, Sibley b Beauclerk 6, Freeman b Beauclerk 2, Crew b Beauclerk 0
Extras b 4
Total 79

MCC First Innings
A. W. Schnabner c J. Sibley 55, D. J. W. Kinnaird b S Carter 1, C. Warren b Taylor
25, E. H. Budd c T Carter 36, E. Bligh b Bentley 6, T. J. Burgoyne run out 0, Lord
Frederick Beauclerk b Taylor 3, G. Osbaldeston b Mowbray 18, W. Ward run out
10, T. Vigne b Bentley 2, J. Poulet not out 1
Extras b 4
Total 161

HERTFORDSHIRE Second Innings
Mowbray b Beauclerk 1, Bentley run out 0, Bruton b Osbaldeston 17, S. Carter st
Vigne 0, Sibley c Budd 1, Taylor run out 2, Denham st Vigne 21, J. Sibley not out 3,
Crew st Vigne 5
Extras b 5
Total 55

A First Hundred at St John's Wood

Run scoring proved no easier on Thomas Lord's third ground than it had on the previous two, but the year after the present ground opened, two batsmen scored centuries in the same match.

At the time, the Epsom Club in Surrey attracted the patronage of some of the biggest names in cricket. These included major MCC personalities such as Beauclerk and Aislabie. The connection with the premier club enabled Epsom to play a number of matches at Lord's. In August 1815, they faced the Gentlemen of Middlesex. There was little indication of the heavy scoring to come when Middlesex were all out for 51. Teenager Algernon Greville top scored with 17. Epsom had two young brothers on their side: twenty-one-year-old Edward and eighteen-year-old Frederick Woodbridge. Frederick scored 107. If the scores have been recorded correctly, this was the first century scored on the present ground at Lord's in any class of cricket.

Felix Ladbroke hit the only hundred of his career in the same innings. 'He does not appear to have excelled much in the art', wrote Haygarth of him later. 'He was however a great admirer and patron of the noble game.' On this one day in 1815, however, he did excel, and in later life he also became High Sheriff of Surrey.

James Dark was later to take over the running of Lord's, but he found it hard to manage the run flow on this occasion. Epsom totalled 476.

The Middlesex team had three men absent when they batted a second time. The former Hambledon batsman Robinson top scored with 30 made out of 67. But for his intervention, they would have been dismissed even more cheaply.

24 August 1815
Epsom beat the Gentlemen of Middlesex by an innings and 358 runs

GENTLEMEN OF MIDDLESEX First Innings
H. Burrows c Vigne 3, H. Repton b Lord 5, A. Greville run out 17, Robinson c Woodbridge 1, Hon. Mr Kinnaird not out 16, Sir Bellingham Graham b Mann 0, T. Burgoyne c Aislabie 2, Capt. Smyth b Tanner 0, T. Lord Esq junior b Mann 0, Ellis c Aislabie 0, J. Dark run out 7
Total 51

EPSOM First Innings
J. Tanner b Dark 17, F. Woodbridge b Ellis 107, H. Lloyd b Robinson 24, A. Schabner b Ellis 10, E. Woodbridge b Lord 70, F. Ladbroke b Ellis 116, T. Vigne b Dark 38, C. Mitford b Robinson 44, N. Mann run out 9, T. Lord not out 10, B. Aislabie c Kinnaird 15

Byes 16
Total 476

GENTLEMEN OF MIDDLESEX Second Innings
H. Burrows b Tanner 1, H. Repton b Vigne 0, R. Robinson c Ladbroke 30,
T. Burgoyne c Woodbridge 30, Capt. Smyth b Tanner 10, T. Lord b Vigne 1, Ellis not
out 11, J. Dark b Tanner 7
Byes 1
Total 67
A. Greville, Kinnaird, Graham absent

A Hundred in Each Innings

Epsom were on the receiving end of the next big run-scoring feat at the new ground. For this match, Sussex called on the services of William Lambert and George Osbaldeston. Without them, they would not have enjoyed such dominance.

This was the first recorded match to produce over 1,000 runs, and it also featured a notable individual feat: William Lambert became the first man to score a century in each innings of a match at the ground. Lambert was considered one of the finest batsmen of the era and had been deemed good enough to play for the Gentlemen in the inaugural match in 1806. 'The bowler instead of attacking him, always seemed to be at his mercy.'

Against Epsom, Sussex were in trouble until he shared a superb stand with Squire Osbaldeston, who also scored a century. Apart from these two, only three other batsmen reached double figures, but Sussex totalled 292.

Epsom totalled 204 in reply.

When Sussex batted again, Lambert made 157. It was a superb effort, and this was the highest score of his career in major cricket.

2–6 July 1817
Sussex beat Epsom by 427 runs

SUSSEX First Innings
J. Broadbridge c Vigne 12, F. Mellersh b Howard 1, J. B. Baker c Budd 0, W. Broadbridge b Howard 14, W. Lambert not out 107, G. Osbaldeston b Howard 106, J. Bray b Budd 7, W. Slater b Vigne 31, C. Andrew b, Howard 2, W. Sturt b Howard 0, W. Battcock b Vigne 1
Byes 11
Total 292

EPSOM First Innings
C. Warren b Lambert 11, W. Barton b Lambert 25, R. Robinson b Osbaldeston 18, E. H. Budd st W. Broadbridge 63, W. Ward b Osbaldeston 0, F. Woodbridge b Lambert 38, T. C. Howard b Lambert 13, B. Aislabie run out 0, E. C. Woodbridge c Sturt 11, F. C. Ladbroke not out 7, T. Vigne c Bray 1
Byes 17
Total 204

SUSSEX Second Innings
J. Broadbridge b Budd 45, F. Mellersh b Budd 0, J. B. Baker b Ward 25, W. Broadbridge b Budd 61, W. Lambert b Budd 157, G. Osbaldeston b Budd 16, J. Bray b Ward 27,

W. Slater b Ward 35, C. Andrew not out 35, W. Sturt b Howard 26, W. Battcock b Howard 0
Byes 18
Total 445

EPSOM Second Innings

C. Warren c Lambert 0, W. Barton run out 7, R. Robinson c Andrew 16, E. H. Budd st W Broadbridge 8, F. Woodbridge st W. Broadbridge 1, T. C. Howard not out 54, B. Aislabie b W. Broadbridge 0, E. C. Woodbridge c Mellersh 6, F. C. Ladbroke c Baker 9, T. Vigne b Lambert 0, W. Ward absent hurt
Byes 5
Total 106

Lambert did not play again at Lord's. He antagonised Frederick Beauclerk, who accused him of involvement in a case of match-fixing at the Nottinghamshire v England match.

WITHOUT RIVAL THE FIRST BAT
OF THE DAY

William Ward was already a batsman of repute by the time he scored the first double century at Lord's. His great innings was played for MCC in a match against Norfolk. Little detail survives about the course of play in the match, but we do know that he put on over 200 runs in a stand with Lord Frederick Beauclerk.

Ward made a staggering 278, not only the highest individual innings played at Lord's by some measure but also the first double hundred made in cricket. He was eventually caught by Felix Ladbroke who, five years earlier, was one of the first century-makers on the new ground.

Beauclerk was unbeaten on 82 as MCC totalled 473.

'It must be observed that Mr Ward's enormous score, the largest but one ever made, was made against some very inferior bowling (bar Budd) and fielding,' noted Haygarth with his usual caution when recording the match in *Scores and Biographies*.

In *The Cricket Field*, it was recorded that he gave the 'easiest possible chance' when he had scored 30. For all that, Ward's innings seems to have really caught the imagination.

Again in *The Cricket Field*, it was noted that one Charles Morse, perhaps one of the earliest cricket collectors, made sure the feat was noted: 'Mr Morse preserves as a relic, the identical ball, and the bat that hit that ball about. A trusty friend (the bat) which served its owner 30 years.'

The bat he used weighed 4 pounds. To this day, the ball remains as part of the collection at Lord's and is believed to be the oldest cricket ball in existence.

The match was noted for the entry of sixteen-year-old Fuller Pilch, who made his debut at Lord's and lined up alongside his older brother, William. Fuller was to become one of the great batsmen of the early nineteenth century, though on this occasion he made 0 and 2.

24–27 July 1820
MCC beat Norfolk by 417 runs

MCC First Innings
J. Tanner b Budd 0, J. Brand b W. Pilch 38, D. G. Stacey b W. Pilch 8 , W. Ward c Ladbroke 278, H. T. Lane b Budd 27, H. J. Lloyd b W. Pilch 22, G. F. Parry b Budd 10, Lord Frederick Beauclerk not out 82, C. J. Barnett b Budd 3, H. C. Lowther c F. Pilch 3, T. O. Bache b Budd 0
Byes 2
Total 473

NORFOLK First Innings

W. J. Brereton b Beauclerk 0, N. Pilch b Beauclerk 5, E. H. Budd b Beauclerk 2, T. Vigne b Beauclerk 11, R. Frost b Beauclerk 10, W. Pilch b Tanner 9, F. Pilch c Stacey 0, F. C. Ladbroke c Beauclerk 28, C. Brunton b Lowther 21, P. Gurdon c Lloyd 6, W. Quarles not out 0
Total 92

MCC Second Innings

J. Tanner c F. Pilch 0, J. Brand c Brunton 13, D. G. Stacey not out 9, W. Ward c N. Pilch 10, H. T. Lane run out 15, H. J. Lloyd c Budd 19, G. F. Parry run out 15, Lord Frederick Beauclerk st Budd 11, C. J. Barnett b F. Pilch 4, H. C. Lowther b F. Pilch 0, T. O. Bache b F. Pilch 9
Byes 3
Total 108

NORFOLK Second Innings

N. Pilch st Bache 52, E. H. Budd c Parry 0, R. Frost b Ward 3, W. Pilch b Stacey 0, F. Pilch b Ward 2, F. C. Ladbroke c Beauclerk 28, C. Brunton b Ward 4, P. Gurdon b Tanner 9, W. Quarles b Ward 2, W. J. Brereton absent hurt, T. Vigne absent hurt. F. C.
Total 72
Ladbroke absent hurt

The record-breaking Mr Ward was born in 1787, the year the first Lord's ground was opened. He, came from a wealthy family and later became a governor of the Bank of England. At one stage, he was also an MP for the City of London. He was steeped in the lore of the club, and his financial acumen and wealth also came to the rescue of the MCC some five years later. Thomas Lord, now approaching his seventieth year, had been listening very seriously to offers from real estate developers. He had permission from the Eyre Estate to develop seven pairs of houses on the ground. Ward offered Lord £5,000 and took over the lease of the ground. Not for the first time, or the last, Lord's was saved. Ward was the hero of the day and was feted in a contemporary rhyme:

> and of all who frequent the ground named after Lord's,
> On the list first and foremost should stand Mr Ward.
> No man will deny, I am sure when I say,
> That he's without rival first bat of the day

Ward's good work so nearly counted for nothing. In the early hours of the morning of 29 July 1825, a fire broke out in the pavilion. At such an hour, it burnt unchecked. Within an hour and a half, all that remained of the pavilion were charred ruins. It had only recently been renovated, and at great expense. How the blaze began remained a mystery, though it was thought to have started at 1.30 a.m. and, as *The Times* lamented, 'from the nature of the materials which were chiefly of wood, the fire in a very short time defied the power of the fire engines and water.' John Bull added a further catalogue of the damage, which included 'a large and valuable stock of wine.'.At least none of the houses adjoining the ground were near enough to be affected by the blaze.

NOT JUST CRICKET

When there was no cricket, the patrons of Lord's looked for other amusements. In 1806, a sprint race over 100 yards was arranged. The participants, described as 'swift footed antagonists' in the words of the *Morning Post*, were Lord Edward Somerset, the third son of the Duke of Beaufort and the Hon. Mr Edward Harbord, who a decade earlier had reported on the corporal punishment meted out to his Harrovian confederates after their illicit cricket match with Westminster. By now, he had already become MP for Great Yarmouth, and was later to inherit the title Lord Suffield. He had some experience of running. In dress, he was described as 'a little recherché and fantastic'. What he wore for this race was not recorded, but it was for 100 guineas a side and 'attracted a numerous course of fashionables'. Lord Frederick Beauclerk was asked to umpire. Lord Edward Somerset was the pre-race favourite, but Mr Harbord won the race by 'a trifling distance.' According to another report, Beauclerk was called into adjudicate after Somerset fell. A long discussion followed and the race was declared void. Even so, this was probably the first athletic contest at Lord's.

The aristocratic patrons of Lord's found another cricket-related discipline on which to bet in 1826. Sir Henry Goodricke struck a wager with Lord Kennedy on a cricket ball throwing contest.

Boxer Dick Defoe was known as 'The Westminster Hope'. He had beaten the splendidly named 'Chelsea Snob' in a bout, but more significantly he had a strong throwing arm. The 100 sovereigns bet was that 'the ball should alight at 100 yards whence it was delivered'. Sir Henry lost his money because Defoe's throw was only 94 yards.

For reasons that have become muddied by time, the score 111 is known as 'Nelson' and considered unlucky. When a batsman or the total score reached 111, or multiples thereof, many cricketers, most notably the late David Shepherd, took great pains never to have both feet on the ground until the score had moved on. It is not recorded whether superstition had a hand in a very strange contest at Lord's. The challenge was 70 yards out and back in 20 hops each way.

Kennedy claimed the prize of 50 sovereigns by default after his opponent did not show.

A more lasting peace in Europe had made possible the resumption of visits from European sportsmen to England.

In the spring of 1828, the press carried notice of a 'Foot Race Extraordinary' to be held at Lord's Cricket Ground. It was to take place at precisely 2 p.m. on Wednesday 23 April.

John Joseph Grandserre, a twenty-year-old French athlete, had arrived in town the previous month. He announced in newspaper advertisements that he had taken rooms at No. 9 Paddington Street. In France, they called him 'Le Velocipide' and he is thought by some to be a cyclist, although contemporary reports refer to his 'run'. The previous November, he had demonstrated his athleticism at the Palace of Fontainebleau in front of Charles X of France.

When he arrived in London, he undertook to make personal calls on the nobility 'to solicit from their generosity a subscription, to be paid only when he had accomplished the task to their satisfaction'.

He, or at least his backers, proclaimed his intention to perform the feat on the outfield at Lord's Cricket Ground, and a bounty of 1,000 guineas was mentioned. Grandserre also made arrangements for tickets to be sold. Entry to the ground cost 2s 6d (approximately 15.5 pence in decimal currency). These could be obtained from his own address.

Intriguingly, the notice also indicated that 'the pavilion would be fitted up for the accommodation of ladies'.

There was a heavy downpour the night before. Grandserre and his father arrived at the ground with a number of other French gentlemen on the scheduled day for the event. 'On going over the ground, it was discovered to be so soft from the rain that fell the previous night as to render it impossible for the race to take place there.'

After some discussion, Grandserre agreed to make the attempt on the perimeter pathway outside the ground. A course from the St John's Wood chapel to the mews at the end of the ground was chosen. The distance was thought to be three quarters of a mile. It was therefore calculated that twenty-seven laps would be necessary to complete the wager.

The delay in rearranging events meant it was by now over an hour after the advertised time. At 3.12 p.m., Grandserre finally set off and completed the first three quarters of a mile in 4 minutes. He continued at the same steady pace, but soon discovered that running on the perimeter of the ground presented its own difficulties. A report of the event said, 'It was beyond the power of the constables to prevent the crowd pressing around him and an unusual number of dogs kept continually crossing his path.'

Grandserre made light of the canine obstacles, but there seemed little doubt that the interruptions had slowed him down. After 2 hours 15 minutes and 30 seconds, he crossed the line to complete the twenty-seventh lap. This was outside the target time and many felt that the bet had therefore been lost.

There were soon claims that the course had been incorrectly measured.

Bets were suspended until a proper measurement had been taken, but if proven it meant that Grandserre had more than succeeded in covering 21 miles in the time allowed. It was reported that 'at the conclusion of his run, he did not appear in the least distressed'.

James Dark and the committee at Lord's must have taken notice of the excitement generated by this event. They also understood that the sodden ground had very nearly caused the postponement of the whole event. Within the next decade, further improvements were made to the ground, including a dedicated track. This appears to have been introduced in time for the 1837 season, for *Bell's Life in London and Sporting Chronicle* reports on athletic contests 'for which purpose the ground has been admirably adapted'.

The ultimate betting sport came to Lord's in the same year. The results of the Pony Race meeting that was held on the ground do not appear to have survived, but to judge by the advertised details, the meeting was ambitious in scope. There were two days of racing. Five silver cups and a tankard were on offer. Each were appropriately themed.

There was even a Cricket Cup for ponies no higher than 13 hands.

THE VARSITY MEN

On 3 June 1827, *Bell's Life in London, and Sporting Chronicle* carried an announcement that 'a grand match will be played tomorrow at Lord's between the resident members of the two universities of Cambridge and Oxford'. It was the start of another long-standing Lord's tradition.

Charles Wordsworth of Oxford University Cricket Club laid down a marker, which was accepted by Herbert Jenner of Cambridge. For the two men, it continued a cricketing rivalry begun during their schooldays at Harrow and Eton. They played against one another in 1822.

Cricketers from Oxford had already played on the old Lord's ground in Dorset Fields. They were from the Bullingdon Club and, in the later eighteenth century, they played MCC home and away. By the time the challenge was laid down by Wordsworth, it claimed to represent not just one of the many dining clubs of Oxford but the entire university.

He soon discovered that it was one thing to lay down a challenge but with the strict rules in force, quite another to obtain permission to leave the university premises to play.

'I had to present myself to the dean to tell him that I wished to go to London – not to play a game of cricket – that would not have been listened to, but to consult a dentist.' Wordsworth described his deceipt as 'a piece of jesuitry'. His confession came some sixty years after the deed, in an article for the *Badminton Library* on cricket.

The match was scheduled for 4 June, but a notice *Bell's Life in London, and Sporting Chronicle* suggested that the match was deferred for a few days 'owing to the unfavourable state of the weather'. However, Wordsworth has no recollection of such a delay.

When the match did finally take place, Jenner was the first man to take a wicket. He bowled Wordsworth for 8.

'We were not a strong side,' said Wordsworth, but he had his own moment to shine with the ball.

'The state of the ground being in favour, I was singularly successful with my left hand twist from the off.' Wordsworth took 7 for 25, but the match was drawn when the rains returned to bring a halt to proceedings.

Two years later, water played a much more positive role in Wordsworth's life. He was a leading light in the University Boat Club and instrumental in another sporting challenge laid down to Cambridge. Wordsworth rowed in the first university boat race, although his hands were apparently so sore that this affected his cricket: 'I was suffering from the effects of my rowing in a way which made it almost impossible for me to hold a bat,' he complained.

The varsity cricket matches continued, though it was not until 1851 that the fixture was permanently established at Lord's.

When the Golden Jubilee of the match was celebrated, the two rivals were remembered in verse:

Fifty years have sped since first,
Keen to win their laurel,
Oxford round a Wordsworth clustered,
Cambridge under Jenner mustered,
Met in friendly quarrel.

4/5 June 1827
Match drawn

OXFORD UNIVERSITY First Innings
C. Wordsworth b Jenner 8, H. E. Knatchbull c Romilly 43, W. W. Ellis b Jenner 12, J. Papillon run out 42, E. Pole b Jenner 11, R. Price b Horsman 71, C. H. Bayley b Kingdon 14, J. W. Bird b Jenner 17, T. Denne b Jenner 4, W. Pilkington not out 12, W. H. Lewis b Horsman 14
Extras b 10
Total 258

CAMBRIDGE UNIVERSITY First Innings
R. H. Webb b Wordsworth 7, S. N. Kingdon b Wordsworth 5, H. Jenner c Bird 47, E. H. Pickering b Wordsworth 3, J. Dolphin b Bayley 6, E. Romilly b Wordsworth 8, J. L. Freer b Wordsworth 3, C. Templeton run out 5, W. Gifford-Cookesley b Wordsworth 0, E. H. Handley b Wordsworth 0, E. Horsman not out 2
Extras b 6
Total 92

In 1839, a combined Oxford and Cambridge team met MCC. The combined university men batted first but had no answer to the bowling of James Cobbett. Even their modest 115 all out seemed a good total when MCC were dismissed for 67. This was Cambridge bowler Edward Sayres' third match at Lord's in the space of a week. He had taken four wickets for his university against MCC, followed up with eight wickets in the varsity match and a five-wicket haul in the first innings of this match. He received valuable support from Godfrey Lee, another success story in the varsity match. When the university men batted again, they were all out for 61. Cobbett claimed a further four victims in partnership with John Bayley, who took six wickets.

Roger Kynaston top scored for MCC in their second innings, but Sayres took a further five wickets as he continued his purple patch at Lord's. Edward Grimston was left high and dry, and Lord's had its first tie. 'The play of several on both sides was excellent,' was the verdict of the correspondent from *Bell's Life in London, and Sporting Chronicle.*

20/21 June 1839
Match drawn

OXFORD AND CAMBRIDGE UNIVERSITIES First Innings
T. A. Anson c Tuck b Cobbett 8, R. A. Bathurst c Buller b Cobbett 10, G. B. Lee b Cobbett 0, J. Grout c Farmer b Cobbett 28, A. Coote b Bayley 13, C. W. A. Napier b Cobbett 10, F. Thackeray b Cobbett 25, C. G. Taylor b Cobbett 6, W. Massey run out 3, J. H. G. Wynne lbw b Cobbett 0, E. Sayres not out 6

Extras b 5, w 1
Total 115

MCC First Innings

H. J. Snow b Lee 4, H. C. Lowther b Sayres 0, E. H. Grimston b Sayres 15, J. Bayley b Lee 2, J. Cobbett b Lee 0, R. Kynaston b Sayres 21, W. C. Buller b Thackeray 13, R. W. Keate b Sayres 1, A. A. Farmer b Sayres 2, W. Bagge b Thackeray 0, T. R. Tuck not out 1
Extras b 4, nb 4, w 2
Total 69

OXFORD AND CAMBRIDGE UNIVERSITIES Second Innings

T. A. Anson c Farmer b Bayley 10, R. A. Bathurst b Bayley 3, G. B. Lee st Bayley b Cobbett 3, J. Grout b Cobbett 0, A. Coote b Cobbett 6, C. W. A. Napier lbw b Bayley 10, F. Thackeray c Grimston b Cobbett 0, C. G. Taylor not out 4, W. Massey b Bayley 4, J. H. G. Wynne b Bayley 20, E. Sayers b Bayley 0
Extras w 1
Total 61

MCC Second Innings

H. J. Snow b Lee 1, H. C. Lowther b Sayres 12, E. H. Grimston not out 26, J. Bayley c Taylor b Sayres 10, J. Cobbett b Taylor 1, R. Kynaston run out 28, W. C. Buller b Sayres 3, R. W. Keate b Taylor 1, A. A. Farmer b Taylor 1, W. Bagge c Grout b Sayres 0, T. R. Tuck b Sayres 8
Extras b 8, nb 2, w 6
Total 107

THE NORTH–SOUTH DIVIDE

'The grandest cricket match of the season' was how the *Morning Post* of 11 July 1836 described the first match between North and South. At this point, international cricket in England was still some forty years in the future, so the big matches relied on domestic rivalry. This was something new and it whetted the appetite.

The paper also carried some important team news: 'The nonpareil bowler Lillywhite was completely knocked up by the intense heat of the weather last week at Lord's. The Southern Players will consequently be deprived of his able assistance.'

The cricketer in question was Frederick William Lillywhite. He had made his debut at Lord's in 1827 and although only 5 foot 4, he had forged an impressive reputation as a batsman and bowler. His place was taken by the forty-year-old John Bayley.

Thomas Barker from Nottinghamshire was the star performer for the Northern bowlers. He took seven wickets and the South were dismissed for 97. When his side batted, he went in first and top scored with 25, although the North lost two early wickets.

'He maintained his position admirably,' wrote the correspondent for *Bell's Life in London, and Sporting Chronicle*. 'He would apparently have continued the same system had he not been so splendidly stumped by Box.'

Fuller Pilch was by now considered the greatest batsman in England. He started his innings with a five, but he was bowled by Bayley for 13.

Sam Redgate's unbeaten 21 included three fours, but he was missed by Taylor. In previous years, he had forged his reputation with a hat-trick. 'We think however that he occasionally played with more confidence than science and in our opinion, and also of many others, it would be better for him if he did not think quite so much of himself.'

This was the first appearance at Lord's by William Clarke, the founder of the Trent Bridge Ground.

The North led by 12 runs on first innings and South's batting collapsed the second time around. Only Richard Mills reached double figures. His innings included one blow for five. As the *Bell's Life in London, and Sporting Chronicle* correspondent wrote 'there was not much execution done' and the South were bowled out for 69.

The North needed only 58 to win and they completed their victory shortly after tea.

11/12 July 1836
The North beat the South by six wickets

THE SOUTH First Innings
R. Mills b Barker 6, W. R. Hillyer c Filch b Redgate 0, J. Cobbett c Jervis b Barker 21, T. Beagley b Redgate 6, E. G. Wenman c&b Barker 19, G. Milliard b Barker 0, Taylor c Vincent b Barker 0, J. Bayley c Pilch b Barker 6, A. Mynn b Barker 0,

W. H. Caldecourt not out 7
Extras b 20, nb 5, w 5
Total 97

THE NORTH First Innings
T. Barker st Box b Bayley 25, E. Vincent b Cobbett 5, T. Marsden b Hillier 3, F. Pilch
b Bayley 13, G. Jervis run out 11, W. Clarke c Beagley b Bayley 4, B. Good c Taylor
b Bayley 0, S. Redgate not out 21, F. P. Fenner b Cobbett 3, D. Hayward c Milliard b
Bayley 0, C. Cresswell lbw b Bayley 2
Extras b 13, w 5
Total 109

THE SOUTH Second Innings
R. Mills b Redgate 13, W. R. Hillyer st Hayward b Barker 6, J. Cobbett b Cresswell
9, T. Beagley b Cresswell 2, E. G. Wenman b Cresswell 8, G. Millyard c Cresswell b
Barker 1, J. Bayley b Barker 0, A. Mynn not out 8, W. H. Caldecourt c Hayward b
Redgate 7
Extras b 6, nb 2, w 3
Total 69

THE NORTH Second Innings
T. Barker not out 12, E. Vincent lbw b Mynn 0, D. Hayward b Mynn 3, F. Pilch b
Mynn 14, F. P. Fenner b Hillyer 3, G. Jervis not out 7
Extras b 14, w 5
Total 59 for four

Many of the Northern players played for Nottinghamshire. It was a sign of things to
come. The match itself 'attracted a numerous and fashionable assemblage on both sides',
and there was clearly an appetite for this type of cricket. A return match was immediately
fixed for Leicester. The following year, the North v South match formed the centrepiece of
celebrations for the club's fiftieth anniversary. The occasion also celebrated the accession
of Queen Victoria and remained a major part of the calendar for the rest of the century.

BOWLING FEATS

The exploits of bowlers were distinctly undervalued in early years, even though they held sway in an era of generally low scores. When the first instance of what later became known as a hat-trick was recorded in 1750, the identity of the bowler was not recorded. There was a long debate over what constituted a legal delivery. In the 1820s, the laws had been modified to allow round arm bowling, but it was not until 1836 that bowlers were to be given the credit for victims caught or stumped. Bowling figures were starting to be recorded in full, but this was not always the case.

By the 1840s, the *Pictorial Times* was reporting an interesting match 'wherein the relative merits of the fast and slow systems of bowling were tried.' This became an annual meeting and, in 1841, began on a midsummer's day, but the weather was unseasonably poor.

'Notwithstanding the unpropitious state of the weather, the ground on each day was well attended and the pavilion was crowded with noblemen,' wrote the correspondent of the *Morning Post* and, almost inevitably, 'Bets of an immense amount were pending on the result of the match.'

Alfred Mynn was in fine form in the first innings and took seven wickets. Only Kent's Ned Wenman and Joseph Guy of Notts saved the Slow XI from complete embarrassment. Mynn top scored for the fast bowlers in their first innings. Apart from his 36, only Fuller Pilch and Tom Box made double figures. Fred Lillywhite took nine wickets.

The bowling was described in the *Morning Post* as 'very scientific'. In the second innings, Mynn dismissed Wenham, Bayley and Cobbett in successive balls. His hat-trick reduced the Slow Bowlers to 29 for 5 in their second innings. Guy and Lillywhite lifted the score to 133. The fast bowlers were set 151 to win. It would have been the highest total of the match, but Lillywhite took another five wickets in the second innings. Fuller Pilch and Nottinghamshire's Sam Redgate both offered a spirited resistance, but they were bowled out for 90 and so Mynn was on the losing side despite his hat-trick.

21–23 June 1841
Slow Bowlers beat the Fast Bowlers by 60 runs

SLOW BOWLERS First Innings
F. W. Lillywhite run out 2, E. Barnett b Redgate 4, G. A. F. Liddell b Mynn 2, E. G. Wenman c Redgate b Mynn 35, J. Guy b Redgate 31, C. G. Taylor c&b Mynn 0, R. Kynaston b Mynn 3, J. Cobbett not out 16, F. Thackeray b Mynn 10, J. Bayley c Redgate b Mynn 0, T. M. Wythe b Mynn 8
Extras b 16, nb 3, w 8
Total 138

FAST BOWLERS First Innings

W. Ward b Lillywhite 0, C. G. Whittaker b Lillywhite 17, A. Mynn c Guy b Lillywhite 36, F. Pilch c Cobbett b Lillywhite 21, T. Box c Cobbett b Lillywhite 12, W. P. Pickering c Guy b Lillywhite 0, S. Redgate b Lillywhite 9, C. W. A. Napier b Lillywhite 6, R. W. Keate not out 8, Price b Lillywhite 6, N. Bland c Bayley b Cobbett 1

Extras b 4

Total 121

SLOW BOWLERS Second Innings

E. Barnett b Mynn 5, J. Bayley b Mynn 12, G. A. F. Liddell b Redgate 2, J. Guy c Whittaker b Mynn 42, E. G. Wenman b Mynn 0, J. Cobbett b Mynn 0, C. G. Taylor c Whittaker b Mynn 9, R. Kynaston b Redgate 6, F. Thackeray b Redgate 0, F. W. Lillywhite not out 40, T. M. Wythe b Redgate 0

Extras b 11, nb 2, w 4

Total 133

FAST BOWLERS Second Innings

N. Bland c Guy b Lillywhite 4, W. P. Pickering b Cobbett 0, W. Ward c Barnett b Cobbett 4, F. Pilch b Lillywhite 39, C. G. Whittaker c Guy b Lillywhite 1, A. Mynn b Cobbett 3, R. W. Keate b Lillywhite 7, T. Box b Bayley 1, S. Redgate b Lillywhite 29, C. W. A. Napier b Bayley 0, Price not out 0

Extras b 2

Total 90

Cricket at Lord's was starting to resemble the modern game. In 1846, a telegraph scoreboard appeared at Lord's for the first time. Two years later, in time for the MCC v Sussex match, a printing tent appeared on the ground to produce scorecards. Sussex won a very low-scoring affair by 24 runs, and the public could take away every detail. Matters in the tent were supervised by Fred Lillywhite.

In the late 1840s, Kent cricket was becoming a force to be reckoned with, and in 1848 a Kent shoemaker, Edmund Hinkly, became the first bowler to take all ten wickets in an innings at Lord's.

Although born at Benenden, Kent, he had played for a while in Watford before making his home in Surrey. *The Times* noted that he was an attendant at the Surrey County Club. Although only 5 foot 6 inches, Hinkly bowled left-arm fast. 'As a bat he does not excel but as a bowler he was first rate', said the writer of *Scores and Biographies*. How he proved it at Lord's!

The Times described the match as 'the greatest attraction'. Some fifty carriages arrived on the first day to watch proceedings. 'On no occasion do we remember to have seen a fuller or more fashionable attendance than this.'

The England team won the toss and James Dean and William Clarke, captain of the All England XI, walked out to open the innings. Both men were very experienced and must have made an intimidating sight for Hinkly on his first appearance at Lord's. If he had any nerves, his first ball betrayed them. It was wide, but not a sign of things to come. Batting progress was slow and after four maiden overs, Hinkly took Clarke's off stump; the first wicket had fallen for four runs. Wicketkeeper Tom Box replaced him and began with a three. The second wicket stand took the score to 53 before Dean was well taken by Kent wicketkeeper William Dorrinton off Billy Hillyer. When Joseph Guy came in, he broke his bat off the first ball. Hinkly had Box caught on the legside by Fuller Pilch for 36, and it proved the top score. He also claimed the wicket of Sewell before the dinner bell rang.

After lunch, he took a catch at slip to dismiss John Wisden and returned to the attack to complete the innings and bowled Lord Frederick Hervey-Bathurst with a shooter.

When Kent batted they found the going no easier.

On the second day, an even bigger crowd turned up. They saw Kent add only five runs to their overnight score before Wisden took the wicket to end the innings.

When England batted again, Hinkly surpassed his performance in the first innings. Roger Kynaston played a maiden over from Hillyer, but when a single to Dean brought him down to face Hinkly, he was bowled for a duck. England were 1 for 0 and Hinkly's great feat had begun. Soon, it was 2 for 2 when he removed Dean. Clarke and Box took the score to 31, but Clarke was smartly stumped by Dorrington, and in Hinkly's next over Box was acrobatically taken in the slips by Hillyer. When Hinkly produced a shooter to bowl Parr, it was 38 for 5 and 'the Kent gentlemen were in high spirits'. Parr was one of the great names of the time, but the notes in *Scores and Biographies* suggested that he had become Hinkly's 'bunny'. 'Hinkly has seldom been opposed to the crack bat of the day without getting his wicket.'

Hillyer had bowled throughout from the other end without success. Despite this remarkable feat, Hinkly still finished on the losing side. Kent had only 105 to chase but were bowled out for 49.

10/11 July 1848
England beat Kent by 55 runs

ENGLAND First Innings
W. Clark b Hinkly 3, J. Dean c Dorrington b Hillyer 21, T. Box c Pilch b Hinkly 36,
J. Guy b Hinkly 2, G. Parr c Dorrington b Hinkly 24, T. Sewell c Adams b Hinkly
3, Wisden c Hinkly b Hillyer 5, O. C. Pell b Hillyer 10, R. Kynaston b Hillyer 2,
F. W. Lillywhite not out 3, F. H. Hervey-Bathurst b Hinkly 0
Extras b 6, w 5
Total 120

KENT First Innings
W. Martingell b Lillywhite 24, W. Pilch b Clarke 1, T. M. Adams b Lillywhite 3,
F. Pilch b Lillywhite 19, A. Mynn b Wisden 8, N. Felix b Wisden 0, W. R. Hillyer b
Wisden 5, W. Dorrington b Wisden 16, C. J. Harenc b Wisden 3, H. E. Knatchbull b
Wisden 0, E. Hinkly not out 7
Extras b 2, nb 1, w 1
Total 90

ENGLAND Second Innings
R. Kynaston b Hinkly 0, J. Dean senior b Hinkly 2, W. Clarke st Dorrington b Hinkly
10, T. Box c Hillyer b Hinkly 18, J. Guy not out 28, G. Parr b Hinkly 4, T. Sewell b
Hinkly 6, J. Wisden c Adams b Hinkly 0, O. C. Pell c Hillyer b Hinkly 2, F. W. Lillywhite
st Dorrington b Hinkly 0, F. H. Hervey-Bathhurst b Hinkly 0
Extras b 4
Total 74

KENT Second Innings

T. M. Adams lbw b Wisden 0, W. Pilch st Box b Wisden 2, N. Felix lbw b Lillywhite 5, F. Pilch b Lillywhite 2, A. Mynn c Sewell b Lillywhite 11, W. Martingell b Wisden 0, E. Hinkly c Dean b Wisden 8, C. J. Harenc b Wisden 2, H. E. Knatchbull b Dean 14, W. Dorrinton b Dean 1, W. R. Hillyer not out 0

Extras b 4

Total 49

The mention of the dinner bell in Hinkly's match suggests that it was already in use, but perhaps in a rather ad hoc fashion. In 1849, the MCC took another step towards streamlining match days at Lord's. Augustus Liddell proposed that 'after each innings, the bell be rung at the expiration of five minutes in order that the players may be ready to resume the game in ten minutes according to the law'. It also specified that the bell would be rung to signify 'when the umpires are to come and pitch the stumps'.

TEEPEES AT THE PAVILION END

Although the major matches attracted big crowds, it seems as though it was a different matter for the lesser fixtures. James Dark continued to search for other attractions and there were few which that could compare with an encampment of American Indians on the ground. This happened for the first time in the summer of 1844, but even though it was a great success, it was never repeated.

The Indians of the Iowa tribe had been brought to England by George Catlin. He was anthropologist and student of Native Americans who had recorded their way of life in a series of paintings. 'Their stay in London must be limited to a very short time as they are on the way to the Continent'. said the publicity in the *Morning Advertiser*.

The encampment numbered fourteen 'including the principal chiefs, braves or warriors, with their squaws, their children and a papoose (infant).'

There was the first chief of the nation Mew Hu She Kaw, or White Cloud, and his wife, Ruton Ye We Ma (Strutting Pigeon). With them came his daughter Tapateme, or Sophia, Neu-Mon Ya, Chief Walking Rain, with him came his ten-year-old son, Watawebukana, and a medicine man, Se Non Yi Yah, or Blisterfeet, six warriors and braves.

'The Indians themselves were highly pleased with the opportunity of enjoying the fresh air and a clear and spacious stage for their sports,' said the man from *The Times*.

While Caitlin offered lectures on the Indian way of life: "The Ioway Indians encamped in their wigwams and also for the better illustration of their domestic life, mode of warfare, peculiar rites and ceremonies and likewise their wild and exciting sports and pastimes,' said *The Age and Argus* on 24 August 1844.

The wild and exciting sports included 'a grand Archery fete to which the members of all the leading archery clubs have been invited to witness the Indians display their skill in shooting with the bow'.

This was probably the first time that archery had been seen at the ground. There was also a demonstration of 'ball play'.

The London press men described a sport that was

different from anything of the sort played in Europe, it is played with sticks having hoops or rings or nooses in the ends in which the players contrive to hook the ball when on the ground or catch it when in the air and throw it out again with great force and to a great distance. There are two parties in the game as in hockey in this country and goals which are to be gained.

The description bears a striking resemblance to lacrosse, a sport developed from the Indian game 'baggataway'.

ANYONE FOR TENNIS?

Of all the non-cricketing activities introduced at Lord's in the mid-nineteenth century, one stood the test of time more than any other. The sport was real tennis, and during the stewardship of James Dark, the decision had been taken to build a court on the ground. It was to be sited in an area that is now occupied by the Mound Stand. MCC secretary Benjamin Aislabie said:

> From the erection of this building, I foretell the most beneficial results. I look forward to the formation of a society of the first noblemen and gentlemen in the land meeting on terms the most amicable, engaging in this elegant game, purely for the amusement it will afford, not impelled by unworthy desire of the gain.

The following spring, the cricketers' register in *Bell's Life in London, and Sporting Chronicle* offered an update: 'The tennis court which has been erected on the right of the entrance to the ground is an extensive and handsome build with various apartments including two excellent billiard rooms for the accommodation of members.' The tables were described as 'first rate'.

The total cost was estimated at £4,000, but new members now clamboured to join.

The tennis court was opened for business on 1 June 1839 and to really set the seal on the enterprise, the first great match was scheduled for 10 July.

The leading European player at the time was Frenchman Edmond Barre, and he faced Edmund Tompkins, the outstanding English player. By a strange coincidence, they had been born within a few months of one another in 1802.

Barre was born at Grenoble in the French Alps, but he had learnt the game at Rue Mazarin in Paris. He was evidently a very quick learner and won his first French championship in 1829. He played at the royal court in front of Emperor Charles V and his reputation soon spread to England. Tompkins originally came from Oxford. He had moved to Brighton where he had opened a court. In tennis circles, he went under the soubriquet 'Peter'.

This grand match attracted a great deal of interest. Among the spectators were the Earl of Uxbridge, the Earl of Verulam, the Earl of Craven, Viscount Grimston, Lord Beresford and Lord Folkestone. Barre was not short of support. The attendance at the match was swelled by several French gentlemen amateurs, who had arrived to watch proceedings.

They witnessed a victory for their countryman. A rematch was swiftly arranged for the following week. This time, the handicap system was to come into play. Barre 'was able to give half thirty and a bisque', which perhaps explained the result. *Bell's Life in London, and Sporting Chronicle* reported that this second match was won by 'Peter' after 'a very severe struggle'. On level terms, Barre was more or less unbeatable for over thirty years.

John Moyer Heathcote, who dominated the tennis scene at Lord's in later years, stated: 'rivals he had none.'

THE GOLD RACQUET

On 15 May 1867, MCC secretary R. A. Fitzgerald made public a new competition that would make Lord's the major centre for tennis: 'It has been decided that two challenge prizes for the best play at tennis shall be given by the Marylebone Club to be played for annually in the court at Lord's by members of the club.'

In the club minutes, Frederick Ponsonby outlined the regulations for the competition:

> Those entered will be tied by lot and the winners of the two ties will play the final match and become respectively the holders of 1. The Gold Racquet and 2. The Silver Racquet … All matches shall be of five sets without vantage sets and shall be subject to the usual rules of the game. The match shall be played out at the time fixed unless the marker shall declare the court unsuitable for want of light or any other cause.

In the early years, the competition was restricted to members of MCC. 'A player not attending at the time named for his match shall be considered to have lost the match.'

Whatever the regulations, the favourite was John Moyer Heathcote. An Etonian, he had gone up to Trinity College Cambridge and had been called to the bar, where he proved outstanding in a court of another kind. He had learnt tennis at Cambridge and was very soon the finest amateur player. He later wrote, 'By 1859 I had begun to give odds to all other amateurs in this country.'

He dominated the MCC Gold Racquet for the first fifteen years of its existence and later told how he received the ultimate compliment from Barre, the Frenchman: 'M. Escot – he never could get nearer than this to the pronunciation of my name – you play too well for gentleman (sic).'

It was not until 1882 that Heathcote was finally beaten by Alfred Lyttelton.

Although the prizes are described as 'racquets', the trophies the winners received were in fact challenge cups. 'The holder of each prize will be responsible for it and must produce it at the MCC anniversary dinner.' It also stipulated that anyone winning the trophy on three occasions would be entitled to keep it.

Real tennis had been an institution at Lord's since the 1830s, but in 1875 an MCC sub-committee was formed to consider the new outdoor game of lawn tennis. Ultimately, though, the headquarters of the new game was established south of the river at Wimbledon.

I ZINGARI
THE GYPSIES PROMOTING
THE SPIRIT OF CRICKET

Sir Spencer Ponsonby Fane, his brother Frederick and their friend John Loraine Baldwin were three enthusiastic members of MCC who decided to found a team. On 4 July 1845, Baldwin had been playing in a match at Harrow School. That night the friends gathered at the Blenheim Club in Bond Street for dinner and decided to form a club to promote the spirit of cricket.

They framed the rules that the entrance fee was nothing and that the club subscription should not succeed the entrance fee. Unlike many clubs at the time, they made it their practice not to hire professional bowlers. They took the name 'I Zingari', the Italian word for gypsies, and the following day they informed some twenty friends that they were now members. They later selected the club colours, black, red and gold, to symbolise the ascent 'out of darkness through fire into light'.

The nature of the club dictated that the majority of their matches were away, but in 1850 they did play at Lord's for the first time against a team made up of both Houses of Parliament. They are named first for this match, which was to become a regular fixture over the next decade.

The match was reported in *Bell's Life in London, and Sporting Chronicle* as part of their cricketers' register. Their correspondent was in an expansive mood. He wrote,

> Without wishing to detract from the merits of the parliamentary whippers in and without wishing to be guilty of a breach of privilege it must be acknowledged that never was a more successful whip made than on Saturday.

Edward Bligh was unable to play for I Zingari because of illness. The Parliamentary team was boosted by the presence of Alfred Diver and Henry Royston who were the only successful bowlers. Herbert Curteis who came on as first change was 'out of time and tune ... wide and triply no-ball, a rare occurrence for him (sic)'.

This, it was suggested, was because the Royal Artillery Band 'put him out of his usual walk up to the wicket while bowling'. The band played to entertain the crowd throughout the afternoon.

It seemed as though Dark excelled himself in laying on entertainment: 'Much praise is due for the admirable manner in which the whole affair was conducted amongst other of his contributions for the comfort of the visitors, his accommodation of the ladies must not be passed over in silence.'

13 July 1850
Match drawn

I ZINGARI First Innings

F. Micklethwaite b Diver 6, C. Morse b Diver 18, S. C. B. Ponsonby b Royston 37, E. Taswell lbw b Royston 0, R. C. Antrobus b Royston 2, R. J. P. Broughton b Diver 23, E. S. E. Hartopp b Royston 6, T. Moncrieff b Diver 9, R. Kerr b Royston 3, A. M. Archdall not out 2, H. G. G. Duff b Royston 0

Extras b 11, lb 2, w 3

Total 122

LORDS AND COMMONS First Innings

Lord C. J. F. Russell b Archdall 8, Earl of Leicester b Archdall 6, Earl of Verulam b Duff 0, Lord Burghley c Broughton b Duff 25, A. J. D. Diver b Antrobus 21, H. M. Curteis b Archdall 1, Lord Guernsey b Archdall 10, H. C. Lowther b Archdall 0, T. E. Taylor b Archdall 7, W. Bagge b Archdall 0, H. Royston not out 3

Extras b 5, lb 1, nb 1, w 9

Total 97

I ZINGARI Second Innings

C. Morse b Diver 28, S. C. B. Ponsonby c Burghley b Diver 49, E. Taswell b Diver 16, R. J. P. Broughton not out 8, E. S. E. Hartopp b Royston 18, R. Kerr not out 8

Extras b 11, lb 1, nb 2

Total 141 for four

The club grew in prominence and, in the late nineteenth century, they were regulars in first-class cricket. They were even accorded a fixture against the Australians in 1884.

THE FIRST INTERNATIONALS

For seventy years, cricket at the three Lord's grounds had been a strictly domestic affair, but all that changed in 1858. The first team to cross the seas to play a match were a team of gentlemen from Ireland.

Cricket had been developing in Ireland since the late eighteenth century. One of the men responsible for its growth was Col. Charles Lennox, one of the original benefactors who had made possible the establishment of Lord's and the MCC. He had served as a soldier in Ireland and in the early nineteenth century, he returned there as Duke of Richmond to take the post of Lord Lieutenant of Ireland. By the 1850s, Irish cricketers were welcoming MCC teams to play in Dublin on a regular basis.

The team that came to Lord's in May 1858 was a strong one. It included Bob Fitzgerald, who five years later became the MCC secretary, and Spencer Ponsonby Fane.

The weather was poor when play began on the first day at noon. The unsatisfactory state of the field was recorded in *Scores and Biographies*: 'The match was played in thick mud.'

MCC batted first. They opened with John Gordon Boothby, once of Charterhouse school, and Alexander Law, who played under the soubriquet 'Infelix', had scored a half-century for Oxford the previous year.

These were the only men to make double figures in the MCC innings. The star bowler for Ireland was Charles Lawrence, who took eight wickets for 32 in 23 overs. All his victims were bowled. MCC were all out for 55. The Irish innings had just begun when proceedings broke for lunch, but the rains returned and no further play was possible on the first day.

The weather was better on the second day and play began on time. The star performers for Ireland were McCormick and Ponsonby. Even so, Ireland were all out for 120. When MCC batted again, last man Halifax Wyatt was unable to play so Francis Compton was permitted to take his place by agreement among the gentlemen.

Lawrence and McCormick bowled unchanged as the Irish completed their victory in front of Lord Carlisle, the Lord Lieutenant.

The bowlers who had brought about the downfall of MCC went on to make their mark in other areas. Lawrence toured Australia with an early English touring party and decided to settle there. In 1868, he returned to England as the manager of an Australian Aboriginal team, which caused a sensation at Lord's and across England.

McCormick was later concerned with matters of state. An Anglican churchman, he became honorary chaplain to the monarch.

17/18 May 1858
The Gentlemen of Ireland beat MCC by an innings and 10 runs

MCC First Innings

J. G. Boothby b Lawrence 12, A. P. Law c Doyle b McCormick 14, A. Haygarth b Lawrence 3, C. Gordon b Lawrence 5, F. T. A Hervey-Bathurst b Lawrence 5, A. F. Payne b Lawrence 0, G. W. Barker b Lawrence 6, A. Payne b McCormick 2, E. G. Hartnell b Lawrence 0, C. S. Hope b Lawrence 1, M. T. H. Wyatt not out 2

Extras b 2, lb 1

Total 53

Bowling

Lawrence 23 overs 32 runs 8 wickets, McCormick 20-152-0, Doyle 2-30-0

GENTLEMEN OF IRELAND First Innings

P. Doyle b Law 6, T. Quinn c Hope b Law 10, J. McCormick b Law 34, W. H. Johnstone c A. Payne b Law 8, C. Lawrence c Boothby b A. Payne 8, S. C. B. Ponsonby run out 18, J. R. Hume c&b Hartnell 0, R. Cooke b Hartnell 0, R. A. Fitzgerald b Hartnell 4, H. Bruen not out 1, W. L. Pakenham b A. F. Payne 0

Extras b 7, lb 3, nb 9, w 12

Total 120

Bowling

A. Payne 30-40-1, Hope 3-8-0, Law 23-29-4, Hartnell 7-9-3, A. F. Payne 3.3-3-1

MCC Second Innings

J. G. Boothby b Mc Cormick 12, A. P. Law b Lawrence 1, A. Haygarth b Lawrence 5, C. Gordon c Cooke b McCormick 1, F. T. A. Hervey-Bathurst b McCormick 0, A. F. Payne run out 11, G. W. Barker c Johnstone b Lawrence 5, A. Payne b McCormick 7, E. G. Hartnell b McCormick 8, C. S. Hope c Ponsonby b Lawrence 1, F. Compton not out 11

Extras b 1, lb 2, w 2

Total 57

Bowling

Lawrence 23-32-4, McCormick 31-27-5

Cricket had also spread into Wales and the South Wales Cricket Club (SWCC) was established by one Samuel George Homfray. The SWCC was not a representative Welsh side as such. It included players from either side of the Bristol Channel. In 1860, the club made a tour of the Home Counties and played at Lord's for the first time. The eleven chosen for the big match also included two Yorkshiremen, who shared the major partnership. South Wales totalled 209, the most successful MCC bowler was Thomas Davis of Nottinghamshire. When MCC batted Belcher and James were among the wickets, but South Wales were just short of a victory when the umpires called time.

12 July 1860

Match drawn

SOUTH WALES

S. Wildgoose b Davis 5, P. Lloyd c&b Davis 5, S. H. Belcher st Kingscote b Martingell 49, S. France b Davis 65, J. N. Wallis b Muttlebury 31, C. W. James c Barnes b Davis 9, G. N. Boldero b Hervey-Bathurst 2 , S. G. Homfray b Davis 3, J. Lloyd c Martingell b Muttlebury 20, V. H. Lee b Muttlebury 1, not out 4

Extras b 2, lb 5, w 9
Total 209

MCC

Earl of Winterton c&b James 0, E. H. Ellis b Belcher 14, A. F. Kingscote b France 3, E. Turnour c Wallis b Belcher 13, F. T. A. Hervey- Bathurst c France b Belcher 0, Davis c&b France 34, G. D. Lacy c James b France 4, C. H. Barnes b France 10, G. A. Muttlebury not out 7, Banbury b France 1
Extras b 8, w 3
Total 97 for nine

The Times described the first visit of a Scottish team to Lord's as 'brought to a conclusion in a very one sided manner'. There was no formal governing body for Scottish cricket at this time. The team is thought to have been organised by thirty-five-year-old David Buchanan, a Scotsman who lived in Warwickshire and had been educated at Rugby. Buchanan bowled fast left-arm and was noted as a slip fielder. At the time, the Free Foresters Club included a number of his compatriots who were drafted into the Scotland team.

Edward Drake, late of Westminster School, and the former Harrow captain Henry Arkwright bowled unchanged for MCC. 'The slow round arm bowling of Mr Arkwright and Mr Drake's underarm peculiars made sad havoc of the Scottish Gentlemen,' observed *Bell's Life in London, and Sporting Chronicle*. Both bowlers took five wickets, Scotland were all out for 23, and no fewer than seven of their batsmen did not get off the mark.

When Scotland fielded, Buchanan starred with the ball and took eight wickets, as MCC were restricted to a modest 134 all out. Drake top scored with 44. Scotland did rather better in their second innings but could only muster 83.

17 July 1865
MCC beat Scotland by an innings and 28 runs

SCOTLAND First Innings
Col. DCR Buchanan c&b E. T. Drake 16, D. Buchanan c Capt. Stephens b H. Arkwright 0 , C. H. N. G. Glassford hit wicket b H. Arkwright 0, J. Mackenzie b H. Arkwright 1 , Capt. J. F. Bennett c M. P. Fitzgerald b H. Arkwright 0, G. P. Robertson st J. Round b E. T. Drake 0, H. N. Tennent c S. H. Churchill b H.Arkwright 0 , W. M. Tennent st J. Round b E. T. Drake 0 , B. A. J. Lawrence c H. E. Bull b E. T. Drake 0 , D. Duff b E. T. Drake 3 , W. F. Traill not out 3
Total 23

MCC First Innings
H. E. Bull b D Duff 0, E. W. Tritton st J Mackenzie b D. Buchanan 9, M. P. Fitzgerald c W. F. Traill b D. Buchanan 17, D. Elphinstone c B. A. J. Lawrence b D. Buchanan 6 , E. T. Drake b W. F. Traill 44 , Capt. Stephens c J Mackenzie b D. Buchanan 22, J. Round b D. Buchanan 5 , Capt. Parnell b D Buchanan 7, A. Infelix b D. Buchanan 7, H. Arkwright not out 8, S. H. Churchill c H. N. Tennent b D. Buchanan 4
Extras b 3, lb 1, w 1
Total 134

SCOTLAND Second Innings

D. C. R Buchanan b E. T. Drake 7 , D. Buchanan b E. T. Drake 9 , C. H. N. G. Glassford run out 8, J. Mackenzie b E. T. Drake 17, Capt. JF Bennett run out 17 , G. P. Robertson c S. H. Churchill b H. Arkwright 13, H. N. Tennent c A Infelix b H. Arkwright 0 , W. M. Tennent not out 5 , B. A. J. Lawrence b E. T. Drake 2, D. Duff b E. T. Drake 2, W. F. Traill st J. Round b H. Arkwright 2

Extras lb 1

Total 83

Umpires: T. Hearne and H. Royston

First Day of Grace

The words were prophetic. He 'promises to be a very good bat and bowls very fairly', predicted Lillywhite of the young cricketer who would become the greatest of the Victorian era.

Three days after his sixteenth birthday in 1864, William Gilbert Grace ('W. G.') played at Lord's for the first time. He had played his first senior game at the age of only fourteen. By the following year, word of his ability had begun to spread through the West Country after he scored a half-century against Somerset.

Grace had been born into a notable cricketing family, and two of his brothers played for England. In 1863, his brother, Edward 'E. M.' Grace, went on the tour of Australia and did not return until the following English summer. 'His absence in Australia gave me my first opportunity to play in a really big match,' said W. G. In 1864, he was was invited to join the South Wales touring team. Despite the name, this was not an exclusively Welsh team. He later wrote, 'Most of the players came from the West Country, and after all my brother and I were only divided from Wales by the Severn.'

He had played one match in London but was very nearly dropped for the next game. One of the senior players approached Henry Grace, the eldest of the Grace brothers, and suggested the youngster be stood down. This proposal was not well received and W. G. kept his place. When he batted, he made 170.

When the South Wales team was announced for what had become the highlight of their annual tour, W. G. was included. So was his brother, E. M. ,who had arrived back from Australia.

The attendance for the first day was described by *The Times* as 'very scanty'.

W. G. walked out to bat at the most famous ground in the world. He was not overawed by his surroundings and described his experience in very matter of fact fashion: 'I went in first wicket down and made 50.'

Lillywhite's *Cricketers' Companion* described it as 'so good an innings he was presented with a bat by the captain of the South Wales Club'.

South Wales eventually led on first innings, with 'a fine hitting innings' of 65 from captain Rhys Jones helping them to reach 211. They were bowled out cheaply in their second innings. Even W. G. scored only two, but MCC were left with not enough time to force the victory and the match was left drawn or, as one reporter described it at the time, the teams 'then tried cricket conclusions but arrived at none'. The second edition of *Wisden Cricketers' Almanack* did not include any prophetic words about the new star. In those early editions, it gave just the scores without any comment.

W. G. did not yet have the beard or the girth that became so well known and so caricatured in later life. As a teenager, he was also an accomplished athlete and won the 440 yard hurdles at the National Olympian Games in 1866.

Two years later, still almost three weeks away from his twentieth birthday, he scored a century at Lord's for the first time for the Gentleman v the Players. He also took ten wickets in the match for 81.

For the next half-century, he was not just the most famous cricketer but arguably the most famous man in England.

21/22 July 1864
Match drawn

SOUTH WALES CRICKET CLUB First Innings
J. J. Sewell b Hearne 3, E. M. Grace b Teape 0, J. Lloyd c Nixon b Hearne 8, W. G. Grace b Teape 50, W. J. Price c&b Hearne 13, F. R. Price b Hearne 27, S. G. Homfray lbw b Hearne 27, R. Jones c Law b Hearne 65, C. C. Bishop b Hearne 10, E. G. Davies b Nixon 2, W. Crawshay not out 0
Extras b 12, lb 12, w 3
Total 211
Fall of wickets 2, 14, 17, 67, 107, 130, 156, 200, 207-23, 129, 131, 145, 149, 164, 183, 186, 186
Bowling
E. M. Grace 34 overs 63 runs 5 wickets, W. G. Grace 37.1 -67-1, W. J. Price 14.3-12-3, Davies 3-6-0, Homfray 3-9-0, F. R. Price 10-18-1

MCC First Innings
E. M. Grace five for 63

SOUTH WALES CRICKET CLUB Second Innings
E. M. Grace b Nixon 4, W. Crawshay b Nixon 7, W. G. Grace c Swain b Hearne 2, J. Lloyd c Royston b Hearne 5, W. J. Price b Hearne 26, F. R. Price c Winslow b Hearne 4, S. G. Homfray b Hearne 5, R. Jones b Hearne 7, J. J. Sewell c Winslow b Teape 3, C. C. Bishop not out 8, E. G. Davies b Hearne 6
Extras b 2
Total 79
Bowling
Hearne 36 overs 45 runs 7 wickets, Nixon 23-20-2, Teape 13-12-1

MCC Second Innings
Total 28 for one

The County Set

The current Middlesex County Cricket Club came into being on 2 February 1864 after a meeting at the London Tavern in Bishopsgate in the city. Brothers John and Teddy Walker were appointed joint captains of the club. That summer, the county played against MCC at Lord's for the first time.

'Middlesex took possession of the wickets but they did not keep them long,' reported *The Times*. They were bowled out in an hour, as James Grundy and George Wootton tore through their batting. Middlesex were all out for 20. Grundy top scored with 33 when MCC batted. Although they only totalled 113, it still represented a first innings' lead of 93. Middlesex batted again and they lost three early wickets, but Thomas Hearne and Arthur Daniel took them to 81 for three by the close. The following day, they took their fourth wicket stand to 87. Of the remaining batsmen, only Ted Pooley and Isaac Walker reached double figures and although the Middlesex total was a great improvement on their first innings, MCC required only 62 for victory.

25/26 July 1864
MCC beat Middlesex by five wickets

MIDDLESEX First Innings
W. Nicholson b Grundy 0, T. Hearn b Wootton 1, A. J. A. Wilkinson c Biddulph b Grundy 1, A. W. T. Daniel c Hone b Wootton 4, R. D. Walker c Wootton b Grundy 0, W. H. Bentall c&b Wootton 0, E. W. Tritton b Wootton 4, V. E. Walker c Sutton b Grundy 1, I. D. Walker c&b Grundy 7, E. W. Pooley c&b Wootton 0, W. Catling not out 0
Extras lbw 2
Total 20

MIDDLESEX Second Innings
154

MCC
113 and 63 for five

Although MCC were keen for Middlesex to take up residence, the county club played most of their early matches in Islington – an echo of the history of the White Conduit Club almost a century before. By 1868, though, they had fallen out with the landlord and turned down an offer from MCC to make Lord's their home. The future of the club looked in doubt. Lillywhite's *Cricketers' Companion* described them as 'homeless and houseless'.

The first county match played by the current Middlesex club was at Lord's in 1869 against Surrey, but they subsequently moved to Lillie Bridge and then Princes Club in Kensington. In 1876, a further disagreement with the proprietors at Princes left Middlesex without a home. MCC were struggling to make Lord's pay and were still keen to have Middlesex as tenants. Secretary Henry Perkins had written to the club's annual general meeting. The Middlesex captain, I. D. Walker, had been doubtful that such a move was financially wise, but eventually he had to give way to those who wanted to move.

It was agreed that Middlesex would play four matches at Lord's in 1877, and would pay all expenses but would also keep the gate receipts.

FROM RAMBLERS TO CROSS ARROWS

As MCC courted Middlesex, those who worked at Lord's on a daily basis also set up a club. There had been teams raised in the early days of the ground. In 1794, Thomas Lord played for the Thursday Club against the Kennington Wednesday Club. In the late 1860s, a more formal team was established. They called themselves St John's Wood Ramblers.

The early years were recorded by William H. Slatter in his memoir *Recollections of Lord's and the Marylebone Cricket*, published in 1914.

'About 1868 we commenced to play at the end of the season what were called ground boys matches often playing a club composed of all men and rarely being on the losing side,' he said. 'The chief promoter and supporter of the club was George Lambert. He was a good cricketer hitting hard on the leg side as most tennis players can.'

The earliest official scorebooks have not survived, but some details were recorded in newspaper accounts.

13 September 1877
(Actual result not recorded)

GREVILLE Innings
W. Heywood b W. Slatter 48, W. Rice c S. Slatter b Hyslop 13, H. Hardy st S. Slatter b Thompson 25, P. Lee not out 31, W. Cusack st S Slatter b Thompson 7, M. Hewitt b Rylott 1, N. Bearte c&b Thompson 0, Reynolds st Slatter b Thompson 3 , H. Cole b Rylott 0 , C. Bedding c Slatter b Thompson 1 , E. Keen b Thompson 2
Extras 8
Total 144

ST JOHN'S WOOD RAMBLERS
H. H. Hyslop c Cusack b Heywood 57, S. Slatter run out 63, Maj. Thompson (?), Dr Gaye c Lee b Heywood 5, W. Tidy lbw b Heywood 17, W. Slatter b Hardy 6, Rylott not out 4, E. Brindley run out 0
Total 152
Did not bat: W. Pearce, Savage and Dark

Fixtures in future seasons included a match against MCC.

In 1880, the Ramblers changed their name to Cross Arrows. Legend has it that before a match at Northwood, someone asked for directions and was told 'it's 'cross 'arrow way'. The origins of the new club were set down by long-time Lord's employee Dick Gaby at the time of the club's centenary in 1880. His account was based on the recollections of his father, known as 'Old Dick', who had been in at the start of the new club.

The First County Cup

Throughout the decade, MCC continued to try and find new ways to develop cricket and, by extension, greater use of their ground.

They proposed the first knockout County Championship ,'with a view to promoting county cricket and bringing counties into contact which might otherwise not have had the opportunity of competing with each other'.

The club minutes of 24 January 1873 record that they had received 'favourable answers from the counties of Notts, Sussex, Middlesex and Kent in respect of the proposed County championship matches at Lord's'.

They were still waiting for an answer from Yorkshire and Lancashire.

Surrey did not support the enterprise, which might have come as a surprise as their secretary was none other than Charles Alcock. He was also secretary to the Football Association (FA) and had been the prime mover behind the establishment of the FA Cup, which began as a challenge competition in 1871/72. Alcock was wary of a similar competition in cricket as a he felt it might be a vehicle for professionals to dominate the game.

The competition was to be staged in its entirety at Lord's, but enthusiasm had cooled before the first match was played. The MCC abandoned the concept before it had even begun. One match was played, however; a meeting between Sussex and Kent.

It did not receive a great deal of prominence in the news, perhaps because W. G. was in action across town at the Oval. *The Times* reported that 'the scoring was small and the attendance to witness it by no means large'.

James Lillywhite and Richard Fillery both returned five-wicket hauls as Kent were bowled out for 122. The runs came at only two an over, but it looked a considerably better effort when Sussex were bowled out for 45. Only Fillery made double figures. George Coles was singled out for special praise by *The Times*, who described him 'as very destructive'.

When Kent went in again on the first day, they found batting conditions had not improved. Lord Harris made only 4 and only Henry Croxford and Fillery reached double figures in a total of 75. Lillywhite took six wickets this time to take his match haul to 11.

There was still time for Sussex to begin their second innings. To win, they needed the highest score of the match but although they lost Walter Humphries, his older brother George was still there at the end of the day as Sussex closed on 37 for one.

The Lord's wicket was described by some as dangerous. *The Times* reported, 'Several of the players received ugly blows in consequence of the unsatisfactory state of the ground between wickets.'

On the second day, Coles was just as hostile as he had been in the first innings. Humphries resumed at 23 not out, but added only nine more before he was forced to retire hurt. Most of the other batsmen were, as the correspondent described it, 'touched up' by the bowling.

Sussex lost their last eight wickets for only 37 runs to give Kent victory.

CRICKETERS FROM AUSTRALIA ABORIGINALS AND 'THE DEMON CRICKETER'

The first visitors from Australia to play at Lord's were not even considered an official team. Though they were led by Charles Lawrence, an Englishman who had settled in Australia, the rest of their number was drawn from the Aboriginal peoples. As such, they did not enjoy any social standing in Australian life.

When the party set out for England from Sydney on the wool ship *Parramatta* in late February 1868, they did not even have a definite date to play at Lord's. One March day at a meeting in the pavilion, the matter was considered by the grandees of the MCC committee. They had received a letter, sent on March 24 from Messrs Kingston and Hayman, who were 'agents for a company of Australians (aborigines) who are coming to this country'.

The letter asked for 'a cricket match on May 20th, and on the following day an exhibition of spear throwing, javelin, boomerang and jumping'. The response it received was all too predictable: 'The committee decided the proposal be kindly declined as it was of the opinion that the exhibition was not suited for Lord's ground.'

In May, the Australian party docked at Gravesend in Kent, and within a day they had 'exhibited their cricketing prowess' in a match. Their arrival generated great curiosity and not altogether sensitive reporting. 'They are the first Australian natives who have visited this country on such a novel expedition', reported *Sporting Life*. 'They are perfectly civilized.'

Although MCC had rejected the idea of a match back in March, it was a different story now that the tourists were actually here and attracting large crowds. The committee realised they could not afford to be quite so high-handed. On May 18, they agreed to a proposal to W. H. James to invite the Aboriginals to play at Lord's.

This was agreed and a sub-committee was formed to organise matters, comprising James himself, Spencer Ponsonby and MCC secretary Bob Fitzgerald. There was one condition imposed on the tourists before the match went ahead. It was stipulated that 'no exhibition except the cricket match shall take place on the ground'.

The date set was a few weeks later than had originally been hoped. This worked in favour of the Aboriginals.

'It was to be expected that after a sea voyage of many thousands of miles, they should want some rehearsal,' said *Bell's Life in London, and Sporting Chronicle*. The English conditions were another matter: 'The clear air and brilliant sky of Australia are very unlike the vapoury atmosphere and cloudy heavens of our own clime. The Aborigines assert that when they commenced playing here, the effect of the light was so peculiar that they saw two balls instead of one, yet they are almost teetotallers.'

By the time the team reached Lord's, they had sampled some of the delights of an English summer and had even watched the Derby at Epsom. More importantly, they were now much more accustomed to English conditions.

While in England, each man played under a soubriquet rather than their given names, which were considered too difficult for English ears. They also wore a different coloured sash for identification.

Ten of them eventually played at Lord's under the leadership of Lawrence:Jungunjinanuke (Dick-a-Dick), yellow; Arrahmunijarrimun (Peter), green; Unaarrimin (Mullagh), dark blue; Zellanach (Cuzens), white; Bripumyarrmiin (King Cole), magenta; Boninbarngeet (Tiger), pink; Bullchanach (Bullocky), maroon; Brimbunyah (Red Cap), black; Murrumgunarriman (Twopenny), drab; Pripumuarraman (Charley Dumas), brown.

MCC batted first and were dismissed for 164.

When the Australians batted, Charles Buller struck early for MCC, but Mullagh's batting was impressive. The *Sporting Life* correspondent wrote about his performance on the first day; it was 'an innings played in capital style, while Lawrence made 31 in good form'. At the close of play, they were 152 for seven, with Mullagh's contribution an unbeaten 57. The following morning, he took his score to 75 as the Aboriginals reached 185.

'We hear that Cuzens and Mullagh show considerable talent and precision in bowling but to use a homely phrase, the proof of the pudding will be in the eating,' wrote the *Sporting Life* correspondent prophetically, at the outset of the tour. The second MCC innings dispelled any doubts about the ability of the tourists in the field.

Both men bowled impressively as MCC were dismissed for 121. Although Cuzens did bowl three wides, he also took six wickets for 65 in 25 overs. Mullagh's 16.1 overs included six maidens and he returned 3 for 19 from a supremely economic spell.

The tourists' first-choice wicketkeeper Bullocky (Bullchanach) was capable of throwing a cricket ball 106 yards. But when his side batted a second time, he was absent for reasons that have never become clear, so the Australians were one short chasing their modest victory target. They had previously proved susceptible to slow bowling. Buller and Thomas Smyth Abraham proved too much for them. Lawrence had strained his leg and needed a runner. Cuzens was chosen to run for him, but he was out of his ground when a sharp return came in from Harvey Fellows and Lawrence was gone for a single. The tourists were all out for 45.

12/13 June 1868
MCC beat the Australian Aboriginals by 55 runs

MCC First Innings
Earl of Coventry b Mullagh 25, N. C. Allix b Mullagh 20, C. Gee b Mullagh 5, C. F. Buller b Mullagh 14, Lt. Col. F. H. Hervey Bathurst b Cuzens 0, R. A. Fitzgerald b Cuzens 50, H. W. Fellows run out 8, Capt. Trevor b Cuzens 10, A. W. Fitzgerald b Mullagh 6, Viscount Down b Cuzens 10, T. Smyth-Abraham not out 3
Extras b 12, lb 3
Total 164
Bowling
Mullagh 43-13-82-5, Cuzens 34.2-15.5-2-4, Lawrence 8-3-15-0

AUSTRALIANS First Innings
Bullocky b Butler 11, Tiger b Smith 0, Cuzens b Buller 0, Redcap b Buller 13, Mullagh b Buller 75, C. Lawrence b Fellows 31, King Cole run out 7, Dick-a-Dick c&b Buller 8, Twopenny b Buller 6, Peter b Smyth 3, C. Dumas not out 0
Extras b 18, lb 3, nb 3, w 7
Total 185

MCC Second Innings

Earl of Coventry b Cuzens 14, N. C. Allix run out 12, C. Gee b Mullagh 12, C. F. Buller c Peter b Mullagh 23, Lt. Col. F. H. Hervey-Bathurst b Cuzens 0, R. A. Fitzgerald b Cuzens 3, H. W. Fellows b Cuzens 1, F. G. B. Trevor b Cuzens 18, A. W. Fitzgerald b Cuzens 16, Viscount Downs not out 9, T. Smyth Abraham b Mullagh 0

Extras b 8, lb 1, nb 1, w 3

Total 121

Bowling

Cuzens 25-5-65-6, Mullagh 16.1-6-19-3, Red Cap 8-0-24-0

AUSTRALIANS Second Innings

Tiger b Abraham 0, J. Cuzens c Hervey-Bathhurst b Abraham 21, Red Cap c Allix b Buller 3, Mullagh c Downs b Buller 12, C. Lawrence run out 1, King Cole b Abraham 0, Dick-a-Dick b Buller 0, Twopenny b Abraham 3, Peter c Trevor b Abraham 0, C. Dumas not out 0

Extras b 1, lb 1, w 1

Total 45

Bullocky absent

Bowling

Abraham 18.3-16-5, Buller 18-26-3

Umpires: Grundy and Farrands

The match was over but not the entertainment. The Australians 'amused the spectators by throwing the boomerang, spears & c and Lawrence exhibited his bat and ball feat, the cleverness of which elicited loud applause'. Lawrence was presented with a bat for his display. The skills displayed by the Aboriginals clearly fascinated the newspapermen:

> The Boomerang claims more notice at our hands, being a novel performance to most English spectators. The motions of the boomerang are so erratic that one can hardly imagine how it can ever be useful in either warfare or the chase.

The other party piece was carried out by Dick-a-Dick, who would dodge cricket balls 'armed only with a long narrow shield shaped like a canoe and with a strangely formed club.'.

A few days later, the Hon. C. Carnegie drew the attention of the committee to what he called 'the boomerang performance.' This, he complained, 'had taken place in violation of the committee's rule'. The committee had bowed to the inevitable and the treasurer admitted 'the performance seemed to give general sat.isfaction and that the public would have been much disappointed if it had not taken place' Edward Chandos Leigh responded that 'it was distinctly understood when the question was discussed that in the event of the match terminating early there should be a performance'.

At all events, the very fact that the Aboriginal team had played at Lord's lent credibility to the whole enterprise. The management were so inundated with requests to play that by the time they returned home, they had played forty-seven matches.

The match at Lord's had a tragic postscript. King Cole contracted pneumonia and died shortly afterwards.

It was over a century before a team of Aboriginal cricketers returned to England. In 1988, a team played in commemoration of the original tour. In 2001, the former

Australian Test player Ashley Mallett brought a party of young Aboriginals and Torres Strait Islanders to Britain. Although this last team did not play at Lord's, it included batsman Barry Firebrace, who was delighted to trace his own ancestry back to the family of Johnny Cuzens, a star performer on the 1868 tour.

The first official Australian touring team came to England in the summer of 1878, and although their programme did not include a Test match, MCC were determined to welcome them in style.

'It was proposed by the Honourable Frederick Ponsonby and seconded by Captain Slaney and carried unanimously that a dinner be given to the Australian team and the eleven who represented the MCC.' The Australians had endured a long sea voyage to reach England and lost their opening match.

Five days later, they arrived at Lord's to play against MCC. It was only the second match of their tour, but this was an encounter that would define their whole summer.

Heavy rain had made the ground 'very dead.'

Play on the first day began at three minutes after noon. Dr W. G. Grace strode out to open the batting with Lancashire's A. N. Hornby. The crowd was horrified when Grace was out to only the second ball of the match, caught by Billy Midwinter off the bowling of Frank Allan. From 4 for one, and it rapidly got worse. Only Hornby reached double figures. He made 19, but six others were dismissed for a duck. The damage was done by Frederick Spofforth, a fast bowler from the Sydney suburb of Balmain. He took six wickets for 4 runs and, incredibly, the cream of MCC batting was blown away for 33.

When Australia batted, Alfred Shaw of Nottinghamshire proved to be almost as irresistible. Only Billy Midwinter got into double figures. Shaw's five victims included Australian skipper, David Gregory, out for a duck. The Australians were all out for 41.

There was no respite from the onslaught and Spofforth was once again the star. Grace was out for a duck and Alexander Webbe followed shortly afterwards. This time, the innings was all over in only fifty-five minutes. 'The decisive victory of the Australians was earnestly applauded by the members of MCC and tumultuously so by the thousands of other Englishmen present,' said Wisden in the report.

As the afternoon progressed, the spectators continued to flock into the ground. The MCC were eventually able to hand over £119 7s in gate receipts to the Australians.

The Australian victory was completed by 6.20 p.m., which left plenty of time for the tourists to dress for the dinner held in their honour, given by MCC president Lord Fitzhardinge. Although 'no particulars' were available according to Wisden, the room must have been buzzing with talk of the performance of Spofforth.

The Victorians delighted in theatrical villains and, with his moustache, Spofforth certainly looked the part. They christened him 'The Demon Bowler'. It was a name that stuck. When he later revealed the secrets of his success, his words were probably of little consolation to the men he had bowled out: 'I never practice, I seldom play in Australia and when I come over here I am seldom much good until the fourth match,' he said. 'By that time, I have got my muscles in trim and my eye in good order.'

A poem appeared in the satirical magazine *Punch*:

The Australians came down like a wolf on a fold
The Marylebone 'cracks' for a trifle were bowled,
Our Grace, before dinner, was very soon done,
And our Grace after dinner did not get a run.

W. G. later reflected on the match:

> The wicket was as bad as it could be and small scoring was expected but no one dreamt for a moment that in the Australian eleven there were two bowlers with the powers which Messrs Spofforth and Boyle possessed.

Unsurprisingly, the defeat was discussed at the MCC meeting on 3 June. The grandees were far from pleased. 'It was resolved to play the Australians in a second match on July 22.'

When they convened again the following month, the secretary informed the committee that it had proved impossible to raise a side on that date 'owing to the numerous county and other fixtures'. Cambridge University came forward and offered to play the Australians at Lord's. The committee agreed and Philip Morton took twelve wickets in the match as the light blues won by an innings and 72 runs.

27 May 1878
Australians beat MCC by nine wickets

MCC First Innings
W. G. Grace c Midwinter b Allan 4, A. N. Hornby b Spofforth 19, C. Booth b Boyle 0, A. W. Ridley c A. Bannerman b Boyle 7, A. J. Webbe b Spofforth 1, F. Wyld b Boyle 0, W. Flowers c&b Spofforth 0, G. G. Hearne b Spofforth 0, A. Shaw st Murdoch b Spofforth 0, G. F. Vernon st Murdoch b Spofforth 0, F. Morley not out 1
Extras lb 1
Total 33
Bowling
Boyle 14-7-14-3, Spofforth 5.3-3-4-6, Allan 9-4-14-1

AUSTRALIANS First Innings
C. Bannerman c Hearne b Morley 0, W. Midwinter c Wyld b Shaw 10, T. Horan c Grace b Morley 4, A. C. Bannerman c Booth b Morley 0, T. W. Garrett c Ridley b Morley 6, F. R. Spofforth b Shaw 1, D. W. Gregory b Shaw 0, H. F. Boyle c Wylde b Morley 2, W. L. Murdoch b Shaw 9, F. E. Allan c&b Shaw 6, G. H. Bailey not out 3
Total 41
Bowling
Shaw 33.2-25-10-5, Morley 33-19-31-5

MCC Second Innings
W. G. Grace b Spofforth 0, A. N. Hornby b Boyle 1, C. Booth b Boyle 0, A. W. Ridley b Boyle 0, A. J. Webbe b Spofforth 0, F Wyld b Boyle 5, W. Flowers b Boyle 11, G. G. Hearne b Spofforth 0, A. Shaw not out 2, G. F. Vernon b Spofforth 0, F. Morley c Horan b Boyle 0
Total 19
Bowling
Boyle 8.1-6-3-6, Spofforth 9-2-16-4

AUSTRALIANS Second Innings
C. Bannerman b Shaw 1, W. Midwinter not out 4, T. Horan not out 7
Total 12 for one

DIAMONDS, STARS AND STRIPES

English cricketers had made their first transatlantic tour in 1859, but in the decade that followed, America had been plunged into civil war. It had consequences for the game of cricket, which lost momentum to another bat and ball game.

A decade later, contact was renewed, but cricketers soon discovered that 'baseball has grown to be in the United States what cricket is in the old country'.

In 1874, Boston Red Sox team manager Harry Wright had sent his star pitcher, Albert Spalding, as an 'avant-courier' to England on a mission. His aim was to encourage interest in a tour of baseball players.

'The reception and encouragement he met with led him on his return to report favourably,' noted *The New York Times*.

The Tour was on!

The tour party was as follows, from the Boston Red Stockings came James White (catcher), Albert Spalding (pitcher), Jim O'Rourke (first base), Ross Barnes (second base), Harry Schafer (third base), George Wright (short stop), Andy Leonard (left field), Harry Wright (centre field), Cal McVey (right field), George Hall (substitute), Thomas Beals (substitute), and Sam Wright (substitute). From the Philadelphia Athletics: John Clapp (catcher), Dick McBride (pitcher/captain), Weston Fisler (first base), Joseph Battin (second base), Ezra Sutton (third base), Mike McGeary (short stop), Albert Gedney (left field), John McMullin (centre field), Cap Anson (right field), Al Reach (substitute), J. P. Sensenderfer (substitute), and Jim Murnane (substitute).

Their arrival was keenly anticipated. *The London Telegraph* reported on the twenty-two men 'whose doings in the next six weeks may well have the result of popularising among us another scientific outdoor game'. The Americans were delighted to learn that, 'it would appear that several English cricket clubs are organising and training nines to play against our champions and an exciting time is anticipated',

The Americans were also to 'engage in games of cricket in all the prominent cities they intend to visit'. Their party included Sam Wright, 'an expert young cricketer'.

The team landed in England and demonstrated their own sport in Liverpool and Manchester before heading to Lord's.

'The marking out of the diamond shaped ground and the subsequent play of the two sides was watched with marked interest by the audience,' noted Wisden. When play got under way, the great record of cricket suggested that 'the spectators were witnessing a modernised, manly and unquestionably improved demonstration of that old game of their boyhood – rounders'.

The match lasted for 2 hours 10 minutes. Spalding, Leonard, O'Rourke and George Wright hit home runs for the the Red Stockings. The progress of each inning was recorded in the *New York Clipper*.

ATHLETICS 3-0-0-0-1-1-1-0-1 *Total* 7
BOSTON 3-7-4-0-5-0-5-0-0 *Total* 24

Umpire: Thomas Beals

When the combined baseball teams played cricket, the bases were certainly loaded in their favour. They were allowed to play eighteen men against the eleven cricketers of MCC. They had the same advantage in all their matches.

3/4 August 1874
Match drawn

MCC
C. E. Boyle b McBride o, A. Lubbock b W. H. Wright 24, J. Round b McBride o, A. C. Lucas c Schafer b McBride 12, G. Bird c McVey b W. H. Wright 15, V. E. Walker b W. H. Wright 27, A. W. Anstruther c Batten b G. Wright o, F. P. U. Pickering b W. H. Wright 9, E. Lubbock b G. Wright o, R. A. Fitzgerald c Hall b G. Wright 4, W. M. Rose b G. Wright o, A. Appleby not out o
Extras b 9, lb 3, w 2
Total 105
Bowling
W. H. Wright 51 overs 43 runs four wickets, McBride 37-34-3, Wright 16-14-4

BASEBALLERS XVIII
W. H. Wright b Rose 2, J. D. McBride b Rose 5, A. G. Spalding b Appleby 23, W. Anson b Rose 2, R. C. Barnes b Pickering 5, G. Wright b Rose 12, E. B. Sutton b Pickering 3, W. Fisler run out 3, A. J. Leonard b Rose 13, S. Wright c A. Lubbock v Anstruther o, C. A. McVey b Pickering 10, J. H. O'Rourke b E. Lubbock 4, J. P. J. Sensenderfer b Pickering o, T. Batten c Appleby b Pickering 4, J. McMullen b Pickering 5, G. W. Hall c Round b Pickering 5, H. G. Schafer c A. Lubbock b Pickering 5, G. Beales not out 1
Extras b 2, lb 2, w 1
Total 107
Bowling
Rose 12-35-5, Appleby 15-26-1, Pickering 15.3-28-8, Anstruther 1-4-1, Lubbock 7-9-0

Umpires: F. H. Farrands and W. Price

Ten years after the 'baseballers' had visited Lord's, another American team set sail for England. The difference was that this group were cricketers first and last. They were called the Philadelphians and all the players were amateurs. MCC secretary Henry Perkins helped draw up their itinerary and they came via Ireland and Scotland.

'Nothing but the cricketing trip of our men is talked of in athletic circles in our city. It promises to be a great success in every way, and from a social sporting point of view the tour has never had its equal,' said one prominent Philadelphian cricketer.

The schedule did not help them prepare for the biggest match of the whole trip against MCC. The team travelled down from Yorkshire over the weekend after their match against

Scarborough, so spending almost the entire first day in the field was not ideal. Charles Studd scored a century for MCC, who totalled 408 by 6.10 p.m. on the first day.

The following day, they were all out 174. The first innings had lasted little more than 1 hour 40 minutes. Poor Scott was out for duck when they followed on and his teammates had no answer to the bowling of Maude and Hugh Rotherham in the second innings. Shortly after four o'clock, they were all out for 61 and MCC had won by an innings.

16/17 June 1884
MCC beat the Philadelphians by an innings and 171 runs

MCC First Innings
A. J. Webbe b Brewster 50, I. D. Walker c Stoever b Brewster 19, C. T. Studd c Scott b Thayer 106, V. Wilson c Clarke b Brewster 15, G. F. Vernon b Lowry 29, R. Miller b Thayer 0, J. S. Russel b Lowry 51, F. W. Maude c Brockie b Lowry 51, F. T. Welman b Clarke 0, H. Rotherham not out 5, A. G. Courage b Lowry 0
Extras b 11, lb 7, w 2
Total 408
Bowling
Law 19-10-36-0, Brewster 58-25-95-3, Stoever 31-11-56-0, Lowry 21.2-4-75-4, Fox 22-9-26-0, Thayer 27-5-66-2, Clark 19-6-32-1

PHILADELPHIANS First Innings
J. A. Scott c Vernon b Studd 44, H. Brown b Rotherham 0, J. B. Thayer b Studd 35, R. S. Newhall c Miller b Courage 5, D. P. Stoever c&b Studd 8, W. Brockie st Welman b Rotherham 17, E. W. Clark b Rotherham 6, J. M. Fox c Rotherham b Studd 8, F. E. Brewster c&b Studd 2, S. Law b Studd 37, W. C. Lowry not out 5
Extras b 5, lb 2
Total 174
Bowling
Studd 50-23-78-6, Rotherham 24-14-37-3, Courage 16-8-28-1, Maude 9-2-24-0

PHILADELPHIANS Second Innings
J. A. Scott b Maude 6, H. Brown b Rotherham 0, J. B. Thayer b Maude 0, R. S. Newhall b Maude 20, D. P. Stoever not out 4, W. Brockie c Russel b Maude 6, E. W. Clark b Rotherham 0, J. M. Fox c Rotherham b Maude 5, F. E. Brewster b Rotherham 8, S. Law b Rotherham 12, W. C. Lowry b Rotherham 0
Total 61
Bowling
Rotherham 22.3-12-26-5, Maude 23-11-35-5

Umpires: F. H. Farrands and W. Price

CANADA

A DESERTER AND THE OTHER W. G.

When the Gentlemen of Canada made their first tour of England in 1880, their captain hid a dark secret from his teammates. His name was Thomas Jordon and he was the outstanding cricketer in the party, but a week before the team were due to play their big match against MCC at Lord's, his secret was revealed. As he walked off the field at Leicester, he was arrested for desertion from the British Army.

'Montreal's cricketers were somewhat mystified, as the name was not to be found on the list of Canadian adepts in the use of the willow,' reported *The Montreal Witness* on 7 June. The mystery was unravelled when Jordon's real identity was revealed. He was in fact Thomas Dale, 'the brilliant professional cricketer' who played for the Peninsular Club in Detroit. He had been born in Yorkshire and served in the Royal Horse Guards. When he was posted overseas, he had deserted from the army. His adventures in the following months were the stuff of Victorian penny dreadful magazines. He made his way to St Louis where he joined the mounted police. He clearly did not lack confidence, for he was even reported as spending a year as a professional with the British Officers team in Halifax Nova Scotia. He seems to have married in Toledo, Ohio. He then settled in Detroit, where he lived in the keeper's house at the club grounds on Woodward's Avenue. By now perhaps a little complacent, he sailed with the Canadian team to England and had taken four Leicestershire wickets in the match before his arrest.

He was hauled before a court martial and sentenced to thirty-six days in prison. As he was being taken away to begin his sentence, he made an attempt at escape. This proved ill-advised, for he was soon recaptured and taken before another court. His sentence was now increased to 336 days and his tour of England was over.

'Poor Tom Dale!' remarked those who knew him, as the painful intelligence spread from mouth to mouth this morning. His days as a cricketer are ended. How could he have been so very reckless?,' wondered *The Montreal Witness*.

An anonymous letter appeared in *The Times* from one who signed himself an 'Old Cricketer': 'Permit me to state that not one of their number had any notion that Jordan was a deserter,' he said, claiming to write with the authority of the secretary of the Canadian team.

The delicious scandal of the matter remained a cause for excitement throughout the summer. Different versions of the story emerged. 'Thomas Dale owes his misfortune to too much matrimony,' said the *Oamaru Mail* in New Zealand and related that he had left his wife in England, then married again when he arrived the United States.

It appears that he divorced his new wife, too. It was rumoured that she had alerted the British authorities and brought about his arrest.

The detention of their star player had a devastating effect on the team. In the build up to the big showpiece at Lord's, they were supposed to play in Swansea and Cardiff, but both these matches were cancelled.

The date of the match at Lord's coincided with the Gold Cup at Ascot, so the crowd was small. This was in keeping with the pattern of the tour, where gate receipts did not cover expenses. Fifteen Canadians took on the MCC XI, who outclassed their visitors.

The home side batted first. Opener Isaac Walker launched into a huge hit off James Gillean, which landed on the pavilion roof. The MCC totalled 192 and were all out at 3.35 p.m. When the Canadians batted, they were overwhelmed. Fred Morley of Nottinghamshire took a hat-trick in the first innings and finished with the figures of 8 for ten. The tourists were all out for 33, and in the second they struggled once again. This time, it was Morley's county teammate Alfred Shaw who did the damage – another hat-trick as part of an astonishing analysis of 10 for 19. The whole sorry business was completed in a further 2 hours 10 minutes. Wisden's verdict was withering:

> If fifty Canadians of the calibre of this fifteen had been brought into the field it is possible even probable that MCC would still have been victorious, so miserable was the display made by the visitors. There was absolutely nothing either in the batting, bowling or fielding of the visitors calling for praise.

The Old Cricketer did not agree. He said,

> The Canadian cricketers have had much to contend against. They are accustomed to hard wicket and good light. They have had to play on soft ground and the light at Lord's on Thursday was literally darkness ... The old country should not despise the efforts of our fellow subjects who without training have made cricket a national game across the Atlantic. Encourage them in their uphill and plucky enterprise.

10 June 1880
MCC beat Gentlemen of Canada XV by an innings and 123 runs.

MCC First Innings
C. I. Thornton c Miller b Henry 22, I. D. Walker c Howard b Gillean 35, C. E. Green b Henry 0, G. Ulyett c Treloar b Gillean 30, M. P. Lucas c Hibberd b Kearney 6, G. F. Vernon c Dewhurst b Henry 27, W. Barnes b Gillean 8, E. F. S. Tylecote lbw b Henry 18, C. J. Lucas c Phillips b Gillean 9, A. Shaw not out 11, F. Morley run out 21
Extras 5
Total 192
Bowling
Henry 33-9-84-4, Gillean 41.3-16 81-4, Kearney 9-1-22-1

GENTLEMEN OF CANADA XV First Innings
J. S. Howard c Tylecote b Morley 4, T. H. Hodgson st Tylecote b Morley 6, T. D. Phillips c Ulyett b Morley 2, J. L. Hardman b Shaw 0, W. Pinkney c C. J. Lucas b Morley 0, F. Henry c Thornton b Shaw 0, J. Dewhurst C. J. Lucas b Shaw 3, A. H. Lemmon c&b Morley 0, J. Smith b Morley 0, R. W. Hibbard c M. P. Lucas b Morley 0, G. F. Hall st Tylecote b Shaw 13, A. S. Treloar b Morley 0, H. Miller not out 3, J. S. Gillean b Shaw 0, E. Kearney absent hurt
Extras 2
Total 33

Bowling
Shaw 21.3-14-21-5, Morley 21-16-10-8

GENTLEMEN OF CANADA XV Second Innings
J. S. Howard c Ulyett b Shaw 8, T. H. Hodgson b Shaw 0, T. D. Phillips b Barnes
0, J. L. Hardman c substitute b Shaw 0, W. Pinkney b Shaw 0, F. Henry c sub b
Shaw 5, J. Dewhurst c&b Shaw 0, A. H. Lemmon not out 14, J. Smith b Shaw 0,
R. W. Hibbard c Tylecote b Shaw 0, G. F. Hall c Walker b Barnes 6, A. S. Treloar b
Shaw 0, H. Miller b Barnes 1, J. S. Gillean c C. J. Lucas b Shaw 0
Extras 1
Total 36
E. Kearney absent hurt
Bowling
Shaw 16-7-19-10, Barnes 15-6-16-3

Umpires: F. Randon and F. Wylde

Three years later, another Canadian team came to Lord's. They were led by a man called
W. G. He was five years older than Grace and his name was William George Beers. His
sport was lacrosse. Like the English W. G., William George Beers had a career in medicine,
but his speciality was dentistry.

The wide space Lord's offered lent itself to this sport. *The Illustrated London News*
reported that it was also exhibited at Lord's in 1867, and played before Queen Victoria, who
was suitably impressed. The fullest account of actual matches of the sport is from 1883.

Beers had written about the sport that he loved in 1869 in *Lacrosse: the National Game
of Canada*. In it he quoted an article from an 1862 edition of *Chambers* magazine.

'It is more varied, more ingenious, more subtle than cricket and it can be played in all
seasons of the year without danger, expense or preparation. I hold that cricket cannot
hold a candle to Lacrosse.'

On Saturday 2 June 1883, Beers and his party were at Lord's to give what *The Times*
described as 'a brilliant exhibition of the national game of Canada'.

Beers himself skippered a team of Canadian amateurs who wore dark blue jerseys,
decorated with the maple leaf. The Iroquois Indians who opposed them were dressed in
bright scarlet, they were led by Scattered Branches', or Big John. The goals were pitched in
the north-east and south-west quarters of the ground, 135 yards apart.

The demonstration lasted two hours and consisted of some eleven games in that time.
Nine were won by the Canadian Amateurs and two by the Indians 'who despite many
instances of good individual play did not appear to be so well together as their adversaries'.

Although cricket remained supreme, Lacrosse did have a foothold at Lord's and was
played on the ground up until the 1950s. Queen Mary once visited the ground to watch
a match.

THE FIRST LORD'S TEST MATCH

The rivalry between England and Australia was by now well established. At this time, the Australians toured England every two years. In November 1883, MCC's committee scheduled the first test match at Lord's for the following summer. 'The terms to be offered were the whole of the gate money to Australia. The admission to be at the usual sixpence.'

The match at Lord's was to be the Second Test of the three-match series, and right from the outset, a tradition was established. 'No cricket match of the present season has been watched with greater interest than the one just concluded,' suggested *The County Gentleman*.

All of the Australian team had played international cricket, and Billy Midwinter and Jack Blackham had both taken part in the first Test match in Melbourne 1877.

Australia batted first and struggled until Henry Scott and Harry Boyle put on 69 for the last wicket. Scott was eventually caught by his own captain, Billy Murdoch, fielding as substitute fielder for W. G. Grace, who had injured his finger. It is hard to imagine such a gesture being made by any captain in the present day. Scott was henceforth known as 'Tup', apparently because he made the most of sightseeing opportunities in London, and the tours by omnibus tended to cost tuppence.

When England batted, Grace was dismissed for 14. 'Mr Grace is by no means yet played out but he has already attained the rank and status of a veteran, although we trust to see him at the wicket for many years, it would be unfair to expect from him a superhuman longevity in the cricket field,' stated *The County Gentleman*. They were some way off the mark, for Grace's Test career lasted a further fourteen years.

England were struggling at 90 for three when Allan Steel went in. His 148, made out of 260 while he was at the wicket, sealed his place in history as the first Test centurion at Lord's. W. G. described it as 'a brilliant innings'. *The County Gentleman* suggested that 'it marks out A. G. Steel as the champion batsman of the future.'

When Australia batted again, George Ulyett bowled superbly, took a great catch, bowled to dismiss Bonnor and finished with 36 for seven.

England won by an innings and 5 runs, the first time any team had won a Test match by such a margin. It ushered in England's most dominant decade in Anglo-Australian cricket. For the rest of the nineteenth century, England dominated proceedings at Lord's, only losing to Australia in 1888 and 1899.

The British press asked themselves 'What was the key to England's success?' *The Country Gentleman* said:

On the whole we are disposed rather to attribute the comparative successes of the English cricketers to a more careful selection of truly representative men, who by natural fitness and acquired skill are specially qualified to cope with the peculiarities of the Antipodean game.

21–23 July 1884
England beat Australia by an innings and 5 runs

AUSTRALIA First Innings
P. S. McDonnell b Peate 0, A. C. Bannerman b Peate 12, W. L. Murdoch lbw b Peate 10, G. Giffen b Peate 63, W. E. Midwinter b Peate 3, G. J. Bonnor c Grace b Christopherson 25, J. M. Blackham run out 0, H. J. H. Scott c sub (Murdoch) b Steele 75, G. E. Palmer c Grace b Peate 7, F. R. Spofforth c Barlow b Grace 0, H. F. Boyle not out 26
Extras b 5, lb 3
Total 229
Fall of wickets 0, 25, 32, 46, 88, 93, 132, 155, 160
Bowling
Peate 40-14-85-6, Barlow 20-6-44-0, Ulyett 11-3-21-0, Christopherson 26-10-52-1, Grace 7-4-13-1, Steel 1.2-0-6-1

ENGLAND First Innings
W. G. Grace c Bonnor v Palmer 14, A. P. Lucas c Bonnot b Palmer 28, A. Shrewsbury st Blackham b Giffen 27, G. Ulyett b Palmer 32, A. G. Steel b Palmer 148, Lord Harris b Spofforth 4, R. G. Barlow c Palmer b Bonnor 38, W. W. Read b Palmer 12, A. Lyttelton b Palmer 31, E. Peate not out 8, S. Christopherson c Bonnor b Spofforth 17
Extras b 15, lb 5
Total 379
Fall of wickets 37, 56, 90, 120, 135, 233, 272, 348, 351.
Bowling
Spofforth 55.1-19-122-2, Palmer 75-26-111-6, Giffen 22-4-68-1, Boyle 11-3-16-0, Bonnor 8-1-23-1, Midwinter 13-2-29-0

AUSTRALIA Second Innings
P. S. McDonnell b Steel 20, A. C. Bannerman c&b Ulyett 27, W. L. Murdoch c Shrewsbury b Ulyett 17, G. Giffen c Peate b Ulyett 5, G. J. Bonnor c&b Ulyett 4, H. J. H. Scott not out 31, W. E. Midwinter b Ulyett 6, J. M. Blackham retired hurt 0, G. E. Palmer b Ulyett 13, F. R. Spofforth c Shrewsbury b Barlow 11, H. F. Boyle b Ulyett 10
Extras lb 1
Total 145
Fall of wickets 33, 60, 65, 73, 84, 90, 118, 133, 145
Bowling
Peate 16-4-34-0, Christopherson 8-3-17-0, Ulyett 39.1-23-36-7, Steel 10-2-26-1, Barlow 21-8-31-1

Umpires: F. H. Farrands and C. K. Pullin

FOR A GOOD CAUSE

A Jockeys' fundraising match had become a regular fixture on the calendar, but the one in 1880 was the first one to be held on the Lord's ground. The funds were to benefit the Hunt Servants' Benefit Association and the Bentinck Benevolent Fund.

Not all were delighted that the match went ahead because the Middlesex v Surrey championship match was abandoned to make space for it.

29 May 1880
Match drawn

HUNTSMEN XIII First Innings
G. Summers (Surrey Union) c&b L'Anson 4, N. Cornish (The Tynedale), L'Anson b Middleton 2, J. Bailey (The Essex) B. Middleton 1, G. Champion (The Southdown) b Jennings 19, Will Dale (The Buxton), L'Anson 0, G. Travers (The Cotswold) run out 3, G. Loader (Crawley and Horsham) b J. Cannon 3, R. Summers (Sir B. Cunard's) c Birkett b J. Cannon 6, T. Goddard (The Craven) b J. Cannon 0, Tom Firr (The Quorn) b J Cannon 0, F. Beers (Duke of Grafton's) run out 8, R. Roake (South Berkshire) c&b L'Anson 12, S. Hills (Old Surrey) not out 0
Extras b 6, w 2
Total 66
Bowling
L'Anson 17.1 overs 11 runs 3 wickets, Middleton 14-17-2, J. Cannon 9-15-4, Jennings 10-15-1

JOCKEYS First Innings
R. L'Anson c Dale b G. Summers 20, J. Cannon lbw b Bailey 7, W. G. Middleton b G. Summers 58, G. J. Cunningham b G. Summers 0, W. Birkett c Champion b Bailey 3, T. Cannon b Bailey 12, R. Shaw b Champion 15, T. McGeorge run out 12, H. Owen b Champion 0, W. Burbidge b Bailey 1, T. Jennings b Bailey 6, J. Adams not out 5, J. Goater c G Summers b Champion 0
Extras b 11, lb 1, w 1
Total 152
Bowling
Bailey 10-64-5, R. Summers 4-13-0, G. Summers 9-37-3, Goddard 2-5-0, Travers 1-9-0, Champion 4-11-3

HUNTSMEN Second Innings
G. Summers b L'Anson 17, N. Cornish c Middleton b J. Cannon 1, J. Bailey b

L'Anson, G. Champion b Middleton 9, W. Dale c Jennings b Middleton 2, G. Travers b Middleton 0, G. Loader run out 4, R. Summers run out 11, T. Goddard c Birkett b R. L'Anson 16, T. Firr c L'Anson b Cunningham 2, F. Beers not out 6, R. Roake not out 4

Extras b 3, lb 1

Total 114 for ten

Bowling

R. L'Anson 20-48-3 wickets, Middleton 11-10-3, Cunningham 7-17-0, J. Cannon 6-1-27-1, Shaw 4-6-0, Burbidge 3-2-0

Umpires: R. Daft and T. Hearne

In 1884, many of those who had taken part in the first Lord's test returned to contest a match, which would never be contemplated today. The teams were selected from players who smoked and those who did not. It was to raise money for the Cricketers' Fund Friendly Society.

The match was the brainchild of Vyall Walker. It provided a rare opportunity to see the men who had contested The Ashes in action against their teammates. Each team was to be drawn from both England and Australia.

The line-ups were slightly weaker than Walker had hoped. By mid-September, the touring party was about to leave, so star players such as James Lillywhite, Arthur Shrewsbury and Alfred Shaw were unavailable for the match.

Even so, the sides were strong. W. G. and E. M. Grace, Billy Murdoch and R. G. Barlow were part of the team of non-smokers. Those who enjoyed lighting up included Lord Harris, the big-hitting C. I. Thornton, William Gunn and 'The Old Demon' bowler himself, Fred Spofforth. The smokers did not have a reliable wicketkeeper, as James Blackham had injured his hand and so was ruled out of the match.

The match began in fine weather and 6,255 people passed through the turnstiles on the first day.

The Non-Smokers batted on winning the toss, and W. G. went out with the Australian Alick Bannerman. Initial progress was slow and W. G. gave a return catch to the Australian Eugene Palmer. The Non-Smokers lost two more early wickets and struggled at 38 for three.

Spofforth had terrorised the English batsmen in Tests, but now he came up against his countryman George Bonnor, 6 foot 6 and 17 stone. Bonnor struck 124. The reporter in *Wisden* observed that 'the manner in which he punished Spofforth was perhaps the extraordinary part of it. The great bowler had never been hit with such astonishing freedom in this country before.'

Bonnor completed his hundred with a blow over the pavilion and out of the ground. Within six years, this structure would be gone, replaced by a much bigger structure that has only once been successfully cleared in well over a hundred years.

He was fourth man out for 124, an innings in which he had struck 17 fours and a six, a thrilling exhibition of hitting.

E. M. Grace helped Barlow bring up the 200, but the Non-Smokers were soon all out for 250. The Smokers were soon in trouble and closed the first day at 25 for four. W. G. took three of the wickets, including Lord Harris for a duck. W. G. was caught by his brother E. M.

The fine weather continued and a further 5,169 spectators made their way into the ground for the second day. The Smokers started steadily but lost three wickets at 76 and things did not improve. They followed on 139 behind. Billy Gunn and C. I. Thornton added 50 for the sixth wicket, but they were still dismissed for 152. Non-Smokers opener Stanley Christopherson scored eight of the 14 runs needed before he was out, but the winning runs came at six o'clock and the fund benefited to the tune of £561 16s 6d.

15/16 September 1884
Non-Smokers beat Smokers by nine wickets

NON-SMOKERS First Innings
W. G. Grace c&b Palmer 10, A. C. Bannerman lbw b Spofforth 22, W. L. Murdoch b Palmer 4, G. J. Bonnor c Harris b Peate 124, R. G. Barlow c Giffen b Peate 39, E. M. Grace b Peate 10, H. J. H. Scott c Harris b Peate 4, T. C. O'Brien c Emmett b Peate 20, W. Wright b Peate 0, S. Christopherson not out 2, R. Pilling b Spofforth 0
Extras b 14, lb 1
Total 250
Fall of wickets 28, 34, 38, 190, 215, 223, 229, 229, 250
Bowling
Palmer 33-11-68-2, Emmett 22-10-23-0, Spoffort 36.1-14-87-2, Peate 23-10-30-6, Giffen 7-2-18-0, Thornton 6-3-9-0

SMOKERS First Innings
C. I. Thornton c Pilling b Barlow 5, P. S. McDonnell b W. G. Grace 7, G. Giffen c&b W. G. Grace 6, Lord Harris c E. M. Grace b W. G. Grace 0, W. Gunn b Christopherson 18, M. P. Bowden run out 29, G. E. Palmer run out 0, F. R. Spofforth b Christopherson 0, C. F. C. Clarke not out 20, T. Emmett c Bannerman b W. G. Grace 7, E. Peate c Pilliing b W. G. Grace 2
Extras b 9, lb 8
Total 111
Fall of wickets 8, 18, 19, 25, 76, 76, 76, 84, 107
Bowling
Barlow 35-2-34-1, W. G. Grace 34-19-29-5, Wright 14-10-5-0, Christopherson 13-6-26-2

NON-SMOKERS Second Innings 15-1

SMOKERS Second Innings
C. F. C. Clarke c Pilling b W. G. Grace 19, P. S. McDonnell b W. G. Grace 14, G. Giffen b Barlow 15, Lord Harris b Barlow 5, W. Gunn not out 43, M. P. Bowden c Wright b Barlow 0, C. I. Thornton c O'Brien b Bonnor 27, G. E. Palmer st Pilling b Wright 4, F. R. Spofforth c E. M. Grace b W. G. Grace 5, T. Emmett b Barlow 7, E. Peate c E. M. Grace b Barlow 1
Extras b 10, nb 2
Total 152
Fall of wickets 26, 45, 53, 54, 54, 106

A First Indian Summer

The Parsees were the first Indian team to visit Lord's. A tour had been planned in 1877 but the organisers became embroiled in a legal case in India and cancellation was inevitable. They tried again in 1886 and this time it was all systems go.

The organisers' trump card was to persuade Charles Alcock, secretary of Surrey County Cricket Club, to act as the agent for the touring team. Alcock had impeccable contacts and was able to help arrange an impressive tour programme. When at last the Indian party was ready to depart, it caused considerable interest throughout the cricket playing world. *The Western Australian* wrote on 22 May, 'We are accustomed to read of our Australian cousins going home and contending for first place in the noble English game of Cricket but never before has the example been followed by our friends from India.' Of course by 'home', they meant England.

The party was made up of twelve players from Bombay and three from Karrache (Karachi) in Sind province. The Parsees spent almost a month at sea on the SS *Clyde*, before reaching Plymouth. Lord Sheffield welcomed them to his estate in Sussex, but their opening match against his Lordship's team was a draw, and that was only because the rains came at an opportune time. In their first innings on English soil, the Parsees were bowled out for a paltry 46. They then travelled up to Lord's to play MCC.

Sir Pherozeshah Mehta, a leading Bombay lawyer and political figure, had said: 'As artists go to Italy to do homage to the great masters, as pilgrims go to Jerusalem to worship at a shrine, so now the Parsees are going to England to do homage to the English cricketers, to learn something of that noble and manly pastime in the very country which is its chosen home.' He might have added that the ultimate destination was Lord's. The Parsi community had been responsible for the first Indian clubs around the year 1850, and Anglophiles as they were, a trip to Lord's was seen as a wonderful honour.

The home eleven was composed entirely of amateurs. Lord Harris had been asked to play but was prevented from doing so by his parliamentary obligations.

Wisden noted that

the Marylebone Club put an altogether unnecessarily strong team into the field. It should be noted that Mr W. G. Grace played at the request of the Parsees who were anxious to have the champion on the opposing side at least once in the tour.

Whether they quite as happy once W. G. had posted 119 for the first wicket with Isaac Walker is not recorded. Grace hit two boundaries and a three in his 65.

MCC totalled 313. Top scorer William Lindsay had been born in India, and was an all-round sportsman who had been capped for England at football and had also won the FA Cup with The Wanderers.

The verdict of Wisden was that, 'from the first, it was seen that the Parsees were utterly overmatched and had not the smallest chance of success.'

When they batted, they simply could not get the MCC bowlers off the square. Having had a chance to study W. G.'s batting at close quarters, they now received a masterclass from the great man with the ball. He bowled eight maidens, and the Indian batsmen had no answer as he finished with 18 for seven. At the other end, James Robertson of Middlesex kept up the pressure. He bowled sixteen maidens and conceded only 4 runs as he took the other three wickets. Only Jal Morenas reached double figures and the Parsees were all out for 23 in their first innings. Almost inevitably, they were asked to follow on. This time it was Walker who ripped out the heart of their batting. He finished with 5 for 28 in 34 overs, of which nineteen were maidens. Grace took another four wickets as the Parsees were dismissed again for 66. *The Times* of India admitted that

The figures perhaps are not very satisfactory, but it was generous in its assessment of the team's performance. If the Marylebone team was a really strong one, the Parsees have certainly done better than was anticipated by cricket experts when they started. To have scored an average of eight runs each at Lord's is under the circumstances, a triumph for the members of the team, to whom the ground, the manner of play, the crowd the surroundings and even the country itself were new.

The tour continued for almost three months, and the final match was staged in Windsor Great Park against a team raised by Queen Victoria's grandson, at which the Indians were 'highly flattered'.

They won only one further match on their tour, but captain D. H. Patel sent a letter of thanks 'to acknowledge the many kindnesses and friendly encouragements they have received at the hands of people of this country'. Wisden's verdict was less charitable: 'From a cricket point of view, a failure.'

27/28 May 1886
MCC beat Parsees by an innings and 224 runs

MCC
313 (Lindsay 74, Grace 65)

PARSEES First Innings
P. D. Dastur c Carter b Grace 2, B. B. Baria b Grace 4, J. M. Morenas c Ross b Grace 10, M. Framjee b Robertson 3, A. C. Major b Robertson 0, D. H. Patel b Grace 0, B. P. Balla b Grace 1, S. N. Bhedwar c Ross b Grace 0, S. H. Harvar b Robertson 0, A. R. Libuwalla c Hargreaves b Grace 1, D. D. Ghambatta not out 1
Extras 1
Total 23
Bowling
Grace 18 for seven, Robertson 3 for four

PARSEES Second Innings
66 (Grace 4 for 26, Walker 5 for 28)

700 UP

In the 1880s, MCC ran up a series of huge scores against Minor County teams. In 1888, they became the first team to score over 700 in a single innings at Lord's.

This match did not have first-class status, but MCC had first use of the wicket perfect for batting. John Russel, a Scotsman, opened with Somerset batsman Edward Sainsbury. Together they gave the club a tremendous start. Russel had hit five fours and run three threes in his 54 before he was forced to retire. The first wicket did not fall until 196 and when Dudley Pontifex was out, Francis Ford joined Sainsbury in a second wicket partnership that was worth 162. He was finally stumped 9 short of his century. However, England test player Wilfred Flowers had reached 83 not out when MCC closed the first day at a monumental 514 for 2. Sainsbury was still unbeaten on 177, an innings that had included eighteen fours. No bowling figures were given in the press, perhaps to spare the blushes of the Wiltshire bowlers in the light of what *The Times* described as 'extraordinary scoring'.

There was no respite when the match resumed, even the third wicket partnership was ended when it had realised 157, though Flowers was dismissed for 88 and Sainsbury added only another 3 runs to his overnight score.

Henry Brougham, who had toured the United States with the Gentlemen of Ireland earlier in the decade, now scored 117 in an innings that included nine boundaries.

The highest total ever seen on the ground in any class of cricket was 735. Sadly, it was probably achieved in front of a smattering of spectators.

13/14 August 1888
Match drawn

MCC First Innings
J. S. Russell retired hurt 54, E. Sainsbury c Marks b Holt 180, D. D. Pontifex c Roff b Malden 54, F. G. J. Ford st Marks b Pinckney 91, W. Flowers b Malden 88, H. Brougham c Marks b Awdry 117, W. R. Collins b Pinckney 28, C. J. H. Cooper b Pinckney 25, G. H. Chandler c Roff b Malden 15, J. H. Farmer not out 8, M. Sherwin b Awdry 4
Extras b 46, lb 17, w 8
Total 735

WILTSHIRE First Innings
A. J. G. Stancomb b Ford 9, F. Marks b Ford 0, F. C. Batson b Flowers 38, W. G. Roff b Flowers 1, F. W. Stancomb b Flowers 21, A. Holt st Sherwin b Flowers 1, H. Awdry b Ford 9, H. Leaf c Sherwin b Ford 8, R. M. Poore b Flowers 16, W. P. Pinckley c Sainsbury b Ford 2, A. R. Malden not out 6

Extras b 17, lb 1, w 1
Total 130

WILTSHIRE Second Innings
A. J. Stancomb not out 22, F. W. Stancomb b Flowers 17, A. R. Malden b Flowers 3,
H. Leaf not out 12
Extras b 6
Total 60 for two

Umpires: R. O. Clayton and G. Hay

HARRY'S GAME

Harry Graham only played six times for Australia but his place in cricket history is assured for, in 1893, he became the first batsman from any country to score a hundred on his Test debut at Lord's. This was Australia's fifth Lord's Test match in eight years.

According to Wisden, England captain Andrew Stoddart 'was placed in an awkward position' when he won the toss. The wicket was damp but likely to improve later in the match. He decided to bat, and England's 334 was based on a superb stand of 137 between Arthur Shrewsbury of Nottinghamshire and the Hon. Stanley Jackson of Yorkshire, who made his Test debut. Shrewsbury batted 250 minutes for his century and was considered by many to be the finest English batsman. Wisden recorded that 'Shrewsbury's batting was marked by extreme patience, unfailing judgment, and a mastery over the difficulties of the ground, of which probably no other batsman would have been capable'. He received the ultimate accolade from W. G. Grace who, when asked which batsman he would most value, said simply 'Give me Arthur'.

Had he not been caught at the wicket off Charlie Turner, Jackson would have been the first man to score a Test debut century at Lord's. As it turned out, the distinction would be achieved by a member of the opposition.

Australia held The Ashes going into this series, but when they batted they struggled against the bowling of England debutante Bill Lockwood, who had qualified for Surrey because he was unable to command a place in his native Nottinghamshire. Lockwood dismissed Joe Lyons and George Giffen on the first evening of the match with only seven runs on the board. When the Australian innings resumed the next day, only 38 runs came in the first hour as they were reduced to 75 for five. All five wickets had fallen to Lockwood.

Now the stage was taken by a Test debutant, twenty-two-year-old Victorian Harry Graham, who seemed unconcerned as he walked to the wicket. He joined Syd Gregory, nephew of Australia's first Test captain. Together, they added 142 for the sixth wicket to change the complexion of the innings. Graham then completed his century, the first batsman from any nation to mark his Test debut with a hundred at headquarters. In all, he was only at the crease for 2 hours and 20 minutes, and his 107 included a five and twelve fours.

England had a modest lead of 65 on first innings. Another fine innings by Shrewsbury enabled Stoddart to become the first Test captain to declare an innings closed. In the event, rain called a halt to proceedings and the match was left drawn.

Graham headed the Australian averages on tour, but he only played five further Test matches after that, though he did score another century against England in 1894/95. It is a measure of his achievement that it was another seventy-six years before his achievement of scoring a hundred on debut was emulated.

'Graham's brilliant debut in English cricket was one of the most notable features of the tour,' said James Lillywhite's *Cricketers' Companion*.

17–19 July 1893
Match drawn

ENGLAND First Innings

334 (Shrewsbury 106, Jackson 91 Turner six for 67) and 234 for eight declared.

AUSTRALIA First Innings

J. J. Lyons b Lockwood 7, A. C. Bannerman c Shrewsbury b Lockwood 17, G. Giffen
b Lockwood 0, G. H. S. Trott c Magregor b Lockwood 33,S. E. Gregory c Macgregor
b Lockwood 57, H. Graham c Macgregor b Mold 107,W. Bruce c Peel b Mold 23,
C. T. B. Turner b Flowers 0, H. Trumble not out 2, J. M. Blackman not out 2
Extras b 15, lb 1
Total 269
Bowling
Lockwood 101 for six, Mold 44 for three

Umpires: W. Hearn, J. Phillips

From High Veldt and Lowlands

The Gentlemen of Holland were the first team from continental Europe to play a match at Lord's. The sport was well established in the Netherlands. English club sides had visited the lowlands and the Dutchmen had already played in Yorkshire. In 1894, a team played a series of matches against clubs in the London area and were also invited to play at Lord's.

The visitors went in first and scored, and lost wickets at a brisk pace. They were all out for 134 in 2 hours 15 minutes. A thunderstorm delayed play for two hours but if the bowlers were hoping it would liven the wicket, they were to be disappointed. A forty-seven year old clergyman, the Revd Percy Hattersley Smith led the way as MCC went from 18 for 1 to 183 in only an hour and a half by the close. Ranjitsinhji had just come in. The following morning, the pair really set about the Dutch bowling and both men went to their centuries. Ranji scored his runs even faster and 246 runs in all came on the Saturday morning by the time the declaration came.

When the Dutchmen went in again, only Solomon prospered. He went in at the fall of the first wicket and took the score from four to 100 in 1 hour and 20 minutes with 13 boundaries. None of the other batsmen had an answer to the bowling of Eton schoolmaster Charles Allcock, who finished with nine wickets in the match.

10/11 August 1894
MCC beat the Gentlemen of Holland by an innings and 169 runs

GENTLEMEN OF HOLLAND First Innings
E. A. Hoeffelman c Latham b Maude 8, J. C. Schroder c Hattersley-Smith b Allcock 18, W. R. Solomon c Latham b Allcock 18, J. E. Weiss b Maude 14, C. J. Posthuma c Allcock b Maude 11, E. G. S. Bourlier b Allcock 3, P. R. Tromp de Haas c Latham b Allcock 21, W. F. Proost b Maude 3, J. W. van den Bosch c Maude b Allcock 16, L. J. van Erp Taalman Kip b Maude 8, W. Coops not out 3
Extras b 9, lb 2
Total 134

MCC First Innings
J. S. Russel b Tromp de Haas 2, F. W. Maude c Weiss b Posthuma 45, C. H. Allcock c van den Bosch b Posthuma 47, Revd P. Hattersley-Smith b Solomon 139, K. S. Ranjitsinhji not out 137, A. M. Latham c Coops b Solomon 6, F. H. Crampton b Solomon 9, J. H. Farmer not out 10
Extras b 20, lb 8, w 6
Total 429 for six declared
Did not bat: H. D. Littlewood, D. C. Lee, E. F. Newton

GENTLEMEN OF HOLLAND Second Innings
E. A. Hoeffelman c Latham b Allcock 1, J. C. Schroder b Maude 7, W. R. Solomon b Maude 84, J. E. Weiss b Maude 0, C. J. Posthuma b Ranjitsinhji 7, E. G. S. Bourlier c Newton b Allcock 1, P. R. Tromp de Haas b Maude 7, W. F. Proost c Newton b Allcock 2, J. W. van den Bosch c Latham b Allcock 12, L. J. van Erp Taalman Kip c Ranjitsinhji b Allcock 0, W. Coops not out 2
Extras lb 2, nb 1
Total 126

'The bad luck has followed them since they began the real work of the tour, that is the matter of the weather and wickets was again in evidence,' said the leading magazine *Cricket*. The first South African tourists arrived at Lord's to be greeted by rain. It prevented even a single ball being bowled on the first day of their match against MCC.

Most had felt the MCC side would be too strong. 'At all events it was a combination which required some beating. The South Africans had to play all they knew to the very last,' said *Cricket*.

Wisden observed that 'for some inscrutable reason', W. G. Grace asked the tourists to bat when he won the toss – the *Almanack* had the benefit of hindsight. Grace had believed that the wicket might improve. It seemed as though the gamble would paid off. Grace bowled himself for much of the innings and took six wickets as the South Africans were bowled out for 126.

When MCC batted, they were in for a rude awakening. American-born Francis Bohlen opened the club innings and was out for a duck. It set the tone. Apart from W. G., who top scored with 47, none of the home batsmen really got a start. 'The credit for the cheap dismissal of MCC rested with Middleton and Rowe,' said *Cricket*.

Mead and Grace skittled the South Africans, the second time around, and MCC chased a modest target of 84 to win. Old Etonian Hylton Philipson hit 33 and, at 6.40 p.m., they were 63 for three, needing only another 21 for victory.

In the next half hour, it all went wrong for the batting side and Middleton and Rowe bowled South Africa to a memorable triumph. It came early in their tour and was 'a thoroughly well earned success which cannot fail to give increased interest to their tour'.

4 (no play), 5 July 1894
South Africans beat MCC by 11 runs

SOUTH AFRICANS First Innings
T. W. Routledge c Thornton b Mead 13, G. Cripps b Mead 0, C. L. Johnson c Thornton b Grace 0, F. Hearne st Philipson b Grace 48, C. O. H. Searle b Mead 1, E. A. Halliwell c Heseltine b Grace 1, A. W. Seccull c Chatterton b Grace 11, H. H. Castens run out 7, G. K. Glover b Grace 13, J. Middleton not out 5, G. A. Rowe c Chatterton b Grace 6
Extras b 16, lb 5
Total 126
Bowling
Mead 22-11-33-3, Grace 25-7-56-6, Chatterton 8-6-4-0, Thornton 5-2-10-0, Heseltine 3-2-2-0

MCC First Innings

W. G. Grace c Hearne b Middleton 47, F. H. Bohlen b Middleton 0, H. Philipson b Middleton 15, W. Chatterton b Middleton 0, T. C. O'Brien c Halliwell b Middleton 19, G. Thornton b Rowe 1, A. M. Sutthery not out 6, J. A. Gibbs b Rowe 0, J. S. Russel c Castens b Rowe 0, C. Heseltine b Rowe 12, W. Mead c Castens b Middleton 0

Extras b 2, lb 1

Total 103

Bowling

Middleton 20.1-5-48-6, Glover 9-2-33-0, Johnson 5-2-9-0, Rowe 6-3-10-4

SOUTH AFRICANS Second Innings

T. W. Routledge c Russel b Grace 4, G. Cripps c Philipson b Grace 3, C. L. Johnson c O'Brien b Mead 0, F. Hearne b Mead 0, C. O. H. Sewell c Philipson b Grace 17, E. A. Halliwell b Grace 21, A. W. Seccull b Grace 8, H. H. Hastens c&b Mead 5, G. K. Glover st Philipson b Mead 1, J. Middleton c Philipson b Grace 0, G. A. Rowe not out 0

Extras b 1

Total 60

Bowling

Mead 12.2-4-22-4, Grace 13-2-37-6

MCC Second Innings

W. G. Grace c Johnson b Middleton 10, F. Bohlen run out 2, H. Philipson c Hearne b Middleton 33, W. Chatterton b Rowe 1, T. C. O'Brien c Halliwell b Middleton 4, G. Thornton not out 2, A. M. Sutthery b Middleton 0, J. A. Gibbs b Rowe 0, J. S. Russel c Secull b Rowe 0, C. Heseltine st Halliwell b Middleton 20, W. Mead st Halliwell b Middleton 0

Extras 0

Total 72

Bowling

Middleton 15-3-35-6, Rowe 14-4-37-3

Umpires: F. H. Farrands and T. Mycroft

OUT OF THE GROUND

Albert Trott was a remarkable player in more ways than one. He played Test cricket for his native Australia and his adopted England, and once took two hat-tricks in a single match at Lord's. Yet he is best known for a single hit out of the ground.

This feat had been achieved in 1868 by Eton batsman Charles Thornton in the annual match against Harrow. Charles Giles had ripped through their batting. He bowled eighteen maiden overs in the innings and tied down the batsmen to such an extent that only two men made double figures. Charles Thornton and George Canning, later to become Lord Harris at least spared Eton total ignominy. The most memorable moment of Thornton's 44 was a straight drive that soared over the pavilion.

Thornton was bowled by the very next ball. Eton were all out 116. Harrow took a first innings, lead but when Eton batted again, Thornton got a rapturous reception. He began in aggressive style, his first three balls brought 11 runs, but he was dismissed within 2 overs. Eton were all out 129 and Harrow knocked off the runs by mid-afternoon.

There were other big hits at the ground, but the construction of a new pavilion by Thomas Verity in 1890 changed the game. The new structure was much taller than the building it had replaced. Built at a cost of £20,000, it was constructed on the site of the old pavilion and dominated the ground. Clearly, it was also a challenge for a mercurial talent like Trott.

He had made his Test debut at the age of only twenty-one, and seemed certain to become a Test regular for Australia. However, when the 1896 tour party to England was chosen, he was left out. Undeterred, he sailed for England independently. By the time the next Australian team came in 1899, Trott had qualified for Middlesex and was there to oppose his former countrymen.

In those days, MCC played the touring team twice. Trott was out for a duck in the first meeting and therefore had plenty to prove when the Australians returned to Lord's for a second encounter later in the summer.

Tourists struck early. MCC were 123 for four when Trott made his way to the wicket and Monty Noble was the bowler from the Pavilion End when he began his assault.

Teammate Warner recalled, 'Trott began with a sighter on to the first balcony and then came his stupendous straight drive, the ball landing in the garden of one of the houses.'

'I was not very sure about it; and the next thing I saw was the ball looking like a pea in the air, and I learned then that it had just touched a chimney and nearly gone out of the ground,' said Trott later in an interview for *Boys' Own*.

Trott was dismissed shortly afterwards for 41, and Noble exacted some measure of revenge having him caught by Darling. Trott was, however, no doubt pumped with adrenaline when the Australian reply began, for he had Jack Worrall caught by Grace before a run had been scored. At last, his bowling efforts had reaped success against Australia. They were reduced to 18 for three in their innings. His victims included the prized wicket of Victor Trumper.

A century from Joe Darling helped the Australians recover.

That winter, Trott played two Test matches for England on their tour of South Africa. He thus became one of the very few to play for Australia and England. A wonderfully talented man, he was greatly troubled and tragically took his own life.

31 July, 1/2 August 1899

MCC First Innings

W. G. Grace c Jones b Noble 3, P. F. Warner b Jones 10, C. L. Townsend c Howell b Trumble 32, K. S. Ranjitsinhji c Worrall b Jones 92, F. G. J. Ford b Jones 9, A. E. Trott c Darling b Noble 41, W. B. Stoddart run out 6, J. H. Board c Trumble b Jones 19, H. I. Young not out 25, W. Roche b Jones 3, W. Mead b Howell 1

Extras b 10, lb 7

Total 258

Fall of wickets 14, 14, 90, 123, 188, 197, 213, 243, 257

Bowling

Jones 41-7-98-5, Noble 28-10-63-2, McLeod 5-1-26-0, Howell 7.4-3-16-1, Trumble 14-3-38-1

AUSTRALIANS First Innings

J. Worrall c Grace b Trott 0, H. Trumble lbw b Trott 6, V. T. Trumper b Trott 4, S. E. Gregory run out 14, M. A. Noble c Ford b Stoddart 27, J. Darling c Board b Townsend 128, C. Hill b Mead 20, C. E. McLeod c Ford b Mead 46, E. Jones b Mead 51, W. P. Howell c Townsend b Mead 0, A. E. Johns not out 1

Extras b 10, lb 11, w 1

Total 319

Fall of wickets 0, 7, 18, 31, 86, 139, 251, 318, 318

Bowling

Young 31-12-66-0, Trott 43-13-109-3, Stoddart 10-2-30-1, Mead 17-7-31-4, Townsend 10-1-40-1, Roche 2-0-8-0, Grace 3-0-13-0

MCC Second Innings

151

AUSTRALIANS Second Innings

92 for one

CARIBBEAN CRICKETERS

The first West Indians came to England at the invitation of Lord Hawke, who arranged their tour programme. They were led by Aucher Warner (brother of future England captain Pelham). The team sailed by the RMS *Trent*, which docked at Southampton in early June.

They found English conditions very trying and lost their three opening matches before arriving at Lord's to play the Gentlemen of the MCC. This side included W. G. Grace, fast approaching his fifty-second birthday, who opened with another former England Test captain, Andrew Stoddart. Lord Harris was also in the team.

Rain wiped out play on the first scheduled day. The West Indies lost the toss for the fourth time in as many matches. When play did begin, MCC scored their runs freely at a rate of 80 an hour. Centurion Ernest Somers Smith was the last man out.

The West Indies reply began at a rapid rate. Seventy-five runs came in the first half an hour from Ollivierre and Learmond. When that stand was broken, so too was the momentum and the tourists closed the first day at 142 for six.

They were unable to avoid the follow-on despite some brisk hitting from Lebrun Constantine and Burton. They began their second innings 189 behind and crumpled to 132 for eight before Constantine and Burton again hit out to good effect. Their efforts did not prevent defeat but they added 162 runs in 65 minutes. Constantine hit 17 fours and a five in his 113, which was not just the first century made by a West Indian at Lord's but the first of the entire tour. Constantine's son Learie would later enjoy even greater distinction.

21–23 June 1900
MCC beat West Indians by five wickets

MCC First Innings
W. G. Grace c Ollivierre b Woods 11, A. E. Stoddart c Ollivierre v Woods 30, J. Gilman b Burton 33, Lord Harris c Burton b Woods 35, E. C. Mourdant b Burton 31, A. Page b Burton 0, E. Somers-Smith b Ollivierre 118, A. B. Reynolds b Woods 37, M. M. Baker b Goodman 26, E. R. De Little b Goodman 0, A. Montague not out 32
Extras b 17, lb 9
Total 379
Bowling
Burton 37-6-118-3, Woods 41-8-109-4, Ollivierre 13.5-2-55-1, Cox 3-0-18-0, Goodman 11-0-49-2, Sproston 1-0-4-0

WEST INDIANS First Innings

C. A. Ollivierre lbw b Grace 21, C. C. Learmond b de Little 52, S. W. Sproston b Grace 14, P. I. Cox b Grace 17, P. A. Goodman c&b Grace 0, W. Bowring b Grace 0, R. S. A. Warner c Gilman b de Little 22, L. S. D'Ade run out 4, L. S. Constantine not out 24, W. T. Burton b Stoddart 18, J. Woods st Reynolds b Harris 0.

Extras b 17, lb 1

Total 190

Bowling

Stoddart 10-2-32-1, Mordaunt 5-1-30-0, Grace 18-3-56-5, De Little 18-3-46-2, Harris 2.3-0-8-1.

WEST INDIANS Second Innings

C. A. Olliviere b Stoddart 32, G. C. Learmond b Stoddart 6, S. W. Sproston c&b Grace 33, P. I. Cox b Stoddart 6, P. A. Goodman b Stoddart 6, W. Bowring b Stoddart 7, R. S. A. Warner b Stoddart 3, L. S. D'Ade b Stoddart 2, L. S. Constantine st Reynolds b Grace 113, W. T. Burton not out 64, J. Woods st Reynolds b Montague 0

Extras b 17, lb 6

Total 295

LORD'S NURSERY GROUND
A FIRST-CLASS ARENA

It was appropriate that Yorkshire, the home county of the founder of the ground, should be part of the first match with first-class status to be played on Lord's Nursery Ground.

Henderson's Nursery had become part of Lord's in 1887, MCC's centenary year. The addition of this ground added another 3½ acres. It had grown pineapples and tulips, but now the nursery was to be used for practice and the development of cricketers.

Only three years later, the ground came under threat. The Manchester & Central Railway, later to become the Great Central, wanted to build a tunnel under the Nursery End and tabled a bill in Parliament. The club vehemently opposed the bill, and eventually a deal was struck to allow tunnelling to proceed. In exchange, the MCC received the land occupied by the Clergy Female Orphanage School, which stood on what is now the site of the Indoor School and English Cricket Board offices.

In the early summer of 1903, it rained heavily. 'The weather has been disheartening,' said the editor of *Cricket: A Weekly Record of the Game* with classic British understatement. A match between MCC and Nottinghamshire had been abandoned without a ball being bowled, and the same fate seemed likely to befall the match with Yorkshire. The players sat in the pavilion for the first two days.

Lord Hawke captained the Yorkshire team and may well have put some pressure to bear.

MCC batted first and Hawke introduced Walker Wainwright to the fray. As a member of the groundstaff at Lord's, Wainwright knew the surroundings and bowled superbly. He took the wickets in 1 over, 'giving great promise of future excellence' as MCC were dismissed for 133.

In the Yorkshire innings, Wilfred Rhodes carried his bat for 98 as they took a healthy first innings lead, but there was too little time to force a result.

11 (**no play**), 12 (**no play**), 13 **May 1903**
Match drawn

MCC First Innings
A. Hearne b Haigh 26, H. Wrathall c Hirst b Wainwright 12, L. C. Braund b Rhodes 35, C. C. T. Doll b Haigh 0, C. S. G. Griffin b Haigh 1, G. J. Thompson c Ward b Wainwright 4, A. E. Trott b Wainwright 37, C. B. Llewellyn b Wainwright 1, G. W. Beldham c Wilkinson b Wainwright 0, J. H. Board lbw b Wainwright 0, J. T. Hearne not out 13
Extras b 4
Total 133
Bowling
Ward 12-3-16-0, Wainwright 16.4-5-49-6, Haigh 11-1-55-3, Rhodes 5-1-9-1

YORKSHIRE First Innings

J. T. Brown b Llewellyn 30, W. Rhodes not out 98, D. Denton b Trott 12,
W. H. Wilkinson c&b Thompson 3, S. Haigh c A. Hearne b Trott 1, W. Wainwright
c J. T. Hearne b Trott 11, L. Whitehead b Braund 10, Lord Hawke b Beldham 4,
D. Hunter c Thompson b Braund 4, F. Ward b Braund 0

Extras b 4, lb 5, nb 2

Total 184

Bowling

Braund 9.5-0-34-3, Hearne 6-0-21-0, Thompson 14-1-53-2, Llewellyn 5-1-17-1,
Trott 12-2-25-3, Beldham 7-1-23-1

Umpires: W. Attewell and G. Bean

OLYMPIAN FIRSTS

Lord's Cricket Ground became very familiar to the 'Olympic Family' when London announced its bid for the 2012 Games, but in fact, the International Olympic Committee (IOC) first visited the ground over a century earlier, and leading MCC personalities played a critical role in organising the first London Olympics.

When, in the summer of 1894, a congress in Paris decided to revive the Olympic Games, the man behind the idea was a French nobleman called Baron Pierre de Coubertin. He drew up a list of potential IOC members, which included the cricketing grandee Lord Harris, though the suggestion was never followed through.

In 1904, the IOC held their annual meeting in London for the first time. The MCC's own committee met on 23 May 1904 and considered a letter from Lord Kinnaird, which suggested that they be welcomed to Lord's. The committee decided they would be 'glad to see a deputation of the St Louis exhibition of about twelve in number in the pavilion.'

During their meetings in London, the IOC assigned the 1908 Olympic Games to Rome and, incredible as it may seem, Coubertin set out plans for a small-scale cricket tournament to be held at the Villa Borghesi in Rome.

The IOC saw the Trooping the Colour ceremony in Horse Guards Parade and came to Lord's to watch play in the Middlesex v South Africans match. They were welcomed by Lord Darnley, C. B. Fry and W. G. Grace.

The match began in frenetic fashion. K. I. Nicholls was out to the first ball he faced, and Middlesex had still not scored a run when the second wicket went down. Johannes Kotze was the bowler who did the damage and it should have been even worse for Middlesex. Frank Tarrant had only scored a single when he was badly missed. Pelham Warner, who opened the innings, tried to repair matters with Bernard Bosanquet who had a narrow escape. *Cricket* magazine reported that 'was caught at slip but given not out on appeal'. Even so, wickets continued to tumble and at lunch Middlesex were 122 for seven.

After the interval, Bosanquet, with only the tail for company, cut loose and raced to a hundred. The last 50 runs of his century came in only 25 minutes. With assistance from Albert Trott, the late order swung effectively, and 149 runs were scored in just over an hour after lunch.

Bosanquet and Jack Hearne were both among the wickets when the tourists batted, but they closed on 170 for four, only 102 runs behind. Mitchell and Llewellyn scored 61 runs briskly before they were parted and South Africa led by 15 on first innings.

Poor Kenneth Nicholls completed a pair, but Warner, Bosanquet and Trott all scored useful runs to set the tourists a victory target of 211.

They closed on 52 for 2, still requiring 150 for victory. The following day, Tancred continued in the same vein, and with Llewellyn also hitting a half-century, South Africa were in a good position.

Lord's Firsts

Warner shuffled his bowlers but at 197 for seven, the tourists looked set for victory. Trott kept his nerve and the match finished as a tie, the first of the twentieth century at Lord's. By this time, though, the IOC party had long since left the ground to view a display of archery in Regent's Park.

20–23 June 1904
Match drawn

MIDDLESEX First Innings
K. I. Nicholl c Halliwell b Kotze 0, P. F. Warner c Sinclair b Llewellyn 34, R. W. Nicholls c Halliwell b Kotze 0, F. A. Tarrant b Kotze 31, C. P. Foley b Kotze 0, B. J. T. Bosanquet b White 110, A. E. Trott c Llewellyn b Kotze 16, J. A. Berners b Llewellyn 5, J. T. Rawlin c Sinclair b Llewellyn 7, C. Headlam c Tancred b Sinclair 44, J. T. Hearne not out 20
Extras b 4, lb 1
Total 272
Fall of wickets 0, 0, 48, 74, 77, 107, 123, 145, 224
Bowling
Kotze 21-2-94-5, Sinclair 17.4-3-68-1, Llewellyn 10-0-64-3, Schwarz 1-0-1-0, White 5-0-40-1

SOUTH AFRICANS First Innings
L. J. Tancred b Bosanquet 29, W. A. Shalders b Hearne 56, C. M. H. Hathorn c Trott b Rawlin 32, F. Mitchell b Hearne 66, J. H. Sinclair b Bosanquet 0, C. B. Llewellyn b Trott 43, R. O. Schwarz st Headlam b Trott 0, G. C. White lbw b Hearne 1, S. J. Snooke b Trott 19, E. A. Halliwell c Headlam b Trott 5, J. J. Kotze not out 7
Extras b 26, lb 3
Total 287
Fall of wickets 66, 115, 145, 160, 231, 231, 232, 257
Bowling
Hearne 30-9-67-3, Rawlin 10-4-17-1, Trott 27.2-6-80-4, Bosanquet 14-1-64-2, Tarrant 8-1-30-0

MIDDLESEX Second Innings
P. F. Warner lbw b Schwarz 38, F. A. Tarrant c Shalders b Kotze 11, J. T. Hearne lbw b Schwarz 16, K. I. Nicholl b Schwarz 0, B. J. T. Bosanquet c Mitchell b Sinclair 44, C. P. Foley b Schwarz 3, C. Headlam b Snooke 14, A. E. Trott c Halliwell b Sinclair 38, R. W. Nicholls run out 30, J. T. Rawlin not out 21, J. A. Berners b Schwarz 0
Extras b 5, lb 4, nb 1
Total 225
Fall of wickets 28, 70, 71, 71, 79, 104, 165, 176, 224
Bowling
Kotze 16-2-69-1 , Sinclair 15-4-44-2, Llewellyn 6-2-26-0, Schwarz 11.5-1-48-5, White 2-0-7-0, Snooke 3-0-21-1

SOUTH AFRICANS Second Innings
L. J. Tancred st Headlam b Trott 75, W. A. Shalders c Headlam b Rawlin 8, C. M. H. Hathorn c Trott b Rawlin 2, E. A. Halliwell c&b Trott 17, F. Mitchell c

Foley b Hearne 10, J. H. Sinclair c Warner b Trott 1, C. B. Llewellyn b Hearne 60,
R. O. Schwarz c Headlam b Trott 19, S. J. Snooke lbw b Trott 3, G. C. White not out
5, J. J. Kotze b Trott 0
Extras b 7, lb 3
Total 210
Fall of wickets 18, 30, 66, 91, 92, 140, 197, 200, 202
Bowling
Hearne 29-8-77-2, Rawlin 17-4-27-2, Trott 22.3-3-75-6, Bosanquet 3-0-15-0,
Tarrant 1-0-6-0

Umpires: W. Attewell and T. Mycroft

The following year, MCC were invited to have a representative at the formation of the British Olympic Association (BOA). Within a year, this fledgling organisation would also be charged with organisation of the 1908 Olympic Games, when Rome withdrew in the wake of the eruption of Vesuvius.

Lord Desborough, a prominent MCC member, was also chairman of the BOA, and in this role he was charged with heading the Olympic organising committee. He had less than two years to make all the arrangements. There were no Test matches in 1908 and MCC made another concession to help the success Games of the IV Olympics.

MCC's committee 'agreed to alter the date for the MCC tennis competition to meet the convenience of Olympic supporters'.

Lord's was not among the venues, but competition in a range of racket sports were held at Queen's Club, where A. E. Stoddart, of Middlesex MCC and England served as secretary. An MCC member also won the first gold medal to be decided. Evan Baillie Noel was a familiar Lord's personality and an outstanding games player. He had represented his school's XI team at Winchester and although he never played first-class cricket, he did appear in the same MCC team as W. G. and overshadowed the great man on one golden occasion in 1906. Noel took eight for 89 in the first innings and nine for 77 in the second innings of the match against the Gentlemen of the Netherlands, and MCC won by eight wickets. He had won the MCC Silver Racquet and entered three Olympic competitions in court games.

The racket singles competition began on 27 April 1908. By this time, Noel was working as sporting editor at *The Times*. He was one of only eight competitors. In the quarter finals, he was up against Vane Hungerford Pennell, who at the time was holder of the MCC Gold Racquet. Noel prevailed and he beat Henry Brougham in the semi-final. That was enough to guarantee him Olympic gold, because Henry Leaf, the other victorious semi-finalist, had injured his hand and was unable to play the final.

Leaf was also his partner in the doubles where they collected bronze after their defeat to Pennell and John Jacob Astor.

A TEST FOR SOUTH AFRICA

South Africa had been a test playing nation since 1889, but it wasn't until their fourth tour of Britain that they were finally rewarded with a Test match at Lord's.

England captain Tip Foster won the toss and batted. In 5 hours and 40 minutes, England scored 428. This was rapid progress by modern standards, but *Wisden* observed 'for the most part batsmen found runs very difficult to get'.

Len Braund stayed four hours for his century, but the impetus to the innings came from Gilbert Jessop, 'The Croucher', who scored a flashing 93 in 75 minutes. 'He drove, pulled and cut with astonishing ease, but though scoring at such pace he was never at all wild or uncontrolled,' said *Wisden*.

On the second day, South Africa were soon in trouble. After half an hour's play, they were 18 for three. Dave Nourse and Aubrey Faulkner set about recovery. Faulkner was put down at 31 by Kent bowler Colin Blythe, who damaged his hand in the process. The tourists lunched at 127 for four, and Blythe returned at the Nursery end bowling with his hand heavily strapped. He soon had Tip Snooke trapped lbw. Ted Arnold came on at the Pavilion End and South Africa crumbled. The last six South African wickets fell in 4 overs. They followed on and George Hirst clean bowled opener Willam Shalders in the 3rd over of the innings. Captain Percy Sherwell now took the fight to the English bowlers and became the first South African to score a test century at Lord's. His runs came in 1 hour and 45 minutes. They were still 103 runs behind with seven second innings wickets to fall, but rain washed out the final day and the test was drawn.

1–3 July 1907
Match drawn

ENGLAND First Innings
C. B. Fry b Vogler 33, T. W. Hayward st Sherwell b Vogler 21, J. T. Tydesley b Vogler 52, R. E. Foster st Sherwell b Vogler 8, L. C. Braund c Kotze b Faulkner 104, G. H. Hirst b Vogler 7, G. L. Jessop c Faulkner b Vogler 93, J. N. Crawford c Sherwell b Schwarz 22, E. G. Arnold b Schwarz 4, A. F. A. Lilley c Nourse b Vogler 48, C. Blythe not out 4
Extras b 24, lb 6, w 2
Total 428
Fall of wickets 54, 55, 79, 140, 158, 303, 335, 347, 401
Bowling
Kotze 12-2-43-0, Schwarze 34-7-90-2, Vogler 47.2-12-128-7, White 15-2-52-0, Nourse 1-0-2-0, Faulkner 12-59-1, Sinclair 6-1-22-0

SOUTH AFRICA First Innings

W. A. Shalders c Lilley b Arnold 2, P. W. Sherwell run out 6, C. M. H. Hathorn c Foster b Hirst 6, A. W. Nourse b Blythe 62, G. A. Faulkner c Jessop b Braund 44, S. J. Snooke lbw b Blythe 5, G. C. White b Arnold 0, J. H. Sinclair b Arnold 0, R. O. Schwarz not out 0, A. E. E. Vogler c Lilley b Sinclair 3, J. J. Kotze b Arnold 0

Extras b 9, lb 2, w 1

Total 140

Fall of wickets 8, 8, 18, 116, 134, 135, 135, 137, 140

Bowling

Hirst 18-7-35-1, Arnold 22-7-37-5, Jessop 2-0-8-0, Crawford 8-1-20-0, Blythe 8-3-18-2, Braund 7-4-10-1

SOUTH AFRICA Second Innings

W. A. Shalders b Hirst 0, P. W. Sherwell b Blythe 115, C. M. H. Hathorn c Fry b Blythe 30, A. W. Nourse not out 11, G. A. Faulkner not out 12

Extras b 15, lb 2

Total 185 for three

Fall of wickets 1, 140, 153

Bowling

Hirst 16-8-26-1, Arnold 13-2-41-0, Crawford 14-0-19-0, Blythe 21-5-56-2, Braund 4-0-26-0

Umpires: A. Milward, A. White

St George, Three Lions and Imperial Echoes

English cricketers had been venturing abroad for over forty years when Pelham Warner was approached by Melbourne Cricket Club secretary Maj. Benjamin Wardill, who suggested he bring a team to Australia the following winter. Although MCC had played a critical role in the government of cricket almost since its foundation, it had not yet sent a touring team in its colours. Warner suggested to the Australians that an approach be made to MCC. He said, 'they are the proper people to send out a team.' Warner was soon carrying a written invitation home to Lord's. The MCC committee responded enthusiastically to the idea: 'I was summoned to the committee room and asked to undertake the captaincy,' said Warner.

At a meeting held at Lord's on 27 July 1903, an important sartorial decision was taken. For the first time, an England team would have a recognisable uniform: 'It had been decided that the colours of the team be a dark blue coat with a narrow MCC trimming and a design of St George and the dragon wired on the front.' The touring sweater was faced with red and yellow and trimmed with thin dark blue. The design stood the test of time and proved a favourite with players.

There was still the question of home Tests. In 1908, a committee meeting talked of 'a cap for all England'. The minutes show 'the design being the three lions under a crown in silver, subject to the consent of His Majesty the King'. The club was confident that this approval would be forthcoming. Forty years earlier, when he was still Prince of Wales, the King had made a donation towards securing the purchase of the freehold at Lord's. An England sweater with the same crest was not introduced until after the Second World War.

In 1907, the South Africans suggested a triangular tournament to feature England, South Africa and Australia. This idea had been rejected by the Australians but in the wake of the successful 1908 Olympic Games in London, interest in encouraging sport in the British Empire had grown.

At the time of the Second Test match in 1909, MCC president Lord Chesterfield chaired what would become the Imperial Cricket Conference. Lord Harris and Lord Lichfield represented the committee and MCC secretary Francis Lacey was also present. Two other Englishmen, George Hillyard and Henry Leveson-Gower. Leveson-Gower, a man known to his friends as 'Shrimp', were at the meeting to represent the South Africans. The sole Australian representative was Les Poidevin, a cricketer who had played Davis Cup tennis. The other would-be Australian representative, Peter McAllister, was unavoidably absent. – he was out on the field playing in the Test match.

Hillyard made the proposal, seconded by Poidevin and it was unanimously agreed that 'the principle of triangular contests is approved'. The first such series was to be staged in England in the summer of 1912. The new body also tried to organise a future tours programme and considered the issue of eligibility and the appointment of umpires. A further meeting on 20 July confirmed these decisions, and the Imperial Cricket Conference was born.

THE DAMP TRIANGLE

The triangular tournament that had been agreed upon featured three Test matches at Lord's; the first time that so many matches had been played on the ground in a single English summer.

England's first match of the tournament came at Lord's against South Africa. Heavy rain throughout the previous week had saturated the playing area. The grass was so wet that it was even decided to use a different wicket to that which had been earmarked.

South Africa had already lost to Australia in their first match of the tournament at Old Trafford, but skipper Frank Mitchell decided to bat. The 12,000 spectators were in for a long wait. The start of play had been scheduled for 11.30 a.m., but it was not until three o'clock that the South African innings began. At least when play began it was dramatic. Sydney Barnes had Gerald Hartigan caught low down at slip and then trapped Herbie Taylor lbw. All this happened in the first 4 overs, and although Dave Nourse and Charlie Llewellyn took the score to 28, Frank Foster now came into his own. He bowled Nourse off stump with a Yorker and 7 runs later, Llewellyn was beaten with a shooter. At 36, Aubrey Faulkner's off stump was uprooted. From then on it was downhill fast for the South Africans and, by 4.30 p.m., they were all out for 58.

Jack Hobbs played on to Nourse early in the England innings, but by the close England were already 64 runs ahead with nine wickets in hand.

Although Wilfred Rhodes departed early on the second day, runs came swiftly for England. Reg Spooner was dropped on 93 but soon brought up his hundred. In all, he made 119 in less than three hours. Plum Warner was warmly received on his home ground and he helped the great Kent left-hander Frank Woolley add 113 in 75 minutes. By lunch, England were 303 for four. After lunch, Pegler came on for the first time at the Pavilion End and reaped immediate success. He hit the stumps four times and took the last six wickets to fall.

Even so, South Africa still conceded a first innings' lead of 279 and endured a wretched start to their second innings. They lost Hartigan, Taylor and Nourse for 36, and a further humiliation seemed likely. Only Charlie Llewellyn offered any real resistance. His 75 included eight boundaries. It was an innings that, according to *Wisden*, 'dwarfed all the rest of the South African batting'. But it did not save them from an innings defeat.

Less than a fortnight later, England were back at Lord's to play Australia. It was the first time they had played two Test matches on the ground in the same summer.

10–12 June 1912
England beat South Africa by an innings and 62 runs

SOUTH AFRICA First Innings

G. P. D. Hartigan c Foster b Barnes 0, H. W. Taylor lbw b Barnes 1, A. W. Nourse b Foster 13, C. B. Llewellyn b Foster 9, G. A. Faulkner b Foster 7, S. J. Snooke b Barnes 2, F. Mitchell c&b Barnes 1, R. O. Schwarz c Foster b Barnes 4, S. J. Pegler b Foster 0, C. P. Carter b Foster 0, T. Campbell not out 0

Extras b 12, lb 3, nb 2

Total 58

Fall of wickets 2, 3, 28, 35, 36, 42, 45, 54, 55, 58

Bowling

Foster 13.1-7-16-5, Barnes 13-3-25-5

ENGLAND First Innings

J. B. Hobbs b Nourse 4, W. Rhodes b Nourse 36, R. H. Spooner c Llewellyn b Nourse 119, C. B. Fry b Pegler 29, F. E. Woolley b Pegler 73, G. L. Jessop b Pegler 3, F. R. Foster lbw b Pegler 3, E. J. Smith b Pegler 2, S. F. Barnes not out 0, W. Brearley b Pegler 0

Extras b 11, lb 9, w 1

Total 337

Fall of wickets 4, 128, 183, 207, 320, 323, 324, 330, 337

Bowling

Nourse 16-5-46-3, Pegler 31-8-65-7, Faulkner 29-6-72-0, Carter 4-0-15-0, Llewellyn 9-0-60-0, Schwarz 20-3-44-0, Hartigan 10-2-14-0

SOUTH AFRICA Second Innings

G. P. D. Hartigan b Foster 1, H. W. Taylor b Barnes 5, A. W. Nourse run out 17, C. B. Llewellyn c Smith b Foster 75, G. A. Faulkner b Barnes 15, S. J. Snooke b Foster 16, F. Mitchell b Barnes 1, R. o. Schwarz b Barnes 28, S. J. Pegler b Barnes 10, C. P. Carter not out 27, T Campbell c Jessop b Barnes 3

Extras b 17, lb 1, nb 1

Total 217

Fall of wickets 5, 17, 36, 104, 132, 135, 147, 176, 197

Bowling

Foster 27-10-54-3, Barnes 35-9-85-6, Brearley 6-2-4-0, Woolley 4-0-19-0, Hobbs 11-2-36-0

Umpires: W. Richards and W. A. J. West

That summer, Lord's staged a third Test. This was the first in which two overseas nations opposed one another. South Africa batted first and reached 263, thanks in part to an unimpressive display in the field from Australia. *Wisden* reported, 'they allowed nine chances of one kind or another to elude them.' The innings owed much to a sixth wicket stand of 97 between Herbie Taylor and Stricker.

When Australia batted, they made a shaky start when Nourse dismissed Jennings and Charles Macartney. Their recovery was fashioned in painstaking fashion by a stand between Bardsley and Kelleway. The following day, the Australian pair seized the inititiative, adding a further 170 runs in two hours. When they were parted, their stand had realised 242. This was a royal occasion at Lord's, King George V was becoming an increasingly regular spectator at sporting events and he was presented to the two teams.

When South Africa batted again, they needed 129 to avoid an innings defeat. Charlie Llewellyn helped them avoid that fate, but they were staring defeat in the face at the end of the day. When play resumed, Taylor was left high and dry when South Africa were all out for 173. They had lost their last six wickets for 39, and Australia knocked off the runs needed for victory without losing a wicket in half an hour.

15–17 July 1912
Australia beat South Africa by ten wickets

SOUTH AFRICA First Innings
G. A. Faulkner b Whitty 5, L. J. Tancred lbw b Matthews 31, G. C. White c Carkeek b Minnett 0, C. B. Llewellyn c Jennings b Minnett 8, A. W. Nourse b Hazlitt 11, H. W. Taylor c Kelleway b Hazlitt 93, L. A. Stricker lbw b Kelleway 48, F. Mitchell b Whitty 12, R. O. Schwarz b Whitty 0, S. J. Pegler c Bardsley b Whitty 25, T. A. Ward not out 1
Extras b 12, lb 14, nb 2, w 1
Total 263
Fall of wickets 24, 25, 35, 56, 74, 171, 203, 213, 250
Bowling
Minett 15-6-49-2, Whitty 31-9-68-4, Hazlitt 19-9-47-2, Matthews 13-5-32-1, Kelleway 11-3-38-1

AUSTRALIA First Innings
C. B. Jennings b Nourse 0, C. Kelleway lbw b Faulkner 102, C. G. McCartney b Nourse 9, W. Bardsley lbw b Llewellyn 164, S. E. Gregory b Llewellyn 5, E. R. Mayne st Ward b Pegler 23, R. B. Minnett b Pegler 39, T. J. Matthews c Faulkner b Pegler 9, G. R. Hazlitt b Nourse 0, W. Carkeek not out 6, W. J. Whitty lbw b Pegler 3
Extras b 24, lb 3, nb 1, w 2
Total 390
Fall of wickets 0, 14, 256, 277, 316, 253, 375, 379, 381
Bowling
Nourse 36-12-60-3, Pegler 29.5-7-79-4, Schwarz 11-1-44-0, Faulkner 28-3-86-1, Llewellyn 19-2-71-2, Taylor 2-0-12-0, Stricker 3-1-8-0

SOUTH AFRICA Second Innings
L. A. Stricker b Hazlitt 13, L. J. Tancred c Bardsley b Hazlitt 19, G. C. White b Matthews 18, C. B. Llewellyn b Macartney 59, A. W. Nourse lbw b Kelleway 10, G. A. Faulkner c&b Matthews 6, H. W. Taylor not out 10, F. Mitchell b Matthews 3, R. O. Schwartz c Macartney b Matthews 1, S. J. Pegler c Kelleway b Macartney 14, T. A. Ward b Macartney 7
Extras b 9. lb 4
Total 173
Fall of wickets 28, 54, 62, 102, 134, 136, 142, 146, 163, 173
Bowling
Whitty 9-0-41-1, Hazlitt 13-1-39-2, Matthews 13-2-29-4, Kelleway 8-1-22-1, Macartney 14.1-5-29-3

AUSTRALIA Second Innings
C. B. Jennings not out 22, E. R. Mayne not out 25
Extras b 1
Total 44 for 0
Bowling
Nourse 6.1-0-22-0, Pegler 4-1-15-0, Faulkner 2-0-10-0

Umpires: J. Moss and A. E. Street

PEACE AND WAR

Although teams from the barracks at Woolwich played at Lord's in the early nineteenth century, it was not until 1908 that the first inter-services match was played there.

The Army batted first and Arthur Jervois Turner's 128 was the first century in this fixture. He had played first-class cricket for Essex and was in a rich vein of form in 1908.

Turner received excellent support from Francis Brooke and Robert Poore, who had played Test cricket for South Africa. Both men made half-centuries, Poore's runs came at a run a minute and although Frank Wilson took four wickets, the Army totalled an impressive 383. The speed at which they made the runs drew plaudits too; they were made in four-and-a-half hours. When the Navy batted, they reached 40 for 2 by the close.

There was no play before lunch on the second day. When play resumed, Arthur Lupton, who would later captain Yorkshire, led the Army bowling attack. Bertram Evans and Wilson both hit half-centuries for the Royal Navy. The Army had the upper hand when water came to the rescue of the Navy on the final day, as rain washed out the match.

15–17 June 1908
Match drawn

ARMY First Innings
P. G. Robinson b Wilson 23, F. R. R. Brooke c Watson b Mornement 53, Maj. or A. J. Turner b Mornement 128, A. H. De Boulay c Montgomery b Wilson 18, Capt. W. N. White b Sinclair 31, Maj. R. M. Poore b Sparkes 62, H. S. Kaye b Mornement 6, G. J. Edwards c&b Sinclair 14, Capt. T. W. Sheppard b Sparks 0, O. C. Mourdant not out 26, A. W. Lupton b Sinclair 0
Extras b 13, lb 5, nb 4
Total 383
Bowling
Sinclair 26.2-5-92-3, Wilson 32-3-110-2, Mornement 25-2-74-3, Montgomery 8-2-21-0, Syfret 7-0-28-0, Causton 4-0-11-0, Sparks 7-2-25-2

ROYAL NAVY First Innings
Lt G. C. Harrison c Turner b De Boulay 11, Surgeon E. P. G. Causton c Brooke b Lupton 4, Cdr B. S. Evans c Lupton b Robinson 63, Lt H. F. Montgomery b De Boulay 16, Lt F. A. Wilson c Brooke b Mourdant 79, Cdr H. D. R. Watson c Brooke b Robinson 0, Capt. W. W. Godfrey b Lupton 10, Cdr J. B. Sparks c Edwards b Lupton 39, Staff Surgeon R. H. Mornement c Mourdant b Robinson 1, Midshipman E. N. Syfret b Lupton 4, Sub-Lt EW Sinclair not out 1
Extras b 12, lb 3, nb 5, w 1

Total 249
Bowling
Lupton 18.3-1-42-4, Mourdant 20-0-85-1, De Boulay 12-1-32-1, Robinson 14-1-50-3, Turner 4-1-20-0

ARMY Second Innings
F. F. R. Brooke c Syfret b Montgomery 41, G. J. Edwards c Mornement b Wilson 1, O. C. Mourdant c Syfret b Montgomery 8, A. W. Lupton not out 0
Extras b 1, lb 2, nb 2
Total 55 for three
Bowling
Sinclair 4-1-7-0, Wilson 12-6-11-0, Mornement 7-1-19-0, Montgomery 3-1-2-2, Spark 1-0-11-0

in 1914, MCC celebrated 100 years of the ground in St John's Wood, but Europe was soon at war. For a while, cricket continued but many found this unacceptable, including W. G. Grace. 'I think the time has arrived when the county season should be closed,' he wrote in a letter to *The Sportsman* in August 1914. This sentiment was echoed a few days later by Lord Roberts who told a recruiting rally: 'This is not the time to play games.' Cricket at Lord's came to an end in August 1914. After a meeting the following January, Lord Hawke announced that the County Championship was suspended. Strangely, football continued that winter and the FA Cup final of 1915 became known as the 'Khaki Final'.

At the annual general meeting, Hawke agreed to continue as MCC president for a further a year. He announced that 2,112 MCC members had already joined the armed forces and the sum of £1,621 had been given to the war fund. In the first full year of the war, the usual schools matches were rescheduled for other venues.

By now, the ground had been taken over for military purposes. The Territorial Artillery, Army Service Corps and Royal Army Medical Corps all stationed units there. Geese were kept at the ground and 'No ducks but Geese at Lord's' made the perfect headline.

'It was gradually realised that any ban on cricket had become illogical,' wrote Pelham Warner. In July 1915, the 2nd Life Guards played against the Royal Horse Artillery. Trooper Massey made 66 out of a total of 197 for the Life Guards. The Horse Artillery were bowled out for 114 to give the Life Guards victory on the first innings. There was till time for both sides to bat a second time.

3 July 1915
2nd Life Guards beat Royal Horse Artillery by 84 runs

2ND LIFE GUARDS First Innings
Maj. R. Ellison b Braithwaite 7, Trooper Haywood lbw b Braithwaite 7, Cpl E. Stephenson c Campbell b Wood 27, A. P. Graves c Lambert b Braithwaite 4, Maj. S. Surtees b Perritt 0, Capt. T. R. Montgomerie c Perritt b Wesley 36, Trooper W. Massey c Lambert b Ironside 66, F. R. Haggie b Braithwaite 39, Capt. F. J. McLintock b Ironside 0, Capt. A. S. Hoare b Perritt 0, Trooper W. F. Taylor not out 9
Extras b 3
Total 198

Bowling
Perritt 11-1-50-2, Braithwaite 7.1-1-24-4, Wood 3-0-22-1, Jupp 9-0-44-0, Wenley 4-0-34-1, Ironside 6-1-21-2.

ROYAL HORSE ARTILLERY First Innings
Capt. S. Armstrong c Massey b Stephenson 1, 2nd Lt J. A. S. Wenley c&b Haywood 35, 2nd Lt C. K. Campbell lbw b Taylor 52, 2nd Lt K. L. Ironside b Haywood 0, 2nd Lt R. L. Jupp c&b Haywood 2, 2nd Lt H. P. Milne b Taylor 12, 2nd Lt J. C. Jack b Haywood 3, 2nd Lt F. Wood b Haywood 0, 2nd Lt W. D. Lambert c Haggie b Haywood 0, 2nd Lt J. L. Braithwaite not out 0, Cpl Perritt b Taylor 0
Extras b 8, lb 1
Total 114
Bowling
Graves 7-1-18-0, Stephenson 8-1-45-1, Taylor 6-0-13-3, Surtees 1-0-10-0, Haywood 4-0-19-6

2ND LIFE GUARDS Second Innings
Maj. R Ellison b Braithwaite 6, A. P. Graves not out 6, Trooper Massey c&b Ironside 24, Trooper W. F. Taylor lbw b Ironside 32
Extras b 4
Total 72 for three declared
Bowling
Perritt 5-0-17-0, Braithwaite 5-0-21-1, Jupp 4-0-18-1, Ironside 3.4-6-12-2

ROYAL HORSE ARTILLERY Second Innings
Capt. S. Armstrong b Stephenson 7, 2nd Lt J. A. S. Wenley b Graves 30, 2nd Lt C. K. Campbell lbw b Stephenson 69, 2nd Lt K. L. Ironside b Graves 0, 2nd Lt R. L. Jupp b Graves 3, 2nd Lt H. P. Milne b Graves 2, 2nd Lt W. D. Lambert not out 7, 2nd Lt J. L. Braithwaite b Graves 4
Extras b 23, lb 3, nb 1
Total 149 for four
Bowling
Graves 9-0-44-5, Stephenson 7-0-28-2, Taylor 4-0-34-0, Haywood 1-0-13-0, McLintock 1-0-3-0

Umpires: E. Whitaker and 2nd Lt W. Tilley

Most other matches were interschool affairs, and even *Wisden* made its annual selection of cricketers of the year from the ranks of schoolboys. There was also a baseball match between Canadians and London Americans and, in 1917, matches for charity were arranged.

When the guns fell silent, the Army Council wrote to Lord's to express 'their deep appreciation of your patriotic action of the Marylebone Cricket Club in so promptly placing their grounds and premises at Lord's at the disposal of the military authorities'.

THE 300

By the early 1920s, no one had yet scored a triple century at Lord's.

Yorkshire had won the County Championship four years in a row and by the time they came to Lord's in early June, they showed every sign of doing the same in 1925. They had won already won five matches, three by an innings. The first day against Middlesex followed a familiar pattern. Middlesex were all out for 118 by 3.30 p.m. as Emmott Robinson claimed five wickets. At the start of the Yorkshire innings, Percy Holmes overshadowed his more famous opening partner Herbert Sutcliffe. He scored 40 out of the first 50 runs and when tea came at five o'clock, Yorkshire were already 102 without loss, only 16 runs behind the Middlesex total.

The pace slowed slightly after the interval. Sutcliffe took a painful blow on the finger and retired hurt when the score was 140.

The new batsman, Edgar Holroyd, did not last long, and he was bowled by Gubby Allen, but Maurice Leyland joined Holmes and, by the end of the day, Yorkshire were firmly in control at 209 for one.

When they resumed on Monday morning, the Middlesex bowlers came in for still more punishment. Holmes cut effectively but maintained his concentration throughout.

In what was at the time a rare post match interview. Holmes said,

> I was using a bat that I usually reserve for a soft wicket. Strangely enough with my soft wicket bat I made the biggest score I have ever made in my life and that on a wicket that was anything but soft. As a matter of fact it was a very hard good wicket.

The milestones came and went for Holmes, who eclipsed William Ward's record of 278, which was made in 1820. Maj. Arthur Lupton did not close the Yorkshire innings until Holmes had passed 300, the first man ever to score a triple century at Lord's. His 315 not out was made out of 538 for six in 155 overs.

When play was over, Holmes was besieged by reporters and autograph hunters, and 'telegram boys were arriving in quick succession' with messages of congratulations from those back home in Yorkshire. He then posed rather self-consciously in front of the pavilion for the Pathé newsreel cameras.

Although Middlesex batted with much more conviction in their second innings, Yorkshire still won by an innings. Holmes had been on the field for the entire match.

Although he opened regularly for his county with Sutcliffe, Holmes played only seven tests for England. It was his misfortune to be around at the same time as Jack Hobbs, who was known simply as 'The Master'. The following summer, Hobbs also set a new record for the highest individual innings made at Lord's with 316. It was hard not to feel sorry for the Middlesex bowlers.

6–9 June 1925
Yorkshire beat Middlesex by an innings and 149 runs

MIDDLESEX First Innings
G. T. S. Stevens c Sutcliffe b Robinson 10, H. L. Dales b Robinson 27, J. W. Hearne b Macaulay 1, E. H. Hendren lbw b Robinson 15, C. N. Bruce b Robinson 25, G. O. B. Allen c Kilner b Macaulay 7, F. T. Mann b Robinson 5, N. E. Haig b Macaulay 5, H. W. Lee c Macaulay b Waddington 5, H. R. Murrell not out 8, F. J. Durston c Robinson b Waddington 2
Extras b 5, lb 1, nb 1, w 1
Total 118
Fall of wickets 41, 44, 44, 85, 88, 94, 103, 104, 112
Bowling
Robinson 27-6-52-5, Macaulay 24-7-54-3, Waddington 2.5-0-4-2

YORKSHIRE First Innings
P. Holmes not out 315, H. Sutcliffe c Murrell b Stevens 58, E. Oldroyd b Allen 8, M. Leyland c Mann b Haig 61, W. Rhodes c Murrell b Durston 0, R. Kilner c Hendren b Stevens 37, E. Robinson c Murrell b Allen 6, G. G. Macaulay not out 21
Extras b 19, lb 7, nb 5, w 1
Total 538 for six declared
Did not bat: A. Waddington, A. W. Lupton, A. Dolphin
Fall of wickets 153, 319, 319, 404, 412, 438
Bowling
Haig 43-11-93-1, Durston 30-6-97-1, Allen 23-2-106-2, Stevens 26-3-89-2, Hearne 31-3-100-0, Lee 2-0-21-0

MIDDLESEX Second Innings
G. T. S. Stevens b Macaulay 65, H. L. Dales b Macaulay 0, J. W. Hearne b Macaulay 91, E. H. Hendren c Robinson b Macaulay 7, C. N. Bruce not out 42, G. O. B. Allen c&b Kilner 2, H. W. Lee b Kilner 0, N. E. Haig b Waddington 32, F. T. Mann c sub b Robinson 7, H. R. Murrell b Robinson 4, F. J. Durston lbw b Robinson 4
Extras b 11, lb 2, nb 4
Total 271
Fall of wickets 2, 144, 158, 180, 183, 183, 233, 240, 259
Bowling
Robinson 21-1-64-3, Macaulay 27-3-94-4, Waddington 11-2-33-1, Kilner 33-15-56-2, Rhodes 5-1-7-0

Umpires: F. Chester and J. A. Cuffe

THE ASHES URN COMES 'HOME'

When Lord Darnley died in 1927, his most famous possession had been hidden from public view for well over forty years. It was a tiny urn that had become the most famous symbol in cricket.

In August 1882, Australia beat England by seven runs at the Oval and a famous advertisement appeared:

> In affectionate remembrance of English cricket which died at the oval on 29th August 1882. Deeply lamented by a large circle of friends and acquaintances.
> NB. the body will be cremated and the ashes taken to Australia.

Back then, Darnley had yet to inherit his title, so it was as the Hon. Ivo Bligh, that he led an England team to Australia in the winter of 1882. During the tour, a presentation of an urn made by an Australian lady called Florence Morphy had been the first stage of a courtship between the pair. Ivo and Florence were soon to wed and Ivo treasured the urn, not as a cricket trophy but more as a symbol of their union.

Bligh remained passionate about the game of cricket long after he had finished his playing career, and duly became MCC president at the turn of the century.

In 1926, England regained The Ashes for the first time since the First World War. The following January, Bligh, by now the 8th Lord Darnley, died at the age of sixty-eight.

On the afternoon of 2nd July 1928, the MCC committee were told 'that the dowager Countess of Darnley has forwarded to MCC the urn containing the Ashes of Anglo Australian Cricket.' It was decided to ask Lady Darnley if she would be able to make the presentation in person.'

On the same day, the new MCC secretary, William Findlay, despatched a letter to Lady Darnley at the family seat at Puckle Hill in Cobham:

> The presentation of the Ashes urn was formally mentioned to the MCC at their committee meeting today and they expressed great gratification. They much hope you and Clifton will be able to present it in person and wonder if you see your way to do so on Monday next during the Oxford v Cambridge match.

If there was a formal presentation then it was very low-key, but the urn was placed in a glass case for display in the pavilion.

Shortly afterwards, Lady Darnley offered to have a silver replica made 'to be held by the winners of each series of Test matches between England and Australia'.

The idea was turned down: 'While appreciating the offer, the committee did not favour the proposal.'

During the Second World War, the urn itself was carefully removed to a place of safety. When peace came, it was returned to the pavilion and then, in 1953, it was installed in a cabinet in the Memorial Gallery.

It has returned to Australia only for special exhibitions. The Australian Cricket Board asked for a new trophy to be made in 1997, and Waterford Crystal agreed to create an outsize replica in glass. It was presented for the first time in 1998/99 and was won again by the Australians at the end of 2013.

'South Americans' at Lord's

William Findlay, the new MCC secretary, had been part of Lord Hawke's team that had toured Argentina in 1912. Some of the matches played had first-class status and contacts were renewed in the 1920s. By this time, Argentina had already started to play international cricket against other South American nations. A tour of Argentina, soon expanded with matches in Uruguay, Chile and Peru, was arranged for the winter of 1926/27.

Meanwhile, an Anglo-Argentine XI was seen at Lord's in the late summer. Although an amateur club match, it was nonetheless reported in full in *The Times*.

The Anglo-Argentine won the toss and batted.

Many of their players had English-sounding names. They were born in South America but returned to school in England. These included Dulwich-educated Carlos Meld, who had played at fly-half for Argentina's first representative rugby side. At one stage, Kenneth Carlisle had been tipped to play Test cricket for England. Both men departed early and the Anglo-Argentine XI was struggling at 38 for four when Clement Gibson and captain William Gardom came together.

Clement Gibson was born in Buenos Aires but educated at Eton. *Wisden* named him as one of the outstanding schoolboy bowlers in their 1918 edition, his abilities also caught the eye of Archie McClaren for his eleven to face Warwick Armstrong's all-conquering Australians in 1921. Gibson took six wickets in a rare victory.

Gibson was now a confident batsman and 'from the first ball to the finish of his innings, dealt severely and faithfully with the bowling'.

Gardom had played against Lord Hawke's 1912 tourists for Argentina. He had a reputation as 'a rather staid player', but on this occasion he made 91.

It was, according to *The Times*, 'the best innings of his life. He deserved a hundred and made the bowling look very much easier than it actually was.'

His side reached 285 and dismissed MCC for 246.

When the visitors batted again, they went for quick runs, none more so than F. A. Bryans who began his innings in sensational style.

From his first thirteen balls he scored 4, 4, 4, 4, 4, 4, 1, 4, 4, 1, 4. He missed the fourteenth ball, his first non-scoring shot in a half-century that came in less than 20 minutes.

H. R. Ferguson took 22 off 1 over. The Anglo-Argentine team declared their second innings closed, and after all the excitement there was no real prospect that MCC would score the runs. Col. Johnson and Capt. Isherwood posted 121 for the first wicket and the match drifted towards a draw.

23/24 August 1926
Match drawn

ANGLO-ARGENTINE XI First Innings

C. T. Mold c Staples b Hill 4, G. A. Simpson b Isherwood 14, H. P. Miles c Sarel b Isherwood 13, K. M. Carlisle c Staples b Hill 2, F. A. Bryans b Hyndson 12, C. H. Gibson b Isherwood 61, W. D. Gardom c Staples b Hough 91, J. E. Curchod run out 14, R. L. Stuart c&b Hill 50, H. R. Ferguson c Staples b Hough 8, H. E. Moffatt not out 2
Extras b 6, lb 6, nb 1, w 1
Total 285
Fall of wickets 21, 21, 32, 38, 78, 152, 178, 273, 283
Bowling
Hill 23.2-4-82-3, Isherwood 25-7-73-3, Hyndson 9-1-52-1, Hough 9-1-33-2, Heseltine 1-0-6-0, Berliner 3-0-21-0, Routledge 2-1-4-0

MCC First Innings

Col. A. C. Johnston b Gibson 22, Capt. L. C. R. Isherwood c Mold b Ferguson 17, H. P. Hunloke c&b Gibson 33, W. G. L. Sarel c Ferguson b Miles 18, P. B. Berliner c Gibson b Ferguson 4, G. L. De Hough not out 98, Capt. J. G. W. Hyndson b Gibson 25, R. H. Routledge c Miles b Gibson 1, G. V. Staples b Ferguson 1, D. V. Hill c Ferguson b Gibson 5, Lt-Col C. Heseltine c Gardom b Ferguson 5
Extras b 13, lb 3, w 1
Total 246
Fall of wickets 35, 49, 94, 118, 145, 203, 213, 218, 241
Bowling
Gibson 22-2-86-5, Ferguson 24.2-5-67-4, Bryans 16-4-51-0, Miles 4-0-25-0

ANGLO-ARGENTINE XI Second Innings

C. T. Mold b Hill 7, J. E. Curchod b Hill 25, H. P. Miles c Johnston b Hough 34, K. M. Carlisle b Hill 20, G. A. Simpson lbw Hough 14, F. A. Bryant st Staples b Hunloke 61, C. H. Gibson c Johnson b Berliner 39, R. L. Stuart c Isherwood b Hill 10, W. D. Gardom not out 20, H. R. Ferguson not out 31
Extras b 11, lb 1, nb 1
Total 283 for eight declared
Fall of wickets 10, 63, 100, 107, 141, 200, 220, 239
Bowling
Hill 14-3-53-4, Isherwood 8-0-38-0, Hough 16-2-79-2, Hyndson 4-1-19-0, Berliner 12-3-42-1, Hunloke 6-0-38-1

MCC Second Innings

Col. A. C. Johnston c Simpson b Curchod 59, Capt. L. C. R. Isherwood c Curchod b Ferguson 57, H. P. Hunloke c Moffatt b Stuart 3, W. G. M. Sarel not out 6, Capt. J. G. W. Hyndson c Carlisle b Bryans 30, P. B. Berliner not out 5
Extras b 5, lb 1, nb 1, w 4
Total 171 for four
Fall of wickets 121, 130, 130, 166/
Bowling
Gibson 13-2-33-0, Ferguson 15-3-49-2, Bryans 6-2-12-1, Curchod 6-0-23-0, Miles 4-0-28-0, Stuart 6-1-15-1

Umpires: T. W. Oates and W. J. A. West

A public subscription raised the funds to enable a team of South Americans to tour England in 1932. Clement Gibson now returned to lead the gentlemen of the South.

When they came to Lord's for their two-day match, they were faced by an experienced MCC team. It included South African Test veteran Herbie Taylor, now forty-three and nearing the end of his playing career, who was spending the season playing in England. He opened with former test player Eddie Dawson and Frederick Seabrook, formerly of Gloucestershire, who twice had to send back to the pavilion for a replacement bat. In the words of a correspondent from *The Times*, he wanted one that 'did not make a noise like a banjo'. The new bat did not bring him luck. He was soon out, but Herbie Taylor helped lift the MCC score towards 250.

At the age of fifty-nine, Plum Warner walked out to great applause at his spiritual home. He wasn't quite as fast as in his prime, and his partner Ian Akers-Douglas was run out. Warner himself made 9 before he was bowled.

It was hard work in the field. *The Times* reported that 'the fielding of the South Americans was as keen as could be but in their anxiety, they sometimes overran the ball and sacrificed accuracy for speed'.

MCC declared at tea and the South Americans began well, but the innings began to unravel after Chilean-born Alfred Jackson was run out at 32.

The MCC captain brought up three slips and left-arm Essex bowler George Reynolds-Brown, bowling off a two-step run-up helped tie down the tourists from the Nursery End. Hearne caused similar problems from the other and South America closed the day at 92 for six. They were still 246 runs adrift.

There was little time for the visitors to ponder their predicament because a gala dinner in the Long Room had been arranged for that night. MCC president Lord Lewisham, and past presidents Sir Kynaston Studd, Lord Bridgeman and Lord Lucan joined the festivities.

The next morning, a leg break from Hearne accounted for Dennet Ayling to leave the score at 97 for seven. It was up to his brother, Cyril, to try and save the follow-on in partnership with his captain Gibson. The skipper responded by hitting 12 runs in 1 over from Ronald Rutter. Cyril Ayling was still unbeaten when the final wicket fell, but the follow-on was accepted. More importantly, they had taken up so much time that it was 3.30 p.m. MCC went for quick runs as Seabrook was joined by Taylor in a brisk partnership in which the South African hit a six into the Tavern.

When the declaration came, the South Americans had no more than an hour and a half to bat to force the draw.

15/16 June 1932
Match drawn

MCC First Innings
F. J. Seabrook b C. E. Ayling 36, E. W. Dawson c Ferguson b C. E. Ayling 20, J. W. Hearne c Stuart b Gibson 85, H. W. Taylor c Knox b Taylor 60, W. G. L. F. Lowndes c Stuart b W. E. Ayling 50, I. S. Akers Douglas run out 40, P. F. Warner b C. E. Ayling 9, J. C. Atkinson Clark b D. E. Ayling 7, P. E. Musgrave not out 6
Extras b 18, lb 4, nb 1, w 2
Total 338 for eight declared

Bowling
Gibson 23-5-76-1, Keen 15-1-58-0, D. E. Ayling 22-3-88-1, C. E. Ayling 24.1-6-72-5, Knox 1-0-5-0, Stuart 3-0-14-0

SOUTH AMERICANS First Innings
H. W. Marshal lbw b Brown 12, A. L. S. Jackson run out 20, R. L. Stuart b Hearne 7, G. W. Ferguson b Brown 1, R. L. Latham c Rutter b Hearne 8, J. Knox lbw b Brown 9, D. E. Ayling c Rutter b Hearne 38, C. E. Ayling not out 95, C. H. Gibson b Rutter 26, F. F. Keen b Brown 22, A. L. Jacobs lbw b Atkinson-Clark 12
Extras b 6, lb 14
Total 270
Bowling
Rutter 24-5-78-2, Lowndes 7-1-22-0, Reynolds-Brown 37-10-74-4, Hearne 238-8-63-3, Akers 2-0-6-0, Atkinson-Clark 3-1-7-1

MCC Second Innings
F. J. Seabrook st Jacobs b D. Ayling 67, E. W. Dawson b D. Ayling 12, H. W. Taylor not out 48, W. G. Lowndes b D. Ayling 0, J. C. Atkinson-Clark not out 15
Extras b 2, lb 2
Total 150 for three declared
Bowling
Gibson 14-1-47-0, Keen 7-1-32-0, D. Ayling 18-3-50-3, C. Ayling 3-0-17-0

SOUTH AMERICANS Second Innings
H. W. Marshall lbw b Reynolds-Brown 0, A. L. S. Jackson lbw b Reynolds-Brown 4, R. L. Stuart b Reynolds-Brown 20, G. W. Ferguson not out 2, F. F. Keen not out 23
Extras b 1
Total 50 for three
Bowling
Rutter 6-2-19-0, Reynolds-Brown 10-5-15-3, Atkinson Clark 4-0-15-0

Umpires: Atfield and Hubble

A KIWI-RUN FEAST

New Zealand's cricketers had to wait until 1927 for their first match at Lord's, but it proved to be a record-breaker. It produced the highest aggregate of any three-day match up to that time.

The Times lamented the poor crowd on the first day: 'Our visitors have not yet acquired the prestige which attaches to Australian touring teams.' Perhaps the chilly weather also had something to do with keeping the spectators away.

The MCC were captained by the fourty-four-year-old J. W. H. T. Douglas, who won the toss and decided to bat.

Charles Titchmarsh made a career best 171 as MCC cracked along to 392 all out. Before the first day was out, New Zealand openers Roger Blunt and Jack Mills reduced the deficit by 57 without loss.

On the second day, Ces Dacre struck a superb 100 for the tourists. It was his second in as many matches on this tour. There was also a century for New Zealand skipper Tom Lowry, and New Zealand scored 434 runs in 519 balls.

In the time that remained on the second day, MCC's openers put on 96 without being parted. Dar Lyon went on to get his century on the final day. Gubby Allen hit an unbeaten century, and Hubert Ashton struck 88 before Douglas declared.

The wicket showed no signs of deterioration and the runs continued to flow. Lowry and Blunt both hit half-centuries in the New Zealand second innings before time was called.

11–13 May 1927
Match drawn

MCC First Innings
M. D. Lyon b Bernau 24, C. H. Titchmarsh b Merritt 171, G. O. B. Allen c Dempster b Henderson 38, H. Ashton c Page b Merritt 4, A. P. F. Chapman c Page b Bernau 18, J. W. H. T. Douglas b Blunt 36, F. S. G. Calthorpe b Blunt 31, H. J. Enthoven b Merritt 0, N. E. Haig c James b Henderson 34, M. Falcon b Merritt 1, W. B. Franklin not out 10
Extras b 15, lb 8, nb 1, w 1
Total 392
Fall of wickets 68, 137, 156, 181, 305, 343, 343, 345, 348
Bowling
Henderson 13.5-1-59-2, McGirr 12-1-42-0, Blunt 25-2-117-2, Bernau 17-5-45-2, Merritt 39-4-104-4

NEW ZEALAND First Innings

R. C. Blunt c Calthorpe b Allen 52, J. E. Mills b Allen 24, M. L. Page b Calthorpe 8, C. S. Dempster c Franklin b Enthoven 2, K. C. James lbw b Allen 33, C. C. R. Dacre c Falcon b Allen 107, T. C. Lowry b Falcon 106, E. H. L. Bernau lbw b Allen 0, H. M. McGirr not out 58, W. E. Merritt st Franklin b Allen 40, M. Henderson b Allen 4

Extras b 11, lb 9, nb 2, w 4

Total 460

Fall of wickets 83, 92, 106, 106, 185, 300, 300, 388, 456

Bowling

Allen 26.3-3-120-7, Haig 27-4-105-0, Calthorpe 15-2-99-1, Falcon 8-1-56-1, Enthoven 10-0-54-1.

MCC Second Innings

M. D. Lyon b McGirr 110, C. H. Titchmarch c James b Blunt 71, G. O. B. Allen not out 104, H. Ashton lbw b Page 88, A. P. F. Chapman c Dempster b Bernau 24

Extras b 18, lb4, nb7

Total 426 for four declared

Fall of wickets 188, 200, 394, 426

Bowling

Henderson 7-1-26-0, McGirr 19-1-78-1, Blunt 14-2-62-1, Bernau 18.1-1-88-1, Merritt 21-1-103-0, Dacre 2-0-8-0, Page 3-0-32-1

Umpires: H. R. Blunt and J. Hardstaff senior

Test Status for The West Indies

Until the mid-1920s, there were only three Test-playing nations. The full membership of the ICC doubled in the space of five years.

The West Indies were the first of the trio to be welcomed into Test cricket. On the night before their first test at Lord's, they were in celebratory mood at Dulwich College as they staged a dinner in honour of West Indies captain R. K. Nunes, an old boy of the school.

England were captained by Percy Chapman, and a Surrey batsman called Douglas Jardine made his debut. Lancashire's Charlie Hallows had scored 1,000 runs before the end of May and he was recalled for his second Test appearance, seven years after his first. In what proved his only innings of the match, Hallows was out for 26. Although Yorkshire star opening bat Herbert Sutcliffe scored 48, he evidently found the fast bowling difficult to come to terms with. Learie Constantine, watching from his position in the field, observed his discomfort: 'Never have I seen a batsman so unhappy.'

England accelerated during the afternoon, thanks in no small measure to a century from George Tyldesley. By the close of the first day, they were comfortably placed on 382 for eight.

They were soon all out on the Monday morning and five years before the Bodyline series that would cement his name in history, Harold Larwood was steaming in from the Pavilion End. Opener Freddie Martin was hit on the side of the head but resumed his innings and posted 86 for the first wicket with George Challenor. The departure of the openers signalled a collapse, and West Indies were soon 96 for five. *The Times* had noted, 'In LN Constantine, they have an all round cricketer of exceptional merit'. But on this occasion, he was out hitting Tich Freeman uppishly to mid-on where Larwood took the catch.

West Indies were all out for 177 and Chapman decided to enforce the follow-on, even though Larwood was injured. Hammond opened the bowling with Tate but it was Freeman who did the damage, reducing West Indies to 44 for six. Late resistance from Clifford Roach, Joe Small and Snuffy Brown lifted West Indies to 166 all out, but England's victory was completed in under three days.

23–26 June 1928
England beat West Indies by an innings and 58 runs

ENGLAND First Innings
H. Sutcliffe c Constantine b Francis 48, C. Hallows c Griffith b Constantine 26,
G. E. Tyldesley c Constantine b Francis 122, W. R. Hammond b Constantine 45,
D. R. Jardine lbw b Griffith 22, A. P. F Chapman c Constantine b Small 50 ,
V. W. C. Jupp b Small 14, M. W. Tate c Brown b Griffith 22, H. Smith b Constantine
7, H. Larwood not out 17, A. P. Freeman b Constantine 1

Extras b 6, lb 19, nb 2
Total 401
Fall of wickets 51, 97, 174, 231, 327, 339, 360, 380, 389
Bowling
Francis 25-4-72-2, Constantine 26.4-9-82-4, Griffith 29-9-78-2, Browne 22-5-53-0,
Small 15-1-67-2, Martin 8-2-22-0

WEST INDIES First Innings
G. Challenor c Smith b Larwood 29, Martin lbw b Tate 44, M. P. Fernandes b Tate
0, R. K. Nunes b Jupp 37, W. H. St Hill c Jardine b Jupp 4, C. A. Roach run out 0,
L. N. Constantine c Larwood b Freeman 13, J. A. Small lbw b Jupp 0, C. R. Browne
b Jupp 10, G. N. Francis not out 19, H. C. Griffith c Sutcliffe b Freeman 2
Extras b 13, lb 6
Total 177
Fall of wickets 86, 86, 88, 95, 96, 112, 123, 151, 156
Bowling
Larwood 15-4-27-1, Tate 27-8-54-2, Freeman 18.3-5-40-2, Jupp 23-9-37-4

WEST INDIES Second Innings
G. Challenor b Tate 0, F. R. Martin b Hammond 12, M. P. Fernandes c Hammond b
Freeman 8, R. K. Nunes lbw b Jupp 10, W. H. St Hill lbw b Freeman 9, C. A. Roach c
Chapman b Tate 16, L. N. Constantine b Freeman 0, J. A. Small c Hammond b Jupp
52, C. R. Browne b Freeman 44, G. N. Francis c Jardine b Jupp 0, H. C. Griffith not
out 0
Extras b 10, lb 5
Total 166
Fall of wickets 0, 22, 35, 43, 44, 44, 100, 147, 147.
Bowling
Tate 22-10-28-2, Freeman 21.1-10-37-4, Jupp 15-4-66-3, Hammond 15-6-20-1

Umpires: L. C. Braund and F. Chester

A RECORD TEST SCORE

Australia are the most regular overseas visitors to Lord's, and throughout the twentieth century they only once lost a Test match at headquarters. In 1930, their batting line-up, already formidable, had a new star. Donald Bradman was very relaxed as he approached his first Test at Lord's and spent the morning before the match in Parliament.

'To the House of Commons and House of Lords shown over,' said the entry in his diary. Bradman, wicketkeeper Bertie Oldfield and cricket writer Trevor Wignall were invited to lunch with the minister for war and the Attorney General. Then it was off to Wimbledon with a ticket for centre court.

'Centre Court a wonderful sight,' he wrote as he watched such stars as Fred Perry, Jack Crawford, Henri Cochet, Thierry Brugnon, Elizabeth Ryan and Helen Wills.

That night, he headed to the latest Noel Coward production, *Bitter Sweet*. It was indeed a relaxed way to build up to a Test match, but he had every reason to feel at ease. He had scored a thousand runs before the end of May and had already played twice that summer at Lord's, so even the imposing surroundings must have appeared familiar enough to a young man brimming with confidence. A month before, he had scored 66 against MCC and also played in the tour match against Middlesex.

There was no live televsion or even radio coverage and, short of waiting for the newsreel coverage, the only way to see the action was to actually be there.

The match began on Friday morning and those without tickets queued overnight outside the ground to pay their 3s (15p) entry. Over the course of the four days, some 110,000 watched the match.

England batted first and raced to 405 for nine by the close of the day, a remarkable scoring rate. Duleepsinhji scored a century.

When Australia batted, openers Bill Woodfull and Bill Ponsford built the innings on firm foundations. They took 162 over three hours. *Wisden* later described their tactics thus: 'The Australians batted to a set plan, Woodfull and Ponsford steadily wearing down the bowling for Bradman later on to flog it.'

Only one thing interrupted the progress of the Australian openers – King George V arrived at the ground and play was halted so that he might be presented to the teams. Shortly after the resumption, Ponsford was out, which brought Bradman to the wicket at 3.29 p.m. He made a brisk start, brought up his half-century out of the 66 runs, and by tea time Australia were already 244 for one. Bradman continued the assault after the interval and, in a further three quarters of an hour, he had his hundred. By the end of play, he was still unbeaten on 155 and had spent only 2 hours 40 minutes at the wicket. Australia closed on 404 for two, only 21 runs behind with eight first innings' wickets still in hand. The rest day followed for the English bowlers, which included debutant Gubby Allen and Maurice Tate.

When the innings resumed on Monday morning, Australia continued in the same remorseless way. Bradman was now joined by Alan Kippax. Their third wicket stand realised 192 runs in less than three hours. As *Wisden* noted of Bradman, 'he scarcely ever lifted the ball.' A glance at the statistics of the innings will bear this out. He struck twenty-five boundaries but not one of them was a hit over the ropes. *Wisden* recorded only two false shots in the entire time he was at the wicket (341 minutes). Bradman's innings was the highest in a Test match at Lord's, a record that stood until 1990.

'The most remarkable thing about his play was the extreme severity with which he dealt with any ball off which he wished to score,' wrote Percy Fender in his account of the tour. Even when Bradman was out, Australia kept on remorselessly. It was the first time that a team had scored more than 700 at Lord's, and it was a record score for a Test match. The declaration came at 729 for six, still a ground record for a first-class match for Lord's.

Even though England captain Percy Chapman scored a hundred on the final day, Clarrie Grimmett took six wickets and England were dismissed for 375. Australia needed only 72 for victory. This time, Bradman scored only a single, before he was taken by Chapman off Tate, but it had been his first masterful innings that had turned the course of the match. As it turned out, the destiny of the entire series had been altered and Australia regained The Ashes.

27–30 June, 1 July 1930
Australia beat England by seven wickets

ENGLAND First Innings
J. B. Hobbs c Oldfield b Fairfax 1, F. E. Wooley c Wall b Fairfax 41, W. R. Hammond b Grimmett 38, K. S. Duleepsinhji c Bradman b Grimmett 173, E. H. Hendren c McCabe b Fairfax 48, A. P. F. Chapman c Oldfield b Wall 11, G. O. B. Allen b Fairfax 3, M. W. Tate c McCabe b Wall 54, R. W. V. Robins c Oldfield b Hornibrook 5, J. C. White not out 23, G. Duckworth c Oldfield b Wall 18
Extras b 2 lb 7 nb1
Total 425
Fall of wickets 13, 53, 105, 209, 236, 239, 337, 363, 387
Bowling
Wall 29.4-2-118-3, Fairfax 31-6-101-4, Grimmett 33-4-105-2, Hornibrook 26-6-62-1, McCabe 9-1-29-0

AUSTRALIA First Innings
W. M. Woodfull st Duckworth b Robins 155, W. H. Ponsford c Hammond b White 81, D. G. Bradman c Chapman b White 254, A. F. Kippax b White 83, S. J. McCabe c Woolley b Hammond 44, V. Y. Richardson c Hobbs b Tate 30, W. A. Oldfield not out 43, A. G. Fairfax not out 20
Extras b 6, lb 8, w 5
Total 729 for six declared
Fall of wickets 162, 393, 585, 588, 643, 672
Bowling
Allen 34-7-115-0, Tate 64-16-148-1, White 51-7-158-3, Robins 42-1-172-1, Hammond 35-8-82-1, Woolley 6-0-35-0

ENGLAND Second Innnings

J. B. Hobbs b Grimmett 19, F. E. Woolley hit wicket b Grimmett 28, W. R. Hammond c Fairfax b Grimmett 32, K. S. Duleepsinhji c Oldfield b Hornibrook 48, E. H. Hendren c Richardson b Grimmett 9, A. P. F. Chapman c Oldfield b Fairfax 121, G. O. B. Allen lbw b Grimmett 57, M. W. Tate c Ponsford b Grimmett 10, R. W. V. Robins not out 11, J. C. White run out 10, G. Duckworth lbw b Fairfax 0

Extras b 16, lb 13, w 1

Total 375

Fall of wickets 45, 58, 129, 141, 147, 272, 329, 354, 372

Bowling

Wall 25-2-80-0, Fairfax 12.2-2-37-2, Grimmett 53-13-167-6, Hornibrook 22-6-49-1, Bradman 1-0-1-0, Mc Cabe 3-1-11-0

AUSTRALIA Second Innings

W. M. Woodfull not out 26, W. H. Ponsford b Robins 14, D. G. Bradman c Chapman b Tate 1, A. F. Kippax c Duckworth b Robins 3, S. J. McCabe not out 25

Extras b 1, lb 2

Total 72 for three

Bowling

Tate 13-6-21-1, Hammond 4.2-1-6-0, Robins 9-1-34-2, White 2-0-8-0

BLACK CAPS AND INDIANS

The New Zealanders had good reason to be confident when they played a Test match at Lord's for the first time in 1931. A month before, they had beaten MCC by an innings and 122 runs.

They won the toss and openers Jackie Mills and Stewie Dempster posted 58. Gordon Lindsay Weir continued the positive start, and by lunch they were 132 for 2. After the interval, they lost momentum and their last eight wickets for 92 runs in an hour and a half. Even so, the score appeared a good deal better when England foundered at 62 for four. Frank Woolley rescued matters with 80 at a run a minute, but England still closed the day at 190 for seven. There was no Sunday play, so Kent wicketkeeper Leslie Ames was joined by Gubby Allen of Middlesex. On Monday morning, together they put on 246, an England record for the eighth wicket. Ames hit eighteen fours and two sixes in his century, and Allen also struck a six as he too went to three figures.

It was a superb exhibition of hitting to set before King George V, who was presented to both teams, resplendent in bowler hat.

Back in New Zealand, the Evening Post in Wellington spoke of a 'tremendous crowd of enthusiasts which attended each day at Lord's.'

England made an immediate breakthrough in the New Zealand second innings. Jackie Mills was bowled for a duck by Allen, but the top order responded to the challenge. Stewie Dempster became the first New Zealander to score a Test century at Lord's. Curly Page followed and Durham-born Roger Blunt fell four short of his hundred.

The New Zealand batting drew high praise from *Wisden*. It was, they said, 'just the sort of cricket the circumstances demanded.'

Skipper Tom Lowry declared, setting England 240 in 160 minutes. England were 94 runs short of victory with five wickets in hand when stumps were drawn.

27–30 June 1931
Match drawn

NEW ZEALAND First Innings
J. E. Mills b Peebles 34, C. S. Dempster lbw b Peebles 53, G. L. Weir lbw b Peebles 37, J. L. Kerr st Ames b Robins 2, R. C. Blunt c Hammond b Robins 7, M. L. Page b Allen 23, T. C. Lowry c Hammond b Robins 1, I. B. Cromb c Ames b Peebles 20, C. F. W. Allcott c Hammond b Peebles 13, W. E. Merritt c Jardine b Hammond 17, K. C. James not out 1
Extras b 2, lb 12, nb 1, w 1
Total 224
Fall of wickets 58, 130, 136, 140, 153, 161, 190, 191, 209

Bowling
Voce 10-1-40-0, Allen 15-2-45-1, Hammond 10.3-5-8-1, Peebles 26-3-77-5, Robins 13-3-38-3

ENGLAND First Innings
A. H. Bakewell lbw b Cromb 9, J. Arnold c Page b Cromb 0, W. R. Hammond b Cromb 7, K. S. Duleepsinhji c Kerr b Merritt 25, D. R. Jardine c Blunt b Merritt 38, F. E. Woolley lbw b Merritt 80, L. E. G. Ames c James b Weir 137, I. A. R. Peebles st James b Merritt 0, G. O. B. Allen c Lowry b Weir 122, R. W. V. Robins c Lowry b Weir 12, W. Voce not out 1
Extras b 15, lb 8
Total 454
Fall of wickets 5, 14, 31, 62, 129, 188, 190, 436, 447
Bowling
Cromb 37-7-113-3, Weir 8-1-38-3, Brunt 46-9-124-0, Allcott 17-3-34-0, Merritt 23-2-104-4, Page 3-0-18-0

NEW ZEALAND Second Innings
C. S. Dempster b Hammond 120, J. E. Mills b Allen 0, G. L. Weir b Allen 40, M. L. Page c&b Peebles 104, R. C. Blunt b Robins 96, J. L. Kerr lbw b Peebles 0, I. B. Cromb c Voce b Robins 14, W. E. Merritt b Peebles 5, T. C. Lowry b Peebles 34, C. F. W. Allcott not out 20
Extras b 23, lb 10, nb 2, w 1
Total 469 for nine declared
Fall of wickets 1, 100, 218, 360, 360, 389, 404, 406, 469
Bowling
Voce 32-11-60-0, Allen 25-8-47-2, Hammond 21-2-50-1, Peebles 42.4-6-150-4, Robins 37-5-126-2

ENGLAND Second Innings
A. H. Bakewell c Blunt b Cromb 27, J. Arnold c&b Blunt 34, W. R. Hammond run out 46, K. S. Duleepsinhji c James b Allcott 11, F. E. Woolley b Cromb 9, L. E. G. Ames not out 17, D. R. Jardine not out 0
Extras lb 2
Total 146 for five
Fall of wickets 62, 62, 94, 105, 144
Bowling
Cromb 25-5-44-2, Weir 5-1-18-0, Blunt 14-5-54-1, Allcott 10-2-26-1, Merritt 1-0-2-0

Umpires: F. Chester and J. Hardstaff snr

In 1932, there was another addition to the ranks of Test match teams. Political independence had not yet come, but All India certainly enjoyed their first hour of international cricket. England's Yorkshire opening pair of Herbert Sutcliffe and Percy Holmes had arrived late the previous evening from a county match. Mohammed Nissar accounted for them both, and when Frank Woolley was run out, England were reeling at 19 for three.

'The wicket was a little more lively right at the beginning but we did get an unfortunate start,' recalled England wicketkeeper Les Ames many years later. It was left to the captain Douglas Jardine, born in India, to steady the innings with 79.

Ames was missed off a stumping chance when he had not scored, but he took the attack to the Indian bowlers. His innings of 65 included nine fours – 'the only English batsman to show that the bowling could be hit,' said *Wisden*. With Walter Robins he added 63 in half an hour.

'The two Indian bowlers created a very good impression with the England team,' he admitted as England were all out for 259.

India's captain C. K. Nayadu was the top scorer in his side's innings. But from a promising 153 for four at lunch on the second day, they lost their last six wickets in an hour for only 36 runs to concede a 70 run advantage on first innings. Yorkshire's Bill Bowes, England's only debutante, took four wickets.

Perhaps it was the visit of King George V that had the unsettling effect. It was often felt that a royal visit would 'get a wicket' for England.

When England batted again, Jahangir Khan came into his own. 'My feeling all the time was that I was a good bowler against left-handers. My ball moved away which the left-handers did not like.' So it proved that Woolley and Eddie Paynter were among his four victims, but not before Paynter had helped Jardine add 89 for the fifth wicket.

The captain again top scored for England, but he unselfishly declared at 12.30 p.m. on the third day, when he was 15 runs short of a century, to try and force the victory. India were set 346 to win. They crumbled to 108 for seven when Amar Singh and Lall Singh came together in the most productive partnership. They added 74 in 40 minutes and Amar Singh moved confidently to a half-century. He was last man out, giving a return catch to Wally Hammond, who finished with three wickets at a cost of only 9 runs.

25–28 June 1932
England beat India by 158 runs

ENGLAND First Innings
H. Sutcliffe b Nissar 3, P. Holmes b Nissar 6, F. E. Woolley run out 9, W. R. Hammond b Amar Singh 35, D. R. Jardine c Navle b Nayadu 79, E. Paynter lbw b Nayadu 14, L. E. G. Ames b Nissar 65, R. V. W. Robins c Lall Singh b Nissar 21, F. R. Brown c Amar Singh b Nissar 1, W. Voce not out 4, W. E. Bowes c Nissar b Amar Singh 7
Extras b 3, lb 9, nb 3
Total 259
Fall of wickets 8, 11, 19, 101, 149, 166, 229, 231, 252
Bowling
Nissar 26-3-93-5, Amar Singh 31.1-10-78-2, Jahangir Khan 17-7-26-0, Nayadu 24-8-40-2

INDIA First Innings
J. G. Navle b Bowes 12, Naoomal Jaoomal lbw b Robins 33, S. Wazir Ali lbw b Brown 31, C. K. Nayadu c Robins b Voce 40, S. M. H. Colah c Robins b Bowes 22, S. Nazir Ali b Bowes 13, P. E. Palia b Bowes 1, Lall Singh c Jardine b Bowes 15, Jahangir Khan b Robins 1, L. Amar Singh c Robins b Voce 5, M. Nissar not out 1
Extras b 5, lb 7, nb 2, w 1
Total 189
Fall of wickets 39, 63, 110, 139, 160, 165, 181, 182, 188

Bowling
Bowes 30-13-49-4, Voce 17-6-23-3, Brown 25-7-48-1, Robins 17-4-39-2, Hammond 4-0-15-0

ENGLAND Second Innings
H. Sutcliffe c Nayadu b Amar Singh 19, P. Holmes b Jahangir Khan 11, F. E. Woolley c Colah b Jahangir Khan 21, W. R. Hammond b Jahangir Khan 12 , D. R. Jardine not out 85, E. Paynter b Jahangir Khan 54, L. E. G. Ames b Amar Singh 6, R. V. W. Robins c Jahangir Khan b Nissar 30, F. R. Brown c Colah b Naoomal Joomal 29, W. Voce not out 0
Extras b 2, lb 6
Total 275 for eight declared
Fall of wickets 30, 34, 54, 67, 156, 169, 222, 271
Bowling
Nissar 18-5-42-1, Amar Singh 41-13-84-2, Jahangir Khan 30-12-60-4, Nayadu 9-0-21-0, Palia 3-0-11-0, Naoomal Jaoomal 8-0-40-1, S. Wazir Ali 1-0-9-0

INDIA Second Innings
J. G. Navle lbw b Robins 13, Naoomal Jaoomal b Brown 25, S. Wazir Ali c Hammond b Voce 39, C. K. Nayadu b Bowes 10, S. M. H. Colah b Brown 4, S. Nazir Ali c Jardine b Bowes 6, Lall Singh b Hammond 29, Jahangir Khan b Voce 0, L. Amar Singh c&b Hammond 51, M. Nissar b Hammond 0, P. E. Palia not out 1
Extras b 5, lb 2, nb 2
Total 187
Fall of wickets 41, 41, 52, 65, 83, 108, 108, 182, 182
Bowling
Bowes 14-5-30-2, Voce 12-3-28-2, Brown 14-1-54-2, Robins 14-5-57-1, Hammond 5.3-3-9-3

Umpires: F. Chester and J. Hardstaff snr

India had to wait until 1986 to finally win a Test match at Lord's. A superb century from Dilip Vengsarkar set up the platform for Kapil Dev to work his way through the England batting. Appropriately, Kapil hit a six to win the match.

ON THE AIR

The media centre has towered above the Nursery End since 1999. Television and radio coverage are such an integral part of cricket that it might seem incredible that ball-by-ball cricket coverage was deemed to be nigh on impossible in the early years.

At the time, the MCC telephone number was not even listed in the directory. In 1926, the Marconi Company had offered to install public address loudspeakers during the Test match. The minutes of 26 April 1926 record simply that this proposition was 'not entertained'.

Yet the following year they did agree to let in the BBC.

'The British Broadcasting Corporation were anxious to broadcast certain matches at Lord's from the pavilion or failing that, from the roof of the bowlers room by the clock tower,' noted the minutes of 25 April 1927.

The makeup of the committee gives a clue to their positive attitude. H. D. G. Leveson Gower and Pelham Warner both made a living writing about the game and no doubt saw a new opportunity beckoning. Another member was Arthur Gilligan, who later became a member of the Test match commentary team.

The committee gave permission for 'the necessary equipment to be erected as an experiment on the roof of the bowlers' room'.

Originally, the broadcast was scheduled for May, but it was put back to June. Perhaps unsurprisingly, Warner was asked to do the broadcast on the Middlesex v Nottinghamshire championship match. His first broadcast was scheduled for 2.15 p.m. that Saturday. There was no shortage of action for him to describe. Nottinghamshire batted well. Gubby Allen took five for 99, and his figures might have been even better as he'd beaten the bat throughout the day. The Nottinghamshire ninth wicket pair put on 123 thanks to 67 from Harold Larwood. After tea, his side added 100 runs in an hour and were eventually all out for 381. In more familiar guise, Larwood sent down a hostile spell before the close, but Middlesex ended the day on 44 without loss. He eventually took nine wickets in the match as Notts won by an innings.

By any standards, it was interesting day of cricket and further requests to broadcast matches were received by the club that summer. Unfortunately, Warner's broadcasting style was soon described as 'melancholy' by those at the BBC. More importantly, it also became apparent that they considered cricket to be unsuitable for live broadcasts. Their opinion may have been coloured by star rugby commentator Teddy Wakelam, who had not relished his own experience broadcasting the game and made his reservations clear to his broadcasting masters.

It was not until 1934 that the BBC were at last prepared to try ball-by-ball commentary again. During previous tours of England, the Australians had shown that it was possible. Their broadcasts were actually carried out from a studio in Australia, where commentators used the ticker tape wire service despatches sent via the Eiffel Tower. These commentaries were known as 'synthetic'.

The BBC now realised they had just the man to mount an operation of their own. He was a former rugby player with a superb broadcasting voice. His name was Howard Marshall.

'It was he who did most to create the style of the test ball by ball commentary,' said E. W. Swanton, a distinguished writer who also became a commentator.

For the first Test match commentary from Lord's on 22 June 1934, the committee decided that the BBC could have 'the use of a room in the hotel'. By hotel, they meant the Tavern. They decided to charge 25 guineas as a facility fee. The BBC beat them down to 20 guineas and Marshall took his place in the Tavern Stand.

'The engineers were very helpful. They were always ready to fetch me a glass of beer or a cup of tea, or get the bowling figures from the scorers,' Marshall recalled later. He outlined his philosophy on broadcasting in an article for the *Radio Times*: 'You chat as you would do to a friend who is interested in cricket.'

England owed their impressive first innings of 440 to a fine sixth wicket stand between Maurice Leyland and Leslie Ames. Centurions both, Ames was the first wicketkeeper to score 100 in Ashes cricket.

Australia were 196 for 2 over the weekend in reply to England's 440 when the rains came. Enter Hedley Verity of Yorkshire, who exploited conditions to the full. Australia crumbled to 284 all out, England enforced the follow-on and he was even more devastating – Australia all out 118. In all, Verity took fourteen wickets on the final day. It made it a testing task, even for the capable Marshall, to keep up in the commentary box.

The dramatic day's play at least had one positive effect; for the next test at Old Trafford, the BBC made sure Marshall had the assistance of a scorer.

By the time the Australians returned to Lord's in 1938, television had started. Ian Orr Ewing, a young producer, was given the job of developing sports coverage. 'Lord's and Wimbledon were easily the most helpful and accommodating,' he recalled later.

The man chosen to do the broadcasts was Capt. Teddy Wakelam, a surprising choice perhaps, given his earlier scepticism. His commentary position was not ideal. It was out in the open at the top of the stand at the Nursery End, adjacent to the Mound Stand. Unfortunately, when the sun was in the wrong position, it was difficult for commentator and cameraman to see what was happening.

It was not until after the Second World War that the cameras took their place in the pavilion. Cameras at the Nursery End were introduced even later.

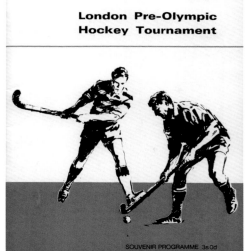

Above left: 1966 Rothmans World Cup programme.

Above right: Hockey at Lord's, 1967.

Below left: An advertisement for the first Prudential World Cup in 1975.

Below right: A brochure produced for the 1976 women's match at Lord's, featuring a blue cricket ball.

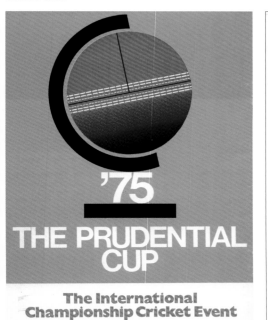

Cricket at the White Conduit Club (WCC) around the time Lord's.

Left: A chaotic scene at lunchtime at Lord's in the Victorian Era.

Below: A match at Lord's in 1857.

Boston and Philadelphia play baseball at Lord's in 1874.

Right: A match at Lord's in 1823.

Below: Oxford *v.* Cambridge cricket match in the eighteenth century.

Above: A grand cricket match on the first Lord's ground in 1793.

Below: Allan Steel returns to the pavilion after scoring a century in the first Lord's Test in 1884.

Above: W. G. Grace sits with his England team mates in 1884.

Below: The Grace Gates at Lord's.

Above: Australians practice at Lord's in 1902.

Left: In 1802, the aeronaut Garnerin hoped to demonstrate his parachute at Lord's.

Opposite: Troon celebrate as the first winners of the Haig Village competition in 1972. (*Courtesy Troon Cricket Club*)

HOWARD MARSHALL

CAPTAIN H. B. T. WAKELAM

D. G. BRADMAN

Above left: Howard Marshall, the first Test match radio commentator.

Above centre: Captain Teddy Wakelam, the first television commentator to broadcast from Lord's.

Above right: Sir Donald Bradman scored 254 out of Australia's 729 for six in 1930, which is still a record score.

Below left and centre: Middlesex twins Denis Compton and Bill Edrich.

Below right: Three Lions: the England cricket cap was introduced in 1908.

D. C. S. COMPTON

W. J. EDRICH

ENGLAND.

Above: A view of the Nursery End in the 1920s.

Below: The Nursery Ground in the twenty-first century.

The Old Grandstand
scoreboard with Father
Time in its original position.

Left: In 1992, the electronic
scoreboard at Lord's showed a
catch by Gary Lineker.

Below: The new media centre
with a cameraman above.

Above: The scoreboard displays congratulations for South Africa as they become the number one Test nation in 2012.

Below: The *Test Match Special* box in the media centre.

Construction of the new media centre offers a backdrop as the 1997 Australians prepare.

Left: Melbourne Cricket Club.

Below: An MCC women's playing section was established in the wake of the 1998 vote. They play at Lord's for the first time as part of the celebrations in 2014.

Above: In 2009, floodlights were used during a Test match at Lord's for the first time.

Below left: Tossing for innings at Lord's: a timeless ritual.

Below right: The Prudential Cup.

Chinese archers at Lord's during the 2007 MCC Cup.

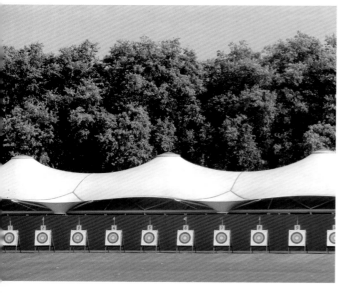

Archery targets on the Nursery Ground.

Japanese cricketers, 2013.

Above: Archery during the Olympic Games of 2012.

Below: Michael Vaughan leads England out at Lord's.

Above: Since her accession in 1952, The Queen has been a regular visitor to Lord's.

Inset: Father Time at Lord's.

Below: England captain Alastair Cook signs autographs.

ENTER THE MIDDLESEX TWINS
AND A BOY CALLED M. C. C.

The names Compton and Edrich first appeared together on a Lord's scorecard in 1936, when both were chosen for the MCC team to face Oxford University. Appropriately, the weather was fair. Denis Compton's first-class debut had come earlier in the season when he was last man in against Sussex, but he had shown promise and, as the correspondent of *The Times* pointed out, he had 'quite rightly been promoted in the batting order'. Compton had made 15 when he smashed Alexander Singleton to mid-wicket where Norman Mitchell Innes took a superb catch. MCC struggled at 74 for four but Bill Edrich walked out to bat at Lord's for the second match in a row. He'd played there for the Minor Counties against India earlier in the week. Waiting to greet him was a Middlesex hero of a previous era. Patsy Hendren was by now forty-five years of age and coming towards the end of his own illustrious career. Together, they turned the course of the innings and the match. The runs came quickly – 102 in 50 minutes at one stage. Edrich took 14 in 1 over off Randall Darwall Smith and when Hendren was eventually dismissed, MCC skipper Percy Fender also hit two big fours in a brief innings and Jim Smith struck a big six onto the pavilion steps. Two wickets in 1 over from Compton wrapped up the Oxford innings, which crumbled from 87 for four overnight to 128 all out. When the students went in again, they were bundled out shortly after three o' clock to give MCC victory.

Although this was their first appearance together at Lord's, they had played together against Beaumont Oratory before Edrich signed up at Lord's.

Compton, still only eighteen, was already an old hand there. He had first played there at the age of twelve and his exploits as a schoolboy eventually led to a place on the MCC groundstaff. His mother was worried about what he should do in the winter months, but she need not have worried. His talent as a footballer had already impressed Arsenal, then arguably the premier club in the country. They were managed by Herbert Chapman, a man years ahead of his time who presided over the first golden era at Highbury. On 21 March 1933, MCC secretary Bill Findlay wrote to Chapman about Compton: 'We have engaged him on the ground staff at Lord's, but we shall not want him until May 1st. I hope this fits in with your arrangements. I am glad to hear what you tell me about him as a footballer.'

Bill Edrich was two years older and also had a career as a footballer, albeit much briefer. He was signed by Tottenham who had been relegated to Division Two. He eventually played thirty-five games for Spurs in 1935/36.

The pair became known as the 'Middlesex Twins'. Both played with great distinction for England, and never more so than in the golden summer of 1947 when they put on 370 for the third wicket against South Africa at Lord's.

20, 22 June 1936
MCC beat Oxford University by an innings and 123 runs

MCC First Innings
R. Aird c Singleton b Darwall-Smith 10, C. Fairservice c Matthews b Mitchell-Innes 6, D. C. S. Compton c Mitchell-Innes b Singleton 15, E. H. Hendren c Barton b Murray-Wood 98, S. A. Block c Mitchell-Innes b Singleton 18, W. J. Edrich b Darwall-Smith 114, P. G. H. Fender c sub b Murray-Wood 13, J. M. Sims c Murray-Wood b Mitchell-Innes 31, C. I. J Smith not out 15, J. T. H. Comber run out 3, J. W. T. Grimshaw b Darwall-Smith 0
Extras b 7, lb 3
Total 333
Fall of wickets 12, 26, 44, 74, 215, 243, 313, 329, 332, 333
Bowling
Darwall-Smith 17.5-4-73-3, Mitchell-Innes 13-3-45-2, Singleton 26-6-91-2, Dyson 13-3-39-0, Murray-Wood 19-4-75-2

OXFORD UNIVERSITY First Innings
N. S. Mitchell-Innes b Smith 44, M. R. Barton b Grimshaw 50, B. H. Belle c Grimshaw b Fender 0, J. N. Grover b Fender 0, M. H. Matthews b Smith 5, R. C. M. Kimpton c Compton b Grimshaw 2, M. M. Walford c Comber b Grimshaw 3, W. Murray-Wood st Comber b Grimshaw 1, A. P. Singleton not out 11, J. H. Dyson c Hendren b Compton 9, R. F. H. Darwall-Smith b Compton 0
Extras lb 1, w 1, nb 1
Total 128
Fall of wickets 80, 81, 81, 86, 88, 98, 107, 113, 128
Bowling
Smith 17-4-19-2, Edrich 4-0-6-0, Sims 7-0-27-0, Grimshaw 12-4-27 4, Fender 11-1-45-2, Compton 1-0-12-2

OXFORD UNIVERSITY Second Innings
N. S. Mitchell-Innes c Comber b Smith 0, M. R. Barton run out 45, B. H. Belle b Smith 0, J. N. Grover st Comber b Edrich 1, R. C. M. Kimpton b Smith 6, M. M. Walford c Hendren b Smith 15, W. Murray-Wood c Aird b Smith 0, A. P. Singleton lbw b Sims 6, M. H. Matthews c Comber b Smith 6, J. H. Dyson not out 1, R. F. H. Darwall-Smith c Comber b Smith 0
Extras b 2
Total 82
Fall of wickets 0, 2, 3, 18, 44, 44, 61, 74, 81
Bowling
Smith 17.3-4-31-7, Edrich 3-2-1-1, Sims 11-1-40-1, Grimshaw 3-0-8-0

Michael Colin Cowdrey was christened with the most famous initials in cricket and, within hours of his birth in Bangalore on Christmas Eve 1932, his cricket-loving father Ernest had put him down for membership at Lord's.

'Whether or not this gave him the idea of giving me the same initials I shall never know. A number of journalists are convinced he did it deliberately, I shall never know. I never once discussed it with him,' he wrote later. Whatever the truth of the matter, many felt it was simply a matter of destiny that he would play at Lord's and, in due course, for England.

His cricketing ability became very clear very soon. In fact, it was so clear that his first appearance at Lord's came in the summer of 1946. Cowdrey was still only thirteen years of age when he was chosen to represent his school., Tonbridge. The match at Lord's against Clifton College was the high point of their season. Gifted cricketer though he was, Cowdrey's memoirs, which were written some thirty years later, revealed the self-doubt that some felt dogged his entire cricketing career.

> I would have given anything to have gone there and watched. I felt sick and ill as I walked out to bat. All I could think about on my way to the wicket was how dearly my father would love me to score a single at Lord's. One run was the limit of my ambitions but heaven alone knew where this single was going to come from.

Cowdrey did indeed get off the mark and then imperceptibly growing in confidence, he reached 75 and was last man out in a Tonbridge total of 156.

His innings drew an accolade from *The Times*: 'A boy of quite exceptional promise. At the end of that innings I knew I was on the way in the game,' he said.

Clifton looked well set for a sizeable first innings' lead at 186 for three, but at this time, Cowdrey was already building a reputation as a leg spin bowler. He took three wickets in quick succession and their first innings' lead was restricted to 58.

In the second innings, his 44 was part of a more convincing Tonbridge display. His efforts were described by one observer as 'batting like a professional seen through the wrong end of a telescope'. Even so, Clifton needed only 118 to win. Opener Thomas Penny had been called away that morning but it was still a modest total to chase. Cowdrey was brought on against a strong wind but, galvanised by his success with the bat, he held his nerve, took a wicket in his first over and also claimed the key scalp of opposition captain Rodney Exton. He finished with five for 59 as Tonbridge edged home.

It was the start of a glittering career in which he played 114 tests for England. He toured Australia six times and wore the club touring colours at the age of forty-two against the fearsome pace of Lillee and Thomson in 1974. Appropriately, 'M. C. C.' became president in the club's bicentenary year of 1987. He would also be elevated to the peerage, truly a Lord at Lord's.

29/30 July 1946
Tonbridge beat Clifton by 2 runs

TONBRIDGE First Innings
D. S. Kemp lbw b Exton 25, G. P. Bowler b Exton 28, M. C. Cowdrey c Lindsay b Exton 75, D. K. Horton c R. K. Green b Penny 3, J. R. Wrightson c Lindsay b Penny 0, C. Macnicol c Penny b Exton 0, A. J. Turk b Penny 0, M. J. Bickmore c Lindsay b Penny 16, J. D. Bickmore c Bishop b Exton 1, J. F. Macmillan b Exton 1, P. N. Kirch not out 0
Extras b 2, lb 2, w 3
Total 156

TONBRIDGE Second Innings
175

CLIFTON
214 and 115

A Healthy and Restful Antidote

When war broke out in 1939, MCC President Stanley Christopherson announced that the adjutant general had asked the club to encourage cricket in every way.

'Cricket provided a healthy and restful antidote to war strain and every year we had a good programme of matches', wrote Sir Pelham Warner.

The ground was to be loaned to service teams that wished to play there. Sir Kynaston Studd suggested that every cricket club should make at least one collection in aid of the Red Cross fund during the season.

The first of nineteen matches planned for Lord's was between the City Police and the London Fire Brigade. This was described as a 'cheerful match and an encouraging start'. Goulbourn took six wickets as the Police were reduced to 98 all out. It didn't take long for the Fire Brigade to pass the total. Hall and Bills posted 75 for the first wicket and the Fire Service took a healthy first innings lead. When the Police batted again, they were 43 for five when the close of play came.

The BBC also played at Lord's in a match against the local barrage balloon squadron. They scored 161. Raymond Glendenning, later one of the corporation's most famous football commentators was out for a duck. The Barrage Squadron included J. C. W. McBryan, who had made one appearance for the England test team in the 1920s. They passed the BBC total and batted on despite a fine bowling performance by Michael Standing, an early cricket commentator. The corporation was soon planning for its first wartime broadcast of a cricket match.

This was to be the first big match between sides of almost Test match strength and was announced for Whitsun. Wally Hammond was by now an officer in the Royal Air Force, but he was granted leave to lead a team of over-30s against Freddie Brown's under-30s. The match was to be broadcast live on the radio. It was announced that the commentator would be Howard Marshall, just as it had been in peacetime.

Over-30s: Flt Lt W. R. Hammond (Gloucs), Flt Lt R. V. W. Robins (Middx), Pilot Officer L. E. G. Ames (Kent), Lt H. Verity (Yorkshire), Sergeant Instructor M. S. Nichols (Essex), Sgt M. Leyland (Yorkshire), Lance Bombardier B. H. Valentine (Kent), Sapper W. E. Bowes (Yorkshire), F. E. Woolley (Kent) R. E. S. Wyatt (Warwickshire) and J. Sims (Middlesex).

Under-30s: Lt F. R. Brown (Surrey), Pilot Officer C. J. Barnett (Gloucestershire), Lt S. C. Griffith (Sussex), Sergeant Instructor L. Hutton (Yorkshire), Cpl C. Washbrook (Lancashire), Cpl N. W. Harding (Kent), Gunner D. V. P. Wright (Kent), Aircraftman W. J. Edrich (Middlesex), H. T. Bartlett (Sussex), A. E. Fagg (Kent), H. E. Dollery (Warwickshire).

It was a match that never took place, as the international situation became ever more serious and minds were concentrated on the evacuation of troops from Dunkirk.

Lord's remained a centre of cricket throughout the war. The scorecards offered advice in the event of air raids. In 1944, a flying bomb flew over the ground. The players flung themselves to the ground and when play resumed, Jack Robertson of Middlesex hit a six after the resumption. When the war finally ended, cricket celebrated with a series of Victory Test matches and as in the First World War; these included games at Lord's.

OUT OF AFRICA

Sarofeem Bey's XI was the first side raised by an Egyptian, and the first from North Africa to play a match at Lord's. Before the First World War, MCC had played a team styled Egypt and the Sudan, but this was a team made up of those who were stationed in the colonial offices. They were predominantly British born. Fares Bey Sarofeem learned his cricket at Victoria College Alexandria and had been one of the founders of a cricket club in Cairo. During the war, Freddie Brown, Bill Bowes and future Australian skipper Lindsay Hassett all served in Egypt.

The year 1951 marked the centenary of the founding of the Alexandria Sporting Club and to celebrate, Bey brought his team to England. He arranged twenty-three matches played over a six-week period. Their itinerary included matches with leading club sides, but none were accorded first-class status. Even so, the tour still attracted the attention of the national press.

'What luck Serofeem Bey and his team will have against English teams remains to be seen, but they will certainly play the game in its true spirit,' said *The Guardian* as they arrived in Britain. Without a doubt, the visit to Lord's was the highlight for the tourists. Bey himself skippered the side, won the toss and chose to bat. The Egyptians scored at a run a minute but Victor Ransom, a bowler who had played briefly for Surrey and Hampshire, took the first wicket to fall and finished with 36 for four. Ian Bedford, a future captain of Middlesex, also took four wickets.

Marro top scored with 41, Bey himself went in at 9 and scored 10 runs in eighteen minutes before he was run out.

When MCC batted they lost early wickets, but there was a famous name to rescue the innings. Reverend Gilbert Jessop was the son of the legendary Test batsman of the Edwardian era. The younger Jessop hit 41. His partnership with Lt-Col John Tresawna revitalised the innings. Skipper Tom Longfield added valuable runs as MCC edged closer to their target.

With 4 runs to win, Bey brought himself on to bowl and Lawson hit his first ball for four to take MCC to make sure of the win.

6 June 1951
MCC beat Fares Sarofeem Bey's XI by four wickets.

SAROFEEM BEY'S XI First Innings
Abdul (Ahmed on scorecard) Fahmey b Longfield 23, Abdou Hassanein b Ransom 5, D. Rall lbw b Bedford 11, B. de Bolton b Bedford 39, R. Barcilon b Ransom 13, R. D. Watt c Ransom b Bedford 13, Marro c Jessop b Ransom 41, Hassan Aly lbw b Bedford 24, Fares Sarofeem Bey run out 10, J. Kayarian not out 1, J. Halaby b Ransom 3

Extras b16, lb1, nb2, w1
Total 204
Fall of wickets 32, 40, 58, 86, 121, 184, 196, 201, 204
Bowling
Ransom 17.1-4-36-4, Crouch 5-2-9-0, Longfield 13-3-32-1, Bedford 18-0-82-4,
Cook 6-0-24-0

MCC

C. J. Harrison c Kayarian b Hussain Aly 10, A. G. Skinner lbw b Rall 3, H. R. Crouch
c de Bolton b Hussain Aly 10, Revd G. L. O. Jessop c Abdul Hassanein b Watt 43,
Lt-Col J. H. A. Tresawna c Bey b Hussain Aly 65, T. C. Longfield b Hussain Aly 25,
Lt-Col W. P. L. Lawson not out 35, V. J. Ransom not out 8
Extras b 6, lb 1
Total 206 for six
Did not bat: P. I. Bedford, S. J. Cook, D. C. G. Raikes
Fall of wickets 4, 19, 34, 111, 159, 160
Bowling
Abdou Hassanein 14-1-49-0, Hussain Aly 21-1-72-4, Rall 7-0-31-1, Watt 11-1-30-1,
Marro 2-0-13-0, Bey 0-1-4-0

A RAINY WELCOME FOR PAKISTAN

Only eight hours play was possible in Pakistan's first Test match at Lord's. The first three days were completely washed out and even the traditional visit by the Queen was cancelled. Instead, the players went to Buckingham Palace.

Play did not start until 3.45 p.m. on the fourth day. England skipper Len Hutton tossed with a sixpence given to him by Prince Philip. It proved a lucky omen. Hutton invited Pakistan to take first innings. When play did start, it was slow going. By the close they had reached 50 for three and Hanif Mohammed had batted throughout the 2 hours 35 minutes for 11 runs. When play resumed, Brian Statham was in fine form. He took three wickets in thirteen balls without conceding a run as Pakistan crumbled to 87 all out. Hanif had taken 3 hours 15 minutes for his 20.

When England batted, Hutton went for a duck but Peter May and Reg Simpson tried to force the pace. Fazal Mahmood and Khan Mohammed bowled unchanged, Godfrey Evans also hit out and England declared on 117 for nine.

Pakistan lost their first wicket to the eighth ball of the second innings, but Hanif was as defiant as ever. He was out to the last ball of the day but an honourable draw was secure.

Pakistan were dogged by bad weather on subsequent visits to Lord's and were forced to wait until 1982 before they won a Test match there. On this occasion, Mohsin Khan became the first Pakistani to score a double century at Lord's, and the medium pace of Mudassar Nazar tore through the England batting.

10–15 June 1954
Match drawn

PAKISTAN First Innings
Hanif Mohammed b Tattersall 20, Ali Muddin c Edrich b Wardle 19, Waqar Hassan c Compton b Wardle 9, Maqsood Ahmed st Evans b Wardle 0, Imtiaz Ahmed b Laker 12, A. H. Kardar b Statham 2, Fazal Mahmood b Wardle 5, Khalid Wazir b Statham 3, Khan Mohammed b Statham 0, Zulfiqar Ahmed b Statham 11, Shujauddin not out 0
Extras b 4, lb 1, nb 1
Total 87
Fall of wickets 24, 42, 43, 57, 67, 67, 71, 71, 87
Bowling
Statham 13-6-18-4, Bailey 3-2-1-0, Wardle 30.5-22-33-4, Tatersall 15-8-12-1, Laker 22-12-17-1

ENGLAND First Innings

L. Hutton b Khan Mohammed 0, R. T. Simpson lbw b Fazal Mahmood 40, P. B. H. May b Khan Mohammed 27, D. S. C. Compton b Fazal Mahmood 0, W. J. Edrich b Khan Mohammed 4, J. H. Wardle c Maqsood Ahmed b Fazal 3, T. G. Evans b Khan Mohammed 25, T. E. Bailey b Khan Mohammed 3, J. C. Laker not out 13, J. B. Statham b Fazal Mahmood 0

Extras b 2

Total 117 for nine declared

Fall of wickets 9, 55, 59, 72, 75, 79, 85, 110, 117

Did not bat: R. Tatersall

Bowling

Fazal Mahmood 16-2-54-4, Khan Mohammed 15-3-61-5

PAKISTAN Second Innings

Hanif Mohammed lbw b Laker 39, Alimuddin b Bailey 0, Waqar Hassan c Statham b Compton 53, Maqsood Ahmed not out 29

Extras 0

Total 121 for three

Fall of wickets 0, 71, 121

Bowling

Statham 5-2-17-0, Bailey 6-2-13-1, Wardle 8-6-6-0, Tatersall 10-1-27-0, Laker 10.2-5-22-1, Compton 13-2-36-1

Umpires: T. J. Bartley and D. Davies

Raiders from the North

a Danish First

Danish cricketers had visited Lord's in 1926, but their visit was only to watch the Test match against Australia. It wasn't until nearly thirty years later that a team of Danes from the cricket section of the Kobenhavn Boldspilklub finally walked out on the field to play a match. MCC had already made five tours of Denmark by this time. The visiting club had impeccable connections and could count the King and Queen of Denmark and Prince Axel among its members.

Back home, they were used to playing on matting wickets. They won the toss and decided to bat. Very soon, they probably wish they hadn't. Before long they were floundering at a 12 for three.

For Eigil Nielsen, the match at Lord's was a return to the city where he'd enjoyed his greatest sporting success. In 1948, he had been a member of the Danish football team that won bronze at the London Olympic Games. He tried to revive the innings but missed a long hop on 40 and was bowled. Svend Morild, one member of a remarkable Danish cricketing family, took the attack to the MCC bowlers and even hit a six, but he was left high and dry on 32.

Pakistan-born Saeed Mohammed led the MCC victory charge with 41, but Morild made sure the Danes would have something by which to remember their first visit to Lord's. He removed Fairbairn and then Lock with a superb ball that pitched middle and hit off before he accounted for Adrian Hill to complete the hat-trick. MCC captain Barrington Hill atoned for the indignity suffered by his brother and took his side home to victory.

10 August 1954
MCC beat Kobenhavn by five wickets

KOBENHAVN
S. B. Eliason c Lock b Bick 21, Kristen Morild b Eckersley 4, Karl Morild b Eckersley 0, E. Nielsen b Bick 11, B. Pockendahl c A. G. W. Hill b B. J. W. Hill 2, S. Morild not out 32, E. Jensen b Grace 10, P. Michaelson c Crace b Grace 6, N. Z. Lorentzen c A. G. W. Hill b Eckersley 1, A. Hartelins c Skinner b Grace 2, W. A. Dorset c Grace b Eckersley 5
Extras b 7, w 1, nb 3
Total 105
Bowling
Crace 8-5-12-0, Eckersley 17.4-10-16-4, Bartlett 12-7-13-0, Bick 8-3-22-2, B. J. W. Hill 5-2-6-1, Grace 11-4-25-3

MCC

D. A. Bick b Dorset 14, Mohammed Saeed st Eliasen b Karl Morild 41, A. Fairbairn b S Morild 27, B. H. Lock b S Morild 0, A. G. W. Hill b S Morild 0, B. J. W. Hill not out 10

Extras b 1, w 1

Total 107 for five

Did not bat: P. L. Eckersley, O. J. Grace, J. N. Bartlett, C. E. Crace

Bowling

Dorset 16.1-5-23-1, Lorentzen 11-3-27-0, S. Morild 13-6-26-3, Karl Morild 8-1-29-1

Umpires: L. Dolding and G. Morton

A Test Hat-Trick at Lord's

For fast bowler Geoff Griffin, his first appearance at Lord's should have been a moment to cherish for a lifetime. He was the first bowler to perform the hat-trick, and also the first player to be no-balled for throwing in a Test on the ground.

The early 1960s were a time when there was great controversy over what constituted a legal action, and Griffin had been no-balled earlier in the tour. After a delayed start to play, he had a wicket in his second over, England's captain Colin Cowdrey caught at second slip. This was a day much interrupted by rain and bad light. Ted Dexter and Raman Subba Row added 96 for the second wicket, and Dexter brought up his half-century off Griffin but was soon out, chopping to slip.

England resumed their innings on the second day at 114 for 2. They added 51 in the first hour before Ken Barrington was out. By the time Subba Row was out for 90, he had been at the crease for five hours and hit only four boundaries. 'He fought extremely well and placed his strokes cleverly,' was the verdict of *Wisden*. At 227 for five, M. J. K. Smith was joined by Glamorgan's all-rounder Peter Walker. Together, they added 120 for the sixth wicket in 2 hours and 20 minutes. Smith was only a single away from a century at Lord's when he was caught at the wicket off Griffin off the last ball of an over.

In the next, Walker went to his half-century, with two sixes off Goddard, and took another single to retain the strike. Griffin had the ball again and removed Walker's off stump. Griffin was now on a hat-trick. Enter Fred Truman who swung and missed and Griffin had made history. He was the first man to take three wickets in three balls in a Lord's Test.

Griffin's complete analysis was 30 overs 7 maidens four wickets for 87, but he also bowled one wide and eleven no-balls.

England declared at their overnight total. A sustained spell from the Pavilion End by Brian Statham reduced South Africa to 96 for six at lunch.

'Everyone is sorry for Griffin in the tribulations his action brings,' said *The Times* correspondent. South Africa were bowled out for 152 and followed on 210 behind. They were 34 for one in their second innings and, after the rest day, play resumed on Monday morning. It was another superb spell from Statham that help reduce South Africa to 72 for six. When Griffin walked in to bat once again, he was summarily bowled by Statham, who in the process broke the top of his middle stump.

Statham's match figures of eleven for 97 were the best of his career, and a match scheduled for five days had ended by 2.25 p.m. on the fourth day. With a sizeable crowd present, not to mention the imminent arrival of the Queen and the Duke of Edinburgh for their traditional visit, the two teams agreed to an exhibition match. The royal party arrived shortly after poor Griffin was no-balled four times in five balls by umpire Syd Buller. It was his only over. In desperation, he switched to an underarm delivery after advice from his captain, Jackie McGlew, and was instantly no-balled again by Frank Lee for failing to advise the batsman that he had changed his action. Some newspapers called for Griffin to be withdrawn from the remainder of the series. Though he attempted to remodel his action, he never did play Test cricket again and was subsequently called for throwing when in action for Rhodesia in a Currie Cup match.

23–25 June 1960
England beat South Africa by an innings and 73 runs

ENGLAND First Innings
M. C. Cowdrey c McLean b Griffin 4, R. Subba Row lbw b Adcock 90, E. R. Dexter c Mclean b Adcock 56, K. F. Barrington lbw b Goddard 24, M. J. K. Smith c Waite b Griffin 99, J. M. Parks c F Smith b Adcock 3, P. M. Walker b Griffin 52, R. Illingworth not out 0, F. S. Trueman b Griffin 0, J. B. Statham not out 2
Extras b 6, lb 14, nb 11, w 1
Total 362 for eight declared
Fall of wickets 7, 103, 165, 220, 227, 347, 360, 360
Bowling
Adcock 36-11-70-3, Griffin 30-7-87-4, Goddard 31-6-96-1, Tayfield 27-9-64-0, Fellows-Smith 5-0-13-0

SOUTH AFRICA First Innings
D. J. McGlew lbw b Statham 15, D. L. Goddard b Staham 19, S. O'Linn c Walker b Moss 18, R. A. McLean c Cowdrey b Statham 15, J. H. B. Waite c Parks b Statham 3, P. R. Carlstein c Cowdrey b Moss 12, C. R. Wesley c Parks b Statham 11, J. P. Fellows-Smith c Parks b Moss 29, H. J. Tayfield c Smith b Moss 12, G. Griffin b Statham 5, N. A. T. Adcock not out 8
Extras b 4, nb 1
Total 152
Fall of wickets 33, 48, 56, 69, 78, 88, 112, 132, 138
Bowling
Statham 20-5-63-6, Trueman 13-2-49-0, Moss 10.3-0-35-4

SOUTH AFRICA Second Innings
D. J. McGlew b Statham 17, T. L. Goddard c Parks b Statham 24, S. O'Linn lbw b Trueman 8, R. A. McLean c Parks b Trueman 13, J. H. B. Waite lbw b Statham 0, P. R. Carlstein c Parks b Moss 6, C. Wesley b Dexter 35, J. P. Fellows-Smith not out 27, H. J. Tayfield b Dexter 4, G. Griffin b Statham 0, N. A. T. Adcock b Statham 2
Extras nb 1
Total 137
Fall of wickets 26, 49, 49, 50, 63, 72, 126, 132, 133
Bowling
Statham 21-6-34-5, Trueman 17-5-44-2, Moss 14-1-41-1, Illingworth 1-1-0-0, Dexter 4-0-17-2

Umpires: J. S. Buller and F. S. Lee

BERMUDAN SHORTS

The first Bermudan team to play at Lord's were not a national team but a club side from the island. MCC first played in Bermuda in 1953, en route to a Test series in the Caribbean against Jeff Stollmeyer's West Indies side. Seven years later, Stollmeyer spent his summer playing for MCC.

In 1961, encouraged by the cricket writer E. W. Swanton, Somerset Cricket Club toured the UK. Swanton enjoyed his role as a cricketing philanthropist. He had toured Bermuda with Sir Julien Cahn's XI in the 1930s and knew all about the island's cricketing heritage. He was an influential figure in the game and no doubt eased the way to a fixture at Lord's, but even he could not do anything about the weather. When the Bermudan team arrived in Scotland early in their tour, their newspapers reported that the players were 'freezing'. Things were a little better in Lancashire and through North Wales before they finally arrived in London.

The team was managed by Alma Hunt, the outstanding Bermudan cricketer of his day.

A week before their own big match at Lord's, they had two days set aside for practice at Lord's and other fixtures arranged in and around London.

On the big day, MCC batted first. Stollmeyer joined the belligerent Essex batsman Dickie Dodds to give them a fine start.

But it was a superb century from Essex left-hander James Purvis that enabled MCC to declare at 299 for six.

When the Somerset club batted, wicketkeeper Simmons hit 55. Stollmeyer took a wicket but also bowled the only wide of the innings. The Bermudans held out to force a draw. The following week, they were back at Lord's but this time it was as spectators to watch play in the second Test as Australia beat England.

17 June 1961
Match drawn

MCC
T. C. Dodds b Edwards 32, J. B. Stollmeyer B. E. Raynor 34, J. H. purves C. Dauphin B. Edwards 130, A. R. Day B E Raynor 10 , C. Griffiths c Simmons b Chas Swan 48, Flt Lt R. Leggett not out 30, Bick D. A. c Carl Swan b Raynor 2
Extras b 5, lb 8
Total 299
Fall of wickets 46, 117, 159, 238, 295, 299
Did not bat: C. B. Howland, Dr C. B. Clarke, H. W. Tilly, A. C. Waite
Bowling
Dauphin 6-0-51-0, Hall 10-1-45-0, Edwards 7-0-29-2, Simmons 11-0-40-0, E. Raynor 12-1-52-2, Durham 2-0-12-0, Charles Swan 9-1-47-1, S Raynor 2.2-0-10-1

SOMERSET CC BERMUDA

J. Stovell b Tilly 0, R. Durham c Howland b Leggett 14, Carl Swan b Waite 9, S. Raynor c Tilly b Stollmeyer 35, E. Raynor lbw b Leggett 0, W. Simmons b Tilly 55 , C. Dauphin c Tilly b Clarke 16, W. Edwards not out 11, A. Hall lbw b Clarke 0, M. Simmons not out 4

Extras b 6, lb 5, nb 0, w 1

Total 156 for eight

Fall of wickets 1, 10, 35, 35, 109, 135, 151, 151

Did not bat: Charles Swan

Bowling

Tilly 16-7-43-2, Waite 10-6-16-1, Leggett 11-5-18-2, Clarke 14-5-45-2, Bick 10-7-11-0, Stollmeyer 6-4-11-1 (bowled one wide)

Umpires: H. P. Sharp and B. L. Muncer

THE ONE-DAY REVOLUTION

In fading light on a September evening in 1963, Sussex captain Ted Dexter raised a trophy after the first limited overs final to be played at Lord's.

The idea of a knockout cup for the counties had first been suggested almost a century earlier without success, but by the 1960s, attendances at traditional county matches were falling and the cricket community realised that something had to be done.

In 1961, the Cricket Advisory Committee finally decided that they should proceed with a one-day competition. There was too little time for the arrangements to be made for 1962, so it was decided that the competition would begin in 1963.

The search for sponsors was on and Gillette wrote to Lord's to express their 'willingness to take an interest in the forthcoming knockout competition by the award of a challenge trophy and any other appropriate awards covering team and individual performances in the course of the competition'.

Discussions went on throughout the summer. Finally, on 26 November 1962, the counties agreed to accept a block grant of £6,500 in sponsorship.

The cup itself was to be made by Garrards. It was a distinctive design in sterling silver and 9 carat gold, featuring the crests of all the counties along the base and surmounted by Father Time, the design borrowed from the familiar Lord's weather vane.

The first competition draw was made in the pavilion at Lord's by MCC secretary Billy Griffith, Donald Carr and James Dunbar. In the first year, only the seventeen first-class counties took part in matches of 65 overs per side.

Individual performances were also to be recognised with a man of the match award. This was to be chosen an adjudicator, drawn from the ranks of former Test players. The award, a medal made by Garrards and a prize cheque for £50, could be won for batting, bowling or fielding and did not have to be given to a member of the winning team.

'Some people I have spoken to are under the impression that the knockout competition will produce cricket which is a cross between a slogging match with sixes constantly flying to all parts of the ground,' mused Essex and England player Trevor Bailey. 'One certainly does not associate a carefree approach with Cup football and I cannot see it applying to cup tie cricket.'

Middlesex were drawn away in the first round, so the first knockout cup tie played at Lord's came in the second round. Opponents Northamptonshire had Colin Milburn, an aggressive batsman never afraid to go for his shots, but on this day he first excelled with the ball. He returned figures of 34 for four as Middlesex were shot out for 129. When Northants batted, he struck 84, which typically included a six and fifteen fours. He put on 102 for the third wicket with Roger Prideaux, and his team swept to victory.

12 June 1963
Northamptonshire beat Middlesex by six wickets

MIDDLESEX

C. D. Drybrough b Larter 5, R. A. Gale c Watts b Larter 3, P. H. Parfitt c Andrew b Larter 0, R. A. White c Lightfoot b Larter 7, R. W. Hooker b Crump 43, F. J. Titmus c Reynolds b Milburn 28, E. A. Clark c Lightfoot b Scott 17, D. Bennett lbw b Milburn 9, J. T. Murray c Andrew b Milburn 2, J. S. E. Price c Ramsamooj b Milburn 4, A. E. Moss not out 4
Extras lb 7
Total (40.1 overs) 129
Fall of wickets 8, 8, 15, 18, 62, 103, 117, 121, 122
Bowling
Larter 11-4-22-4, Crump 9-2-14-1, Milburn 10.1-1-34-4, Lightfoot 5-0-31-0, Scott 5-1-21-1

NORTHAMPTONSHIRE

B. L. Reynolds c Hooker b Moss 1, M. E. J. C. Norman lbw b Moss 4, C. Milburn b Drybrough 84, R. M. Prideaux c Clark b Titmus 30, A. Lightfoot not out 2, D. Ramsamooj not out 9
Extras lb 2
Total (39 overs) 132
Fall of wickets 3, 12, 114, 122
Did not bat: P. J. Watts, B. S. Crump, M. E. Scott, K. V. Andrew, J. D. F. Larter
Bowling
Moss 12-2-23-2, Price 7-1-36-0, Hooker 7-1-24-0, Bennett 4-1-19-0, Drybrough 5-1-22-1, Titmus 4-2-6-1

Umpires: O. W. Herman and J. G. Langridge

Frank Woolley, the great Kent cricketer, had an easy choice for the first Lord's 'man of the match'. He returned to undertake the same task on the first Saturday in September at the first cup final. E. W. Swanton told his *Daily Telegraph* readers that this was a 'new and exciting venture'.

The finalists were Worcestershire and Sussex. Neither county had ever won a major trophy.

It seems strange now, but in those days the ground was in use for a county championship match on the day before a major final. The Middlesex v Derbyshire match in the county championship was very soon abandoned, which left the way clear for the groundstaff to do what they could to protect the surface from further damage.

The following day, the match began on a playing area liberally covered with sawdust. Sussex captain Ted Dexter won the toss and decided to bat. Sussex had reached 62 before they lost their first wicket, but the introduction of Norman Gifford, a slow bowler, put a stop to their progress. Dexter had made only 3 when he edged at Martin Horton and Bob Broadbent dived forward to take a superb catch at slip. The Sussex innings was rescued by another England Test player, wicketkeeper Jim Parks. He top scored with 57 but many believed 168 was not enough, especially when Worcester reached 80 for two in their innings. Fast bowler John Snow and Tony Buss brought about a middle order collapse, but an unbeaten 33 from wicketkeeper Roy Booth threatened to guide Worcester to an unlikely victory. In the end, they fell just short.

The presentations were made on a platform in front of the pavilion and MCC president Lord Nugent handed the trophy to 'Lord 'Ted'. Gifford's 33 for four in the Sussex innings earned him the man of the match award.

7 September 1963
Sussex beat Worcestershire by 14 runs

SUSSEX
R. J. Langridge b Gifford 34, A. S. M. Oakman c Slade b Gifford 19, K. G. Suttle b Gifford 9, E. R. Dexter c Broadbent b Horton 3, J. H. Parks b Slade 57, L. J. Lenham c Booth b Gifford 7, G. C. Cooper lbw b Slade 0, N. I. Thomson lbw b Flavell 1, A. Buss c Booth b Carter 3, J .A. Snow b Flavell 10, D. L. Bates not out 3
Extras b 9, lb 10, nb 3
Total (60.2 overs) 168
Fall of wickets 62, 67, 76, 98, 118, 123, 134, 142, 157
Bowling
Flavell 14.2 -3-31-2, Carter 12-1-39-1, Slade 11-2-23-2, Gifford 15-4-33-4, Horton 8-1-20-1

WORCESTERSHIRE
D. J. Kenyon lbw b Buss 1, M. J. Horton c&b Buss 26, R. G. A. Headley c Snow b Bates 25, T. W. Graveney c Dexter b Oakman 29, D. W. Richardson c Parks b Thomson 3, R. G. Broadbent c Bates b Snow 13, R. Booth not out 33, D. N. F. Slade b Buss 3, N. Gifford b Snow 0, J. A. Flavell b Snow 0, R. G. A. Carter run out 2
Extras b 8, lb 9, nb 2
Total (63.2 overs) 154
Fall of wickets 7, 38, 80, 91, 103, 128, 132, 133, 133
Bowling
Thomson 13.2-4-35-1, Buss 15-21-39-3, Oakman 13-4-17-1, Suttle 5-2-11-0, Bates 9-2-20-1, Snow 8-0-13-3

The following season, each innings was reduced to sixty overs per side.

In the first two years of the competition, no one scored a hundred in the final and the portents were not good in 1965. Rain had fallen for the preceding twenty-four hours. The Lord's grounds staff led by Ted Swannell asked for help in personnel and equipment from the Oval. On the day of the match, a large crowd had gathered but captains Mickey Stewart (Surrey) and Brian Close (Yorkshire) were uncertain that conditions were fit for play. MCC secretary Billy Griffith summoned both to his office and persuaded them to try.

Stewart won the toss and sent Yorkshire in, hoping that the slow outfield would inhibit the batsmen and counter the problems his bowlers might face in drying a wet ball. To start with, the plan seemed to be working when, by the twelfth over, Yorkshire had only reached 22. Then, David Sydenham had Ken Taylor caught by Ken Barrington. The other opener, Geoffrey Boycott, had only scored a single off his first nineteen balls. He was 'wary and intense', according to the great sportswriter Ian Wooldridge.

Enter Yorkshire skipper Close. A brief discussion with Boycott followed, and then the two began the stand that would change the entire course of the match.

Boycott took 10 off 1 over from Geoff Arnold (normally the most difficult to hit) and another 12 off David Gibson.

The pace increased significantly so that when lunch came at 23 overs, Yorkshire were one for 87. Boycott was 53, Close 21. After lunch, they moved into top gear. When they were finally parted, they had put on 192 before Close was out for 79. Yorkshire kept up the pressure, Fred Trueman came in at number four and hit 24. He was followed by John Hampshire, who hit three sixes in successive balls. Ken Barrington eventually had Boycott caught by Stuart Storey, but he had made 146; an innings that included fifteen fours and three sixes.

When Boycott returned to the pavilion, Lord's rose as one to acclaim him.

Yorkshire's 317 for four was a record one-day total. Most gave Surrey no chance of scoring the 318 needed for victory, and Trueman had John Edrich caught by Ray Illingworth. He removed Bill Smith and Ken Barrington before a further run had been added. Stewart made a brave 33 and Ron Tindall hit a half-century, but Illingworth came into his own with the ball. He took five of the last six wickets to fall. Surrey were all out for 142 with almost 20 overs still to be bowled.

4 September 1965
Yorkshire beat Surrey by 175 runs

YORKSHIRE
G. Boycott c Storey b Barrington 146, K. Taylor c Barrington b Sydenham 9, D. B. Close c Edrich b Gibson 79, F. S. Trueman b Arnold 24, J. H. Hampshire not out 38, D. Wilson not out 11
Extras b 3, lb 4, nb 3
Total (60 overs) 317 for four
Fall of wickets 22, 214, 248, 292
Did not bat: D. E. V. Padgett, P. J. Sharpe, R. Illingworth, R. A. Hutton, J. G. Binks
Bowling
Arnold 13-3-51-1, Sydenham 13-1-67-1, Gibson 13-1-66-1, Storey 13-2-33-0, Tindall 3-0-36-0, Barrington 5-0-54-1

SURREY
M. J. Stewart st Binks b Wilson 33, J. H. Edrich c Illingworth b Trueman 15, W. A. Smith lbw b Trueman 0, K. F. Barrington c Binks b Trueman 0, R. A. G. Tindall c Wilson b Close 57, S. J. Storey lbw b Illingworth 1, M. J. Edwards b Illingworth 0, D. Gibson lbw b Illingworth 0, A. Long b Illingworth 17, G. G. Arnold not out 3, D. A. D. Sydenham b Illingworth 8
Extras b 4, lb 4
Total (40.4 overs) 142
Fall of wickets 27, 27, 27, 75, 76, 76, 76, 130, 132
Bowling
Trueman 9-0-31-3, Hutton 8-3-17-0, Wilson 9-0-45-1, Illingworth 11.4-1-29-5, Close 3-0-12-1

Umpires: J. S. Buller and C. S. Elliott

COLONIAL TIES

Legend has it that Rhodesian Prime Minister Ian Smith was among the small crowd at Lord's to watch Mashonaland and Districts take on the Cross Arrows in 1964. At that time, they were the first side from what became Zimbabwe to play at Lord's – Mashonaland and Districts were still part of Southern Rhodesia. Prime Minister Smith would make his unilateral declaration of independence (UDI) within a year.

The tourists batted first and were effective down the order. The MCC bowling attack included Harry Latchman, who later enjoyed a career with Middlesex and Nottinghamshire, but even he went for 5 an over as Mashonaland raced towards a declaration. They set Cross Arrows a victory target of 239.

Mike 'Pasty' Harris top scored with 78 for the home side. Future MCC president Mike Griffith was then a twenty-one-year-old making his way with Sussex. He hit one boundary before he was out to leave MCC 51 for three. David Constant of Leicestershire, better known later as a Test umpire, added 82 for the fourth wicket with Harris. Donald Carr added a brisk 11, but a flurry of wickets left Cross Arrows hanging on for a draw. Former Middlesex batsman turned scorer Harry Sharp was now 46, but he made an unbeaten 22 as MCC held out.

11 September 1964
Cross Arrows drew with Mashonaland and Districts

MASHONALAND AND DISTRICTS

R. Duncan lbw b R Stewart 4, P. Densen run out 39, K. Curran c D. Carr b Latchman 45, J. Kitcat not out 89, D. Bailey c Constant b Jones 49, R. Lees not out 1
Extras b 10, lb 2, nb 3
Total 238 for five declared
Fall of wickets 17, 52, 52, 160, 207.
Did not bat: G. Deney, C. Bray, M. Williams, C. Postlethwayt
Bowling
White 9-0-26-0, Stewart 15-3-36-1, Jones 10-3-62-3, Latchman 12-2-60-1, Constant 4-0-21-0, Carr 3-1-19-0

MCC

C. Pugh b Postlethwayt 0, M. J. Harris c Arnott b M. Williams 78, R. Pearman c Duncan b Williams 17, M. Griffith c Deary b Gray 4, D. J. Constant c Postlethwayt b Bray 43, D. G. Carr b Postlethwayt 11, H. P. Sharp not out 22, H. C. Latchman lbw b N. Williams 8, P. Jones b Williams 4, T. White st b Williams 0, R. Stewart not out 4

Extras b 1, nb 2, w 1
Total 195 for nine
Fall of wickets 13, 44, 51, 133, 154, 160 185 190 190
Bowling
Postlethwayt 13-4-27-2, Williams 20-5-54-5, Deary 13-4-38-0, Bray 11-0-59-2,
Kitcat 1-0-13-0

Umpires: L. Gray, G. Dorman

THE OTHER 1966 WORLD CUP

In the summer of '66, everything stopped for football. The Test series against the West Indies was scheduled to avoid a clash. It proved a wise decision as England's footballers captivated the entire country with their progress to the World Cup final. Geoff Hurst's hat-trick in the final has never been equalled and he remains the only World Cup-winning footballer to have played first-class cricket. But in September, Lord's had a three-match World Cup of its own. England, West Indies and the Rest of World were the participating sides.

The Rest of the World XI were to be led by Australian captain Bobby Simpson. The sponsors decided that the other ten members of the side would be chosen by an unusual selection committee. The choice would be made by a vote among the readers of the *Radio Times*. The magazine printed some 'Hints on Selection' by International Cavaliers president Denis Compton, a man who would have been ideally suited to one-day cricket.

'This year you must bear in mind that the Rothmans world cup matches will be played over knockout rules. Some of the famous names may well be better suited than others to this particular form of Cricket,' he warned.

Voting forms appeared over a month at the start of the season, and the BBC were clearly delighted with the response. They claimed ballot forms had come in from as far afield as Egypt, India and even the Bahamas.

Graeme Pollock received more votes than any other batsman. This may have been because viewers remembered his stunning Test century the previous summer. His brother Peter was the most popular choice as a bowler.

Australian Doug Walters unwittingly gave the organisers an administrative problem. He had been on the shortlist of players, but he was called up for military service and was unable to play.

The *Daily Express* cricket correspondent, Crawford White, wrote,

> The important thing for cricket is that this World cup in miniature could be the pilot scheme, the exploratory rocket in space for the far more ambitious world level tournament s big cricket will surely have to stage in the near future.

The three matches were to be played over 50 overs a side, each bowler limited to 11 overs.

'From the cream of the world's cricketers and Rothmans have flown players thousands of miles to England,' claimed the breathless publicity.

Although the matches were played in mid-September, the sun shone. Colin Cowdrey won the toss, so John Edrich of Surrey and Peter Parfitt of Middlesex walked out to open the England innings in the first match against the Rest of the World.

Edrich was soon out for a duck, bowled by Peter Pollock. Graham McKenzie had Parfitt caught by Hanif and, in the tenth over, Simpson brought on leg-spinner Mushtaq

Mohammed in what John Arlott described as 'a breach of knockout practice'. It paid immediate dividends. Cowdrey misread the googly and England were only 39 for three. Dexter and Jim Parks fought their way out of trouble before Basil D'Oliveira set about the bowling to the patent delight of Arlott. 'D'Oliveira batted with brilliant invention and phlegmatic power,' he wrote. A few years earlier, Arlott had been a key figure in arranging for D'Oliveira to come to England from South Africa.

The Rest of the World chased 202 to win. They started briskly and looked on course until D'Oliveira struck with the ball to remove Graeme Pollock and Colin Bland. Ken Higgs and Barry Knight completed the clean-up operation.

10 September 1966
England beat the Rest of the World by 82 runs

ENGLAND
J. H. Edrich b P. M. Pollock 0, P. H. Parfitt c Hanif Mohammad b McKenzie 11, E. R. Dexter st Murray b Nadkarni 32, M. C. Cowdrey lbw b Mushtaq Mohammad 10, J. M. Parks c P. M. Pollock b Nadkarni 42, B. L. D'Oliveira c Mushtaq Mohammad b P. M. Pollock 49, J. T. Murray b Nadkarni 25, B. R. Knight not out 16, F. J. Titmus not out 6
Extras b 4, lb 6
Total (50 overs) 201 for seven
Fall of wickets 9, 15, 39, 88, 105, 165, 184
Did not bat: K. Higgs
Bowling
P. M. Pollock 11-1-51-2, McKenzie 11-3-45-1, Mushtaq Mohammad 8-0-32-1, Bland 9-0-32-0, Nadkarni 11-2-31-3

REST OF THE WORLD
R. B. Simpson lbw b Knight 38, Hanif Mohammad c Knight b Higgs 20, G. Thomas c Parks b Higgs 4, R. G. Pollock c Cowdrey b D'Oliveira 10, K. C. Bland c Murray b D'Oliveira 5, M. A. K. Pataudi b Higgs 13, Mushtaq Mohammad b Knight 3, D. L. Murray b Higgs 12, R. G. Nadkarni b Higgs 2, P. M. Pollock c Higgs b Knight 1, G. D. McKenzie not out 0
Extras b 2, lb 9
Total (36.3 overs) 119
Fall of wickets 35, 52, 81, 83, 87, 90, 114, 118, 119
Bowling
Snow 3-0-19-0, Higgs 11-0-34-5, Titmus 10-1-21-0, Knight 8.3-1-19-3, D'Oliveira 4-1-15-2

Umpires: C. S. Elliott, A. E. Fagg

In the second match of the series, the West Indies beat the Rest of the World by 18 runs, despite half-centuries from Hanif and Pollock. The other batsmen could not cope with Wes Hall. The result of these matches meant that the first limited overs match between two Test playing teams would decide the destiny of the trophy. It was to all intents and purposes the first one-day international but was never officially recognised.

Although everyone got a start for England, the scoring rate seems modest by the standards of today. Only 26 runs came from the first 14 overs. Edrich and Parks were joint top scorers with 33.217 from 50 overs, which was considered a competitive total.

West Indies started brightly but Knight removed Rohan Kanhai and Basil Butcher in the same over to leave them struggling at 28 for three. Edrich missed a chance given by Seymour Nurse seven runs later. Nurse went on to score 58 before he was trapped by Higgs.

Cowdrey had strained a leg muscle, so England were captained in this final match by Double Gillette Cup-winning captain Ted Dexter. The experience he had gained in placing a field for one-day matches paid dividends. Some tight bowling from Higgs, Fred Titmus and John Snow made sure that even the great Garfield Sobers could not break clear. He was in for 6 overs and scored only 3 runs. When D'Oliveira bowled Rawle Brancker, West Indies had been dismissed for only 150.

13 September 1966
England beat West Indies by 67 runs

ENGLAND
J. H. Edrich run out 33, P. H. Parfitt c sub b Lashley 25, E. R. Dexter b Hall 26, J. M. Parks st Kanhai b Carew 33, B. L. D'Oliveira c Hunte b Lashley 14, M. C. Cowdrey b Lashley 19, J. T. Murray b Hunte 26, B. R. Knight not out 10, F. J. Titmus not out 19
Extras b 4, lb 8
Total (50 overs) 217 for seven
Fall of wickets 36, 83, 104, 140, 144, 181, 189
Did not bat: K. Higgs, J. A. Snow
Bowling
Sobers 11-2-28-0, Hall 11-2-29-1, Lashley 10-0-46-3, Gibbs 11-1-54-0, Carew 5-0-30-1, Hunte 2-0-18-1

WEST INDIES
C. C. Hunte c Parks b Snow 27, M. C. Carew c Murray b Higgs 1, R. B. Kanhai b Knight 14, B. F. Butcher c Murray b Knight 0, S. M. Nurse lbw b Higgs 58, G. S. Sobers c Knight b Snow 3, P. D. Lashley c Higgs b Titmus 9, W. W. Hall b Higgs 0, R. C. Brancker c&b D'Oliveira 20, J. L. Hendriks b Higgs 0, L. R. Gibbs not out 6
Extras lb 12
Total (40.4 overs) 150
Fall of wickets 9, 28, 28, 65, 92, 118, 118, 118, 124
Bowling
Higgs 11-1-50-4, Knight 6-2-17-2, Snow 11-0-34-2, Titmus 11-2-32-1, D'Oliveira 1.4-0-5-1

Umpires: C. S. Elliott, A. E. Fagg

Pre-Olympic Hockey

For hockey players, the path to the 1968 Mexico Olympics went via the St John's Wood Road. It was billed as the first big international hockey event in England since the 1948 Games. Middlesex had in fact beaten Surrey in a county championship match on the ground in 1905, but this was the first time that international hockey had been held at Lord's.

Although not a formal qualification tournament, all the teams were aware that when invitations to take part in Mexico were issued, performances in this tournament would be taken into account.

The details for a twelve-team competition had been announced in January by the Hockey Association. The tournament had the backing of the Fédération Internationale de Hockey, the international governing body. 'With hockey perhaps being one of the most impecunious of amateur games, it is a brave venture,' suggested the correspondent of *The Times* when details were announced. He estimated that English hockey clubs would have to raise around £15,000 to stage the competition.

A six-day tournament was planned. All matches were scheduled to take place at the Oval or Lord's. The tournament was also to be televised. Two pitches were laid out at Lord's. One ran from the Tavern to the Warner Stands and the other was at the Nursery End.

Great Britain were drawn to meet the reigning Olympic champions India in their opening match. The home team were managed by Leonard Jones, who had given up his job to take charge of the team. 'The whole world knows that India and Pakistan are no longer unbeatable,' he said.

The Duchess of Kent was presented to both teams, but within a few minutes, rain swept across the ground and made conditions unpleasant for both sides. Despite the rain, Great Britain struck first. After 16 minutes, Timothy Lawson from Tulse Hill became the first man to score an international goal at Lord's. Shortly before half-time, Jerry Barcham of Dulwich made it 2-0. The manager's confidence seemed well-founded. That dream was short-lived as the Indians hit back in the second half with two goals in quick succession. The winning goal came from V. J. Peter.

GB: D. A. Savage (Oxton), D. Prosser (old Kingstonians) (captain), R. Oliver (Hounslow), G. Nott (Tulse Hill), A. Ekins (Southgate), P. Wilson (Oxford City); M. Crowe (Tulse Hill), T. Lawson (Tulse Hill), M. Read (Dulwich), C. Donald (ICI Grangemouth), J. Barcham (Dulwich).

India: S. Laxman, Gurbux Singh (captain), Vinod Kumar, R. H. B. Krishnamoorthy, Jagjit Singh, Harmik Singh, Balbir Singh, V. J. Peter, Harbinder Singh, Inder Singh, Joginder Singh.

Meanwhile, two nations who had never been seen on a cricket field walked out at the Nursery End. The Spanish may have felt at home when they looked up to see an MCC flag flying – the colours were the same as their national flag. Their opponents were East Germany, known officially as the German Democratic Republic (GDR).

'As they played at the same time as Great Britain and India, I could only have a glimpse of what looked a hard struggle that might have gone either way,' wrote Brian Lewis in *The Times*.

The German goalkeeper Hans Dietrich Sasse may well have forged his own place in Lord's history. He wore a protective face mask, perhaps the first instance of a 'helmet' at Lord's, a full decade before they were seen in cricket.

Karl Heinz Freiberg and Lothar Lippert scored the East German goals, while Jordi Fabregas, one of a pair of brothers, offered the only reply for Spain.

Spain: T. Rodriguez, A. Nogues, T. Solaun, F. Fabregas, N. Ventallo (captain), J. Salles, A. Masana, T. Alvear, F. Amat, J. Fabregas.

GDR: Hans Dietrich Sasse, A. Thieme, K. Vetter, K. Traumer, E. Wolloseck, H. Dahmles, H. Lippert (captain), D. Ehrlich, K. H. Freiberger, A. Klaub, H. Brennecke.

Throughout the afternoon, heavy rain took its toll on the outfield at both Lord's and the Oval, so the organisers' back-up plan came into force on the second day. Matches were hastily switched to Chiswick and Richmond to give the turf some respite.

Later in the week, the competition returned to Lord's. Australian Tom Golder had his own unwanted place in Lord's lore as the first man to be sent off. Despite his exit, his side beat France.

Britain did not win any of their matches in the tournament.

Despite Britain's disappointing results, those at Lord's were delighted and minutes of the MCC meeting record 'the pre-Olympic tournament had proved a great success' with remarkable attendances. They were even more pleased at the news that it had made a profit of £750.

Thus encouraged, they wanted more. From 1969, the university hockey match found a home on the ground and some England internationals were also played there. But by the mid-1970s, the sport had moved into a new era. The top level of the game was played on synthetic surfaces and the era of hockey at Lord's was at an end.

A DAY FOR PLAYERS

In 1969, Sunday became a Lord's Day, with the introduction of the Player's League.

Throughout the 1960s, the star-studded Rothmans International Cavaliers had travelled the country, attracting huge crowds and television audiences to watch limited overs cricket.

The Cavaliers did not play at Lord's until 1967, but when they did so some 15,000 people swarmed into the ground, even though the matches were televised on BBC2.

'I have always said the cavaliers have done a wonderful job for Cricket and have shown the way to make Sunday cricket a success,' said MCC secretary Billy Griffith as he announced arrangements for the new league. Matches were to be televised. The first would be from Lord's as Middlesex took on Yorkshire.

The new competition was sponsored by a tobacco company and was initially known as the Player's League. Later, the title was changed to the John Player League (JPL). Matches were to be of 40 overs per side, with no bowler permitted more than 8 overs. The entertainment began shortly before two o'clock each Sunday. The bowlers' run-ups were restricted to ensure that the matches were completed without interrupting evening television schedules.

Despite the attraction of television, there were still some 5,000 spectators inside the ground for the start of play on that first Sunday.

Yorkshire restricted Middlesex to a modest 137 for nine in their 40 overs. Skipper Peter Parfitt top scored with 34 and shared the best stand of the match: 55 for the third wicket with Clive Radley. The real sensation occurred when Yorkshire went into bat. Phil Sharpe departed for a duck to a fine diving catch by Parfitt off Alan Connolly, the Australian Test player. It was the first over he'd bowled in Middlesex colours since joining the club as an overseas player. Then Doug Padgett called Geoffrey Boycott for a sharp single. Fast bowler John Price responded sharply to run out Boycott. Then, in more conventional style, he proceeded to tear into the Yorkshire top order. At one stage, they were 26 for six. Don Wilson added 48 for the seventh wicket with wicketkeeper Jimmy Binks in the best stand of the innings. Wilson's 46 included three sixes; this gave him an immediate claim on a share of a £1,000 bounty for sixes. The bounty had been introduced by the sponsors and was to be proportionately divided at the end of the season between all those who'd cleared the ropes. On this day, however, Wilson's efforts were in vain as Middlesex won by 43 runs.

'It convinced me completely of the entertainment potential of this type of cricket,' wrote John Arlott in *The Cricketer*.

27 April 1969
Middlesex beat Yorkshire by 43 runs

MIDDLESEX

W. E. Russell c Binks b Hutton 2, M. J. Smith run out 5, P. H. Parfitt c Hutton b Old 34, C. T. Radley b Wilson 23, J. T. Murray c Sharpe b Old 4, F. J. Titmus c Close b Balderstone 17, R. W. Hooker run out 12, K. V. Jones not out 32, R. S. Herman c Balderstone b Nicholson 1, A. N. Connolly not out 4

Extras b 1, nb 2

Total (40 overs) 137 for eight

Fall of wickets 6, 8, 63, 71, 73, 94, 106, 118

Did not bat: J. S. E. Price

Bowling

Nicholson 8-1-32-1, Hutton 7-0-33-1, Close 5-1-23-0, Old 8-3-18-2, Wilson 8-1-18-1, Balderstone 4-0-10-1

YORKSHIRE

G. Boycott run out 3, P. J. Sharpe c Parfitt b Connolly 0, D. E. V. Padgett c Murray b Price 1, J. H. Hampshire c Jones b Price 9, D. B. Close c Radley b Price 6, J. C. Balderstone run out 5, J. G. Binks b Hooker 22, R. A. Hutton b Hooker 0, C. M. Old c&b Jones 0, D. Wilson c Smith b Jones 46, A. G. Nicholson not out 0

Extras lb 1, w 1

Total (32.2 overs) 94

Fall of wickets 2, 3, 4, 10, 26, 26, 74, 74, 94

Bowling

Price 8-0-18-3, Connolly 5-2-5-1, Herman 8-2-16-0, Hooker 7-2-18-2, Titmus 3-0-27-0, Jones 1.2-0-8-2

Umpires: A. E. Fagg and A. Jepson

HAMPSHIRE FROM YORKSHIRE

For some reason, Lord's had always seemed to inspire teams from overseas more than it did the home team. It took over ninety years for an Englishman to score a century on his Test debut at the ground.

John Hampshire had been part of the successful Yorkshire county side of the 1960s, but he had to wait until he was almost twenty-eight to be included in the England squad. He finally got his chance when Tom Graveney was dropped as a punishment for playing in a benefit match on the rest day of the first test.

Hampshire spent his first day as a Test cricketer in the field as the West Indies got away to a great start. Roy Fredericks hooked his way to 53 by lunch supported by Steve Camacho.

Their opening stand of 106 was then a West Indies record in England. They continued to play aggressively and they totalled 380. Charlie Davis scored a century, but their talismanic captain Garfield Sobers had been run out by Geoffrey Boycott for 29.

England reached 19 for 0 before Edrich was caught by Fredericks, and Sobers had both Parfitt and D'Oliveira caught.

'Gary loved Lord's he'd failed with the bat and had got his tail up he was bowling pretty quick,' said Hampshire, who was watching from the pavilion balcony as England's top order crumbled.

'He'd done the damage no doubt about it and of course they had Vanburn Holder and Grayson Shillingford. They were pretty sharp if not in Holding's class,' he said. 'Garry was as fast as those first spell, he used to swing the ball about and had a nasty habit of not telling you which way the ball was going to move.'

When Boycott was caught at the wicket off John Shepherd, England were 37 for four. What a time for the debutant to make his way out to the middle.

He said:

It was a strong side but I was almost starting the tail ... It was frightening experience because we were in a lot of bother. I was not particularly anxious to get out there. There was no chance of bad light, there wasn't a cloud in a thousand miles, so you just had to get on with it.

At the wicket, Hampshire was at least greeted by a familiar face in Yorkshire teammate Phil Sharpe. Together the pair survived to the close but a score of 46 for four did not make for restful slumber.

'I'd put chewing gum in my mouth and it went to very much the texture of Weetabix,' said Hampshire.

Sharpe was dismissed early the following day to leave England 61 for five. Now they were in real danger of having to follow on. Out came Kent wicketkeeper Alan Knott, who had made defiant 73 not out when England clung on for a series -clinching draw in the Caribbean in 1968. Knott had now established himself and together they set about a recovery. Their efforts were priceless. Knott made 53 out of a stand of 128 for the sixth wicket.

Hampshire was now joined by his captain Illingworth. They took the score to 249 before Hampshire was at last out for 107, lbw to John Shepherd.

He said later of his innings,

> From an artistic point of view I have no fondness for it ... I won't say my confidence grew because it didn't but other people around me played very, very well ... I'll be quite honest, it was as bad a knock as I'd played in my life. I either played and missed or I nicked it. I don't think I middled anything.

His assessment was a little harsh. In fact, Hampshire hit 15 boundaries in his innings.

'You just felt, I've got to stick it out and keep going. In the end it was a pretty good day for us.'

It was only the eleventh first-class century of his career and *Wisden* later described Hampshire's innings in glowing terms. 'Now Hampshire produced the courage and ability to match the occasion which most Yorkshiremen knew he possessed.'

It proved a good match for Yorkshire-born cricketers. Captain Ray Illingworth shepherded the tail to good effect and when he was last man out for 113, England were only 36 runs behind. Clive Lloyd and Sobers batted aggressively in West Indies' second innings before the declaration at 295 for nine.

England were left with a victory target of 332, but although Boycott made a second-innings century, both he and Sharpe departed in quick succession. At the close, England were 37 runs short of victory with three second innings wickets in hand.

There was no doubt that Hampshire was the headline maker, but he did not read them.

> It never did dawn on me I did not know until the middle of the following winter when I think I'd got flu. Now I've never been one for saving photographs or cuttings and my wife had saved these press clippings and said, 'Here cheer yourself up.'

26–30 June, 1 July 1969
Match drawn

WEST INDIES First Innings
R. C. Fredericks c Hampshire b Knight 63, G. S. Camacho c Sharpe b Snow 67, C. A. Davis c Knott b Brown 103, B. F. Butcher c Hampshire b Brown 9, G. S. Sobers run out 29, C. H. Lloyd c Illingworth b Brown 18, J. N. Shepherd c Edrich b Snow 32, T. M. Findlay b Snow 23, V. A. Holder lbw b Snow 6, L. R. Gibbs not out 18, G. C. Shillingford c Knott b Snow 3
Extras b 5, lb 4
Total 380
Fall of wickets 106, 151, 167, 217, 247, 324, 336, 343, 376
Bowling
Snow 39-5-114-5, Brown 38-8-99-3, Knight 38-11-65-1, D'Oliveira 26-10-46-0, Illingworth 16-4-39-0, Parfitt 1-0-8-0

ENGLAND First Innings

G. Boycott c Findlay b Shepherd 23, J. H. Edrich c Fredericks b Holder 7, P. H. Parfitt c Davis b Sobers 4, B. L. D'Oliveira c Shepherd b Sobers 0, P. J. Sharpe b Holder 11, J. H. Hampshire lbw b Shepherd 107, A. P. E. Knott b Shillingford 53, R. Illingworth c&b Gibbs 113, B. R. Knight lbw b Shillingford 0, D. J. Brown c Findlay b Shepherd 1, J. A. Snow not out 9

Extras b 1, lb 5, nb 10

Total 344

Fall of wickets 19, 37, 37, 37, 61, 189, 249, 250, 261.

Bowling

Sobers 26-12-57-2, Holder 38-16-83-2, Shillingford 19-4-53-2, Shepherd 43-14-74-3, Gibbs 27.4-9-53-1, Davis 1-0-2-0, Butcher 3-1-6-0

WEST INDIES Second Innings

R. C. Fredericks c Hampshire b Illingworth 60, G. S. Camacho b D'Oliveira 45, C. A. Davis c Illingworth b D'Oliveira 0, C. H. Lloyd c Knott b Snow 70, J. N. Shepherd c Sharpe b Illingworth 11, G. S. Sobers not out 50, T. M. Findlay c Sharpe b Knight 11, V. A. Holder run out 7, L. R. Gibbs b Knight 5

Extras b 4, lb 7, nb 1

Total 295 for nine declared

Fall of wickets 73, 73, 128, 135, 191, 232, 263, 280, 295

Bowling

Snow 22-4-69-1, Brown 9-3-25-0, Knight 27.5-6-78-2, D'Oliveira 15-2-45-2, Illingworth 27-9-66-3

ENGLAND Second Innings

G. Boycott c Butcher b Shillingford 106, J. H. Edrich c Camacho b Holder 1, P. H. Parfitt c Findlay b Shepherd 39, B. L. D'Oliveira c Frederick b Gibbs 18, P. J. Sharpe c Davis b Sobers 86, J. H. Hampshire run out 5, R. Illingworth not out 9, A. P. E. Knott b Shillingford 11, B. R. Knight not out 1

Extras b 9, lb 5, nb 5

Total 295 for seven

Fall of wickets 1, 94, 137, 263, 271, 272, 292

Bowling

Sobers 29-8-72-1, Holder 11-4-36-1, Shillingford 13-4-30-2, Shepherd 12-3-45-1, Gibbs 41-14-93-1

Umpires: J. S. Buller, A. E. Fagg

THE WORLD AT LORD'S

In 1970, Lord's was the first ground to stage an official ICC sanctioned match against the Rest of the World. It was the first of a five Test series and replaced the scheduled tour by South Africa. Two years before, the South African government refused to accept Basil D'Oliveira as part of the England Test team. As a result, the 1968/69 MCC tour was cancelled. Even so, the reciprocal tour remained on the schedule until very late in the day.

Demonstrators had targeted the Springbok rugby tour, and barbed wire and floodlights around the square at Lord's signalled that it, too, was a target. The anti-apartheid protests were coordinated by the 'Stop the Seventy Tour' campaign led by Peter Hain. Gradually, the pressure was building.

The United Nations condemned the tour and it was announced that the Queen would not make her traditional visit to the Lord's Test. Finally, on 22 May 1970 , it was called off.

Within a month, a replacement series against the Rest of the World had begun at Lord's. The matches were to have Test match status, although this was later revoked.

The Rest of the World team included three South Africans, and England gave a debut to Glamorgan's Alan Jones. He slashed the first ball of the match over the slips for four, but was soon caught at the wicket off Mike Procter.

Against an inexperienced batting line-up, Sobers found movement on the first morning as England were reduced to 44 for seven by lunch. England captain Illingworth did his best to rescue the innings with 63. His eighth-wicket stand with Derek Underwood added 50 in forty minutes, but England were all out for 127 and already chasing the game.

Rest of the World openers Eddie Barlow and Barry Richards put on 69 in 17 overs for the first wicket. Barlow completed his half-century as they reached 115 for 2 by close of play. There was no play on the next day, a Thursday, because of the General Election. Unusually, the match would have two days of rest.

Barlow completed his hundred and, with Graeme Pollock, took the score to 215 by lunch.

They were both out soon afterwards, but the defining innings of the match was played by Sobers. By the close, he had hit 25 fours and a six in an unbeaten 147, part of a seven-wicket stand of 177 with Pakistan's Intikhab Alam. The following day, the Rest of the World innings finally came to an end at 546.

The unfortunate Jones was out to the first ball of the England second innings, but Brian Luckhurst and D'Oliveira put on 101 for the third wicket. Even so, they still closed the third day on 228 for five. Illingworth and Knott advanced the score by 65 on the Monday morning without losing a wicket. It was not until 25 minutes after the lunch interval that they were parted, but after Knott was dismissed, the last four wickets went for only 26 runs.

England eventually lost the series 4-1. Later, the Test status of these matches was rescinded, which was particularly unfortunate for Alan Jones who had made his only appearance for England in these matches.

17, 19/20, 22/23 June 1970
Rest of the World beat England by an innings and 80 runs

ENGLAND First Innings

A. Jones c Engineer b Procter 5, B. W. Luckhurst c Richards b Sobers 1, M. H. Denness c Barlow b McKenzie 13, B. L. D'Oliveira c Engineer b Sobers 0, P. J. Sharpe c Barlow b Sobers 4, R. Illingworth c Engineer b Sobers 63, A. P. E. Knott c Kanhai b Sobers 2, J. A. Snow c Engineer b Sobers 2, D. L. Underwood c Lloyd b Barlow 19, A. Ward c Sobers b McKenzie 11, K. Shuttleworth not out 1
Extras lb 5, nb 1
Total 127
Fall of wickets 5, 17, 23, 23, 29, 31, 44, 94, 125
Bowling
McKenzie 16.1-3-43-2, Procter 13-6-20-1, Sobers 20-11-21-6, Barlow 4-0-26-1, Intikhab 2-0-11-0

REST OF THE WORLD First Innings

B. A. Richards c Sharpe b Ward 35, E. J. Barlow c Underwood b Illingworth 119, R. B. Kanhai c Knott b D'Oliveira 21, R. G. Pollock b Underwood 55, C. H. Lloyd b Ward 20, G. S. Sobers c Underwood b Snow 183, F. M. Engineer b Ward 2, Intikhab Alam b Ward 61, M. J. Procter b Snow 26, G. D. McKenzie c Snow b Underwood 0, L. R. Gibbs not out 2
Extras b 10, lb 5, nb 7
Total 546
Fall of wickets 69, 106, 237, 237, 293, 298, 496, 537, 544
Bowling
Snow 27-7-109-2, Ward 33-4-121-4, Shuttleworth 21-2-85-0, D'Oliveira 18-5-45-1, Underwood 25.5-8-81-2, Illingworth 30-8-81-3

ENGLAND Second Innings

A. Jones c Engineer b Procter 0, B. W. Luckhurst c Engineer b Intikhab 67, M. H. Denness c Sobers b Intikhab 24, B. L. D'Oliveira c Lloyd b Intikhab 78, P. J. Sharpe b Sobers 2, R. Illingworth c Barlow b Sobers 94, A. P. E. Knott lbw b Gibbs 39, J. A. Snow b Intikhab 10, D. L. Underwood c Kanhai b Intikhab 7, A. Ward st Engineer b Intikhab 0, K. Shuttleworth not out 0
Extras b 4, lb 8, nb 6
Total 339
Fall of wickets 0, 39, 140, 148, 196, 313, 323, 334, 338
Bowling
McKenzie 15-8-25-0, Procter 15-4-36-1, Sobers 31-13-43-2, Barlow 7-2-10-0, Intikhab 54-24-113-6, Gibbs 51-17-91-1, Lloyd 1-0-3-0

CLUB TIES

As Knockout cricket was now growing in popularity on the club scene and a new competition had started in 1969. Clubs across the country competed for the Derrick Robins Trophy and the first final was played at Edgbaston and won by Hamptead. In 1970, the teams had an added incentive: the final would be at Lord's.

Stockport, from the Central Lancashire League, reached the final and started as favourites – all the more so when Indian Test opener Ashok Mankad struck a fighting 83. They scored 169 from 45 overs.

Cheltenham needed 24 to win off the last 5 overs with three wickets in hand, but they won the match with a six off the last ball by Gloucestershire second XI player David Locke.

29 August 1970
Cheltenham beat Stockport by three wickets

STOCKPORT
A. V. Mankad not out 83, T. Hodson lbw b Rutter 3, N. O'Brien c Coley b Brown 18, N. Barlow b Finch 39, H. Walker b Rutter 1, J. Speak not out 13
Extras 12
Total (45 overs) 169 for four
Fall of wickets 11, 38, 135, 138
Did not bat: P. Speak, A. Brown, R. Bunting, G. Greenop, M. Lennie
Bowling
Rutter 8-2-32-2 , Dredge 8-4-15-0, Brown 8-0-34-1, Locke 8-3-18-0, Adams 5-0-40-0, Finch 8-1-18-1

CHELTENHAM
R. S. Mudway c Hodson b Walker 7, J. W. Goode run out 48, M. Adams c&b O'Brien 20, C. Smith b Greenop 8, N. Furley b Lennie 22, M. Finch b O'Brien 5, D. W. J. Brown st Hodson b Mankad 19, C. J. Coley not out 8, D. Locke not out 21
Extras 14
Total 172 for seven
Did not bat: R. Rutter, C. G. Dredge
Bowling
Walker 8-1-24-1, Lennie 8-1-18-1, Brown 8-0-19-0, Bunting 6-0-36-0, O'Brien 8-0-25-2, Greenop 3-1-13-1, Mankad 4-0-23-1

Umpires: J. F. Crapp and O. W. Herman

GOLD AWARDS

At a meeting at Lord's on 21 October 1971, the cricketing powers announced a new limited overs competition for the third time in nine years.

'It would be idle to deny that the institution of this fourth annual county competition owes itself to financial necessity,' wrote E. W. Swanton, who accepted 'an increase in patronage was essential to the survival of certain of the counties'.

The sponsorship was worth £160,000 over the first three years, of which £130,000 was to be distributed directly to the counties.

The new arrival, the Benson & Hedges Cup, soon became known as the 'B&H'. The first stage of the competition was played across four mini groups of five, organised on geographical lines.

Unfortunately, rain swept across England on Saturday 29 April competition and wiped out every single match, including the first match at Lord's. Play eventually began on Monday. Middlesex skipper Mike Brearley won the toss and asked Kent to bat.

It was a familiar face who took charge of the innings. Colin Cowdrey had not expected to play, but when Alan Ealham was unfit he responded with a hundred, the first to be scored in this competition. It included nine fours and three sixes and earned him the first 'gold award for the outstanding individual performance'. The cash prize for this performance was a princely £25.

When Middlesex batted, opener Mike Smith top scored with 75. The middle order all added useful runs and, before Fred Titmus joined, wicketkeeper John Murray knocked off the winning runs with eight balls to spare.

29 April and 1 May 1972
Middlesex beat Kent by three wickets
KENT 234 for five of 55 overs (Cowdrey 107)
MIDDLESEX 235 for seven off 53.4 overs (M. J. Smith 73)

The early season weather had not been kind to the new one-day competition, so organisers breathed a sigh of relief when the final day dawned fine.

The final was between Leicestershire and Yorkshire, who both went into the match with injury concerns. The Yorkshire captain, Geoffrey Boycott, missed the final with a hand injury, which was ironically sustained in a Gillette Cup match, and Yorkshire were further weakened by Richard Hutton was nursing an injured Achilles and the absence of Don Wilson.

They batted first, but Richard Lumb had his off-stump removed by Graham McKenzie. Phil Sharpe went to a superb catch by wicketkeeper Roger Tolchard, who dived in front of first slip Barry Dudlestone to take the catch to leave them 21 for two. Barry Leadbetter top scored for Yorkshire. He hit a four and a six off Brian Davison, who went for 11 in his first over. His stand of 39 for the third wicket with John Hampshire proved the best of the entire innings as Yorkshire struggled throughout. Only 12 runs came in a period from the 25th to the 37th over. Leicestershire skipper Illingworth gave away only 21 runs in his 10-over spell and after 55 overs, Yorkshire had only reached 136 for nine.

They still harboured hopes of an unlikely victory when Barry Dudleston and Roger Tolchard were both taken by 'keeper David Bairstow to leave them at 24 for 2. The asking rate was still only a shade over 2 an over, so what Yorkshire really needed was to bowl out their opponents. It was not to be. Mick Norman's 38 took Leicestershire halfway to their prize. The job was completed by an unbeaten 41 from Chris Balderstone, which earned him the gold award. It was a first major trophy for Leicestershire.

22 July 1972
Leicestershire beat Yorkshire by five wickets

YORKSHIRE
P. J. Sharpe c Tolchard b Higgs 14, R. Lumb b McKenzie 7, B. Leadbetter run out 32, J. H. Hampshire lbw b McKenzie 14, R. A. Hutton c Spencer b Steele 8, J. D. Woodford c Spencer b Illingworth 1, C. Johnson b Higgs 20, C. M. Old lbw b Illingworth 6, D. L. Bairstow c Tolchard b McKenzie 13, H. P. Cooper not out 7, A. G. Nicholson not out 4
Extras lb 9, nb 1
Total (55 overs) 136 for nine
Fall of wickets 17, 21, 60, 65, 77, 83, 113, 122, 124
Bowling
McKenzie 11-2-22-3, Higgs 11-1-33-2, Spencer 7-2-11-0, Davison 11-2-22-0, Illingworth 10-3-21-2 , Steele 5-1-17-1

LEICESTERSHIRE
B. Dudlestone c Bairstow b Nicholson 6, M. E. J. C. Norman c Sharpe b Woodford 38, R. W. Tolchard c Bairstow b Cooper 3, B. F. Davison b Cooper 17, J. C. Balderstone not out 41, R. Illingworth c Bairstow b Hutton 5, P. R. Haywood not out 21
Extras b 2, lb 2, nb 1, w 4
Total (46.5 overs) 140 for five
Fall of wickets 16, 24, 58, 84, 97
Did not bat: J. F. Steele, G. D. McKenzie, K. Higgs, C. Spencer
Bowling
Old 9.5-1-35-0, Nicholson 9-2-17-1, Hutton 11-1-24-1, Cooper 9-0-27-2, Woodford 8-1-28-1

Umpires: D. J. Constant and T. W. Spencer

The wheel turned full circle on tobacco sponsorship in 1997. The Revd Malcolm Gingold, a Woolwich clergyman, proposed a smoking ban in the Lord's pavilion. The motion was carried, over a century after Smokers v Non-Smokers had been such an important fundraising match.

MASSIE'S ATTACK

No bowler before or since has made a Lord's debut with such devastating effect as Robert Arnold Lockyer Massie. His sixteen-wicket haul in his first test may never be equalled but, for all that, his performance did not come as a surprise to two very distinguished judges.

'I happened to see him bowl in a match in Australia and happened to mention this to Sir Donald Bradman the next time I saw him that I had been impressed,' wrote Richie Benaud in *The Cricketer* in 1972. 'You're in good company then,' said the Don. 'Care for a little more of this excellent claret?'

Massie had put in the hard yards in preparation. He spent three years at Kilmarnock getting used to conditions in the British Isles and, crucially, he also learnt to exploit the type of ball that was used in England.

The early summer of 1972 was unusually soggy and, with an expectant crowd at Lord's all ready for play, the weather ran true to form. It began to drizzle shortly before play was due to start on the opening day. Eventually, shortly before noon, the match began. It was still cool enough for Massie to come in from the Nursery End wearing a sleeveless sweater. England openers Geoffrey Boycott and John Edrich put on 22 for the first wicket in 48 minutes of play. Then, Massie struck to claim an illustrious first Test victim. He bowled Boycott for 11 with a delivery he later described as 'a bit of a fluke'.

When his Western Australia teammate Dennis Lillee reduced England to 28 for three, England had lost those wickets for six runs in a quarter of an hour. Massie took every other wicket to fall on the first day. He walked off with five for 75 from 28 overs as England closed 249 for seven. He soon tidied up the loose ends the following morning.

Greg Chappell led the way in Australian reply with what John Arlott described as 'a composed and faultless century', after Snow had bowled Bruce Francis in the first over of the innings. John Price began his opening spell with a wicket as Australia now struggled at 7 for 2. Chappell was still there at the close on 105 not out in his first Test innings at Lord's. Such was the excitement on Saturday that the gates were closed at 11.10 a.m. with 31,000 inside the ground. Chappell was dismissed for 131, but wicketkeeper Rodney Marsh ensured they would have a first innings' lead of 36.

When England batted again, Lillee accounted for Boycott and Luckhurst. Edrich, missed off Lillee, was taken by Marsh off Massie, and when D'Oliveira snicked Massie to Greg Chappell, England were still eleven runs behind at 25 for four. It was a helter-skelter start to the innings and had all but decided the match. They still had not erased the deficit when Tony Greig was caught in the slips by Ian Chappell. Massie, who operated from the Nursery End unchanged, reduced England to 86 for nine by the end of the day. For the experts, his impact recalled that of Frederick Spofforth and his rest day must have been sweet indeed.

Australia completed the victory on the fourth day to level the series.

'You could have thrown in any batsman in any era and they would have had the same problems with Massie,' said Benaud. He also noted the late swing that invited favourable comparisons with Alan Davidson, the great Australian bowler, so it was fitting that he was there to add his congratulations.

22–26 June 1972
Australia beat England by eight wickets

ENGLAND First Innings
G. Boycott b Massie 11, J. H. Edrich lbw b Lillee 10, B. W. Luckhurst b Lillee 1, M. J. K. Smith b Massie 34, B. L. D'Oliveira lbw b Massie 32, A. W. Greig c Marsh b Massie 54, A. P. E. Knott c Colley b Massie 43, R. Illingworth lbw b Massie 30, J. A. Snow b Massie 37, N. Gifford c Marsh b Massie 3, J. S. E. Price not out 4
Extras lb 6, nb 6, w 1
Total 272
Fall of wickets 22, 23, 28, 84, 97, 193, 200, 260, 265
Bowling
Lillee 28-3-90-2, Massie 32.5-7-84-8, Colley 16-2-42-0 , G. Chappell 6-1-18-0, Gleeson 9-1-25-0

AUSTRALIA First Innings
K. R. Stackpole c Gifford b Price 5, B. C. Francis b Snow 0, I. M. Chappell c Smith b Snow 56, G. S. Chappell b D'Oliveira 131, K. D. Walters c Illingworth b Snow 1, R. Edwards c Smith b Illingworth 28, J. W. Gleeson c Knott b Greig 1, R. W. Marsh c Greig b Snow 50, D. J. Colley c Greig b Price 25, R. A. L. Massie c Knott b Snow 0, D. K. Lillee not out 0
Extras lb 7, nb 2
Total 308
Fall of wickets 1, 7, 82, 84, 190, 212, 250, 290, 290
Bowling
Snow 32-13-57-5, Price 26.1-5-87-2, Greig 29-6-74-1, D'Oliveira 17-5-48-1, Gifford 11-4-20-0, Illingworth 7-2-13-1

ENGLAND Second Innings
G. Boycott b Lillee 6, J. H. Edrich c Marsh b Massie 6, B. W. Luckhurst c Marsh b Lillee 4, M. J. K. Smith c Edwards b Massie 30, B. L. D'Oliveira c G. Chappell b Massie 3, A. W. Greig c I. Chappell b Massie 3, A. P. E. Knott c G. Chappell b Massie 12, R. Illingworth c Stackpole b Massie 12, J. A. Snow c Marsh b Massie 0, N. Gifford not out 16, J. S. E. Price c G. Chappell b Massie 19
Extras w 1, nb 4
Total 16
Fall of wickets 12, 16, 18, 25, 31, 52, 74, 74, 81
Bowling
Lillee 21-6-50-2, Massie 27.2-9-53-8, Colley 7-1-8-0

AUSTRALIA Second Innings
K. R. Stackpole not out 57, B. C. Francis c Knott b Price 9, I. M. Chappell c Luckhurst b D'Oliveira 6, G. S. Chappell not out 7

Extras lb 2
Total 81 for two
Fall of wickets 20, 51
Bowling
Snow 8-2-15-0, Price 7-0-28-1, Greig 3-0-17-0, D'Oliveira 8-3-14-1, Luckhurst 0.5-0-5-0

Umpires: A. E. Fagg and D. J. Constant

A VILLAGE AT LORD'S

Not since the fabled Hambledon Club took on the MCC in the late eighteenth century had the spotlight shone so brightly on village cricket.

The idea for a national competition came from publishing executive Ben Brocklehurst, who was in charge of *The Cricketer* magazine. In early 1971, he made the announcement:

> The object is to promote the best in village cricket, give the village cricketer the opportunity to compete in a national event and recognise the value of the village game by applying to have the final at Lord's.

The competition was open to any 'rural community of not more than 2,500'.

In order to keep the game true to the character of village cricket, 'ambitious clubs will be discouraged from enlisting ex-Test stars or hired assassins for the event,' said Brocklehurst whimsically. More seriously, there was the stipulation that 'no-one ever having played first class cricket will be eligible to take part'.

Entries poured in, despite a postal strike in the early months of 1971.

The whisky distillers John Haig agreed to become sponsors after their boss heard a radio broadcast giving details about the competition.

The following spring, the competition began with a series of knockout matches on regional lines. That was no mean administrative operation in itself.

Down in Cornwall, Troon Cricket Club secretary Maurice Bolitho told his club's annual meeting, 'Gentlemen, Next year I shall be reporting on our win, having played at Lord's.'

His words caused mirth at the time but they proved to be prophetic. Troon reached the final. Their opponents were Astwood Bank from the Midlands.

Entry to Lord's on final day was for the princely sum of 25p, and advance tickets were even cheaper. It promised to be a day when much of Cornwall would decamp to London and the club even chartered a train. Unfortunately, a derailment in Dawlish tunnel meant the train never made it beyond Devon, although some intrepid supporters switched transport and completed the journey by car.

Astwood Bank captain John Yoxall had scored a century earlier in the competition, and he started the match in impressive style. The official scorebook reveals that the first 50 came up in 49 minutes from 12.3 overs.

Organisers had arranged for the band of the Royal Green Jackets to play. The problem came when the music continued during play. Troon captain Terry carter said 'I told the Umpires, we are not so keen on this, we are here to play a serious cricket match,' Astwood Bank batsman Brian Spittle did not relish the soundtrack either. When the music stopped, he hit two sixes in a bright 36. After such a lively start, a total of 166 seemed within Troon's reach, especially as they were used to chasing down totals.

Among the crowd was Australian Test batsman Ian Redpath. He had not been selected for that summer's touring party, but he followed the village competition.

'I called Ian Redpath my talisman,' said Carter, who had made runs when the Australian was present at a previous match. His presence had the same positive effect in the final. Carter made an unbeaten 79 in an hour. It included eight fours and two sixes. Fourteen runs came in 1 over, and he finished off proceedings with a four and a six.

Haig had commissioned a special trophy. It stood 15 inches high, was shaped like a whisky bottle, made of sterling silver and featured crossed cricket bats.

Carter didn't even have time to return to the dressing room before collecting it. He said, 'I just laid my bat and gloves on a table in the long room. There can't be too many cricketers who have done that.'

'All newspaper correspondents including myself made reference to the absence of braces, blacksmiths and other traditional rustic trappings. It would have been delightful to see such a picture at Lord's but I doubt if such a village scene is to be found any more in England,' wrote former England bowler Ian Peebles.

There was, however, one nod to the village game of universal imagination. The sponsors arranged a competition for throwing the cricket ball. The winner was seventeen-year-old Michael Richardson from Belsay Cricket Club in Northumbria.

9 September 1972
Troon beat Astwood Bank by seven wickets

ASTWOOD BANK
J. E. Yoxall c W. E. Carter b Edwards 36, J. Robinson b Thomas 30, B. J. Spittle b Johns 36, R. F. Davies st Rashleigh b Duncan 30, M. Wedgebury lbw b Johns 0, C. P. Robinson b Johns 3, J. Crumpton not out 16, J. Poole lbw b Johns 0, T. C. Bird b Johns 1, R. O. Nash not out 2
Extras b 5, lb 6
Total (40 overs) 165 for eight
Fall of wickets 69, 69, 139, 139, 141, 148, 148, 162
Did not bat: F. Morrall
Bowling
Johns 9-1-25-1, Edwards 9-2-35-2, Thomas 9-0-35-0, Moyle 4-0-25-0, Dunstan 9-1-34-1

TROON
J. M. Spry c Poole b Morrall 2, T. Edwards b Morrall 45, G. B. Carter lbw b C. P. Robinson 19, W. T. Carter not out 79, J. Vincent not out 14
Extras lb 8, nb 2, w 1
Total (33.4 overs) 170 for three
Fall of wickets 14, 50, 117
Did not bat: M. Sweeney, P. Johns, B. Moyle, D. Rashleigh, G. J. Dunstan, P. Thomas
Bowling
Morrall 9-2-25-2, Crumpton 9-1-39-0, Yoxall 4-0-26-0, CP Robinson 6.4-1-41-1, Spittle 4-0-23-0, Bird 1-0-5-0

Umpires: L. H. Gray and H. E. Robinson

THE MEN FROM THE PRU

The first official one-day international at Lord's was at the end of the summer of 1972. It was sponsored by Prudential Assurance and was part of a three-match series for a futuristic trophy. The advertising said that matches would be under 'Gillette rules'. In fact, they were played over 55 overs per side, the same as the new B&H competition. In order to explain what was happening, some newspapers described the matches as 'mini Tests'. The England players who took part received a special sweater and cap, emblazoned with a single lion.

England captain Ray Illingworth had been the first captain to lift a trophy in 55 overs of cricket, but he had not recovered from an injury received in the final Test at the Oval. The choice of Somerset captain Brian Close to replace him was a surprise. Five years before, Close had been relieved of the England captaincy after controversial slow play in a county match. In 1970, he had also been sacked as Yorkshire captain, and one of the reasons that had been given was his attitude to one-day cricket.

'I don't say it does the game any good, especially as far as the development of class players goes, but it is part of the game now and we have to accept it,' said Close at the time.

A total of 22,000 came through the gates at Lord's to see if Australia could bounce back after losing the first match of the series.

Australia lost in Manchester after batting first but, this time, Chappell won the toss and put England in. Lillee removed Boycott's middle stump to provide one of the most spectacular sights of the entire summer. Close promoted himself to number three, and picked up the momentum by hitting David Colley for six over square leg. He had reached 43 made from forty balls, when a misunderstanding with Dennis Amiss left him stranded. England lunched at 110 for three but lost three wickets in 4 overs for 7 runs shortly afterwards. From 121 for six, Tony Greig and Alan Knott's seventh-wicket stand made sure England's total of 236 would be at least be competitive.

In the context of one-day cricket, the time would usually have been more than enough, had it not been for some uncharacteristically loose bowling by John Snow and Geoff Arnold. They conceded twelve extras as Australia raced to 44 in the first 5 overs. Ross Edwards was taken low down by wicketkeeper Alan Knott off John Snow, but Australia's second-wicket pairing of Keith Stackpole and Ian Chappell advanced the score to 112 at 5 an over. Greg Chappell and Paul Sheahan shared a stand of 102 in 22 overs to take their side home.

26 August 1972
Australia beat England by five wickets

ENGLAND

G. Boycott b Lillee 8, D. L. Amiss b Mallett 25, D. B. Close run out 43, K. W. R. Fletcher c Stackpole b G. S. Chappell 20, J. H. Hampshire st Marsh b Mallett 13, B. L. D'Oliveira c I. M. Chappell b Lillee 6, A. W. Greig b Massie 31, A. P. E. Knott c Mallett b Massie 50, R. A. Woolmer run out 9, J. A. Snow not out 5, G. G. Arnold not out 11
Extras b 1, lb 10, nb 3, w 1
Total (55 overs) 236 for nine
Fall of wickets 11, 65, 87, 114, 121, 121, 198, 217, 218
Bowling
Lillee 11-0-56-2, Massie 11-1-35-2, Colley 11-1-72-0, Mallett 11-2-24-2, G. Chappell 11-0-34-1

AUSTRALIA

K. R. Stackpole lbw b D'Oliveira 52, R. Edwards c Knott b Snow 6, I. M. Chappell c Knott b Woolmer 31, G. S. Chappell lbw b Snow 48, A. P. Sheahan c Knott b Snow 50, G. D. Watson not out 11, R. W. Marsh not out 6
Extras b 6, lb 4, nb 4, w 12
Total (51.3 overs) 240 for five
Fall of wickets 44, 112, 116, 219, 224
Did not bat: D. J. Colley, A. A. Mallett, D. K. Lillee, R. A. L. Massie
Bowling
Snow 11-2-35-3, Arnold 11-0-47-0, D'Oliveira 11-0-46-1, Greig 9-1-29-0, Woolmer 9.1-0-47-1

Umpires: A. E. Fagg, and T. W. Spencer

In 1975, it snowed in the first week of June. Only two days later, Lord's played host to the greatest gathering of international cricketers ever in one place, and the sun shone. The first World Cup, known officially as the Prudential Cup, had attracted eight participating teams. They went first to Buckingham Palace to meet the Queen and then to Lord's. The decision to stage a competition had been taken in 1972 in a meeting room a few yards from where the players now happily mingled on the grass. The sixteen-man England squad was joined by players from Australia, India, Pakistan, New Zealand and the West Indies. Also taking part were Sri Lanka, not yet a Test-playing country, and East Africa, made up from players in Kenya, Uganda and Tanzania. The only absentees were South Africa; their presence had made impossible by the Apartheid regime. From a cricketing perspective, it meant that great players such as Barry Richards, Mike Procter and the Pollock brothers would be missing from this great festival. 'There was only one starting point for a venture of this magnitude, the ancient headquarters of cricket,' wrote E. W. Swanton, the doyen of English cricket writers at the time.

Saturday 7 June dawned with scarcely a cloud in the sky. Over 16,000 bustled excitedly along St John's Wood Road that morning. England captain Mike Denness walked out for the toss and the coin came down in his favour, so openers Dennis Amiss and John Jameson, both of Warwickshire, were soon padding up. It was a warm summer day. Very few of the Indians felt the need for a sweater. There were no helmets but Amiss wore a cap against the sun. Jameson said,

It was a fairly normal day for me because I was opening with Dennis who was my county partner. So there wasn't any worry about whether we were going to run each other out. I think the great excitement was walking out at Lord's … I don't think it really registered that this was the first World cup match.

Jameson faced the first ball from Indian seamer Madan Lal. Progress was sedate by modern standards but considered text book at the time. England raised the 50 in the tenth over.

'In the early overs, when defence is important, the stealing of well judged singles gives bustle and purpose,' wrote former England captain Tony Lewis in the official tournament programme.

Jameson nicked a ball to slip with the score at 54, but Amiss was now joined by Keith Fletcher of Essex, another specialist in the one-day game. They lifted the score to 150 for one off 35 overs by the lunch interval. Amiss was 98 not out. It seems quaint now that a one-day innings be interrupted by lunch. Amiss completed the first one-day international hundred seen at Lord's in the thirty-seventh over of the innings. When he was finally out, he had faced 140 balls for his 137.

Enter Yorkshire's Chris Old, a fast medium bowler with a reputation for big hitting. With Denness, he added 89 in the last 10 overs as England reached 334 in their 60 overs. It was a ground record in this type of cricket.

Sunil Gavaskar began the Indian reply with Eknath Solkar. 'Right from the start we knew that the chase was out of the question,' said Gavaskar. After 6 overs, India had scored only 8 runs, after 10 overs, the total was 17, and the Indian fans, mostly in the old mound stand, were starting to show their irritation.

Matters became even worse after the interval. Gavaskar later described it as 'a complete mental block as far as I was concerned'.

Indian fans ran on to the field to plead with the batsmen to become more attacking. Their entreaties were in vain. Gavaskar said,

I can understand the crowd's reaction … I am very sorry for spoiling their day. I am the first to admit I deserved to be censured for my slow scoring. It was by far the worst innings I have ever played.

When the 60 overs were finally complete, India had reached 132 for three. The whole affair had also taken the gloss off the day for the victorious England team. Jameson said,

It was amazing actually we were fielding and wondering just what was going on. He just carried on blocking and blocking, at the end of the day we were probably trying to get through the overs quickly and get off the field because it almost became embarrassing in the end.

Indian team manager G. S. Ramchand told reporters, 'I was more than disappointed, I made my views known to Gavaskar.'

RUN RATE COMPARISON
After 5 overs ENGLAND 15 for 0, INDIA 7 for 0
After 10 overs ENGLAND 42 for 0, INDIA 18 for 0
After 25 overs ENGLAND 100 for one, INDIA 52 for two
After 35 overs ENGLAND 150 for one, INDIA 83 for two

After 45 overs ENGLAND 208 for one, INDIA 114 for three
After 55 overs ENGLAND 271 for four, INDIA 128 for three
60 overs ENGLAND 334 for four, INDIA 132 for three

7 June 1975
Prudential World Cup Group A
England won by 202 runs

ENGLAND
J. A. Jameson c Venkat b Armanath 21, D. L. Amiss b Madan Lal 137, K. W. R. Fletcher
b Abid Ali 68, A. W. Greig lbw b Abid Ali 4, M. H. Denness not out 37, C. M. Old not
out 51
Extras lb 12, nb 3, w 2
Total (60 overs) 334 for four
Fall of wickets 54, 230, 237, 245
Did not bat: B. Wood, A. P. E. Knott, J. A. Snow, P. Lever, G. G. Arnold
Bowling
Madan Lal 12-1-64-1, Ghavri 11-1-83-0, Armanath 12-2-60-1, Venkataraghavan
12-0-41-0, Abid Ali 12-0-58-2, Solkar 1-0-12-0

INDIA
S. M. Gavaskar not out 36, E. D. Solkar c Lever b Arnold 8, A. D. Gaekward c Knott
b Lever 22, G. R. Vishwananath c Fletcher b Old 37, B. P. Patel not out 16
Extras lb 3, nb 6, w 1
Total (60 overs) 132 for three
Fall of wickets 21, 50, 108
Did not bat: M. Armanath, F. M. Engineer, S. Abid Ali, S. Madan Lal,
S. Venkataraghavan, K. Ghavri
Bowling
Snow 12-2-24-0, Arnold 10-2-20-1, Old 12-4-28-1, Lever 16-0-16-1, Greig 9-1-26-0,
Wood 6-2-4-0, Jameson 2-1-3-0

Umpires: D. J. Constant and J. G. Langridge

On the longest day of 1975 (21 June), Lord's became the first ground to stage an official
World Cup final in men's cricket. Over the preceding fourteen days, not a minute of play
had been lost to bad light or rain. The tournament was already being hailed as a great
success before the two leading nations took the field in front of a packed ground on a
glorious midsummer's day.

Australia's Ian Chappell won the toss and sent West Indies in. Some questioned this but
West Indies captain Clive Lloyd later admitted 'it was a decision I was glad I did not have
to make'.

West Indies' left-handed opener Roy Fredericks hooked one ball into the stand for
six, but as the many Caribbean supporters roared their approval, his foot slipped in and
dislodged a bail. Alvin Kallicharran had smashed Dennis Lillee to all parts of the Oval
seven days earlier in a group match, but this time he too was out cheaply. The innings
tottered at 50 for three. It was just the sort of stage that West Indian skipper Clive Lloyd
relished. He drew on his own experience of cup final cricket with Lancashire. Fellow

Guyanan Rohan Kanhai, his immediate predecessor as West Indies captain, kept the runs flowing as they set about the Australian bowlers.

Lloyd brought up his hundred with a flashing boundary. It was the second time in three years he had scored a century in a major final at Lord's. Lloyd said afterwards, 'my innings must have been one of the best I have played in limited overs cricket ... We knew we had to get a really big score when we were put in.'

Lloyd eventually touched Gilmour to wicketkeeper Rod Marsh. Vivian Richards, playing an international at Lord's for the first time, was dismissed cheaply for 5. It was a rare failure in a golden career. His one-day average when batting at Lord's would later reach the high eighties.

The West Indies' score of 209 for six was not yet a total for to defend with confidence but, thanks to some useful late hitting by bowlers Bernard Julien and Keith Boyce, they reached 291 for eight. No team had yet successfully chased such a total to win a one-day match, let alone a World Cup final.

Although Richards had failed with the bat, he excelled in the field. He threw down the stumps from midwicket with Australian opener Alan Turner short of his ground. He ended a dangerous stand between the Chappell brothers by running out Greg. A swift return to his skipper also ran out Ian when the Australian skipper was in full flow with Doug Walters.

At 233 for nine, the chance seemed to have gone for Australia, but the longer Dennis Lillee and Jeff Thomson batted, the more the improbable became possible. Thomson hit a catch to midwicket and the crowd surged on to the field, unaware that a no-ball had been called. Lillee and Thomson kept running before umpires Dickie Bird and Tom Spencer restored control. It was 8.21 p.m. when at last wicketkeeper Deryck Murray ran out Thomson. The West Indies had won by 17 runs. In the words of John Woodcock of *The Times*, 'a piece of theatre; of drama, tragedy, carnival and farce all rolled into one.'

A few minutes later, the trophy was set out on a presentation dais in front of the pavilion. Styled on the work of eighteenth-century silversmith Paul de Lamerie, it stood 18½ inches high and contained 89½ ounces of sterling silver.

Clive Lloyd, man of the match of course, stepped up to receive the cup from Prince Philip, president of MCC. It had truly been a match to set before a prince.

21 June 1975
Prudential Cup Final
West Indies beat Australia by 17 runs

WEST INDIES
R. C. Fredericks hit wicket b Lillee 7, C. G. Greenidge c Marsh b Thomson 13, A. I. Kallicharran c Marsh b Gilmour 12, R. B. Kanhai b Gilmour 55, C. H. Lloyd c Marsh b Gilmour 102, I. V. A. Richards b Gilmour 5, K. D. Boyce c G. Chappell b Thomson 34, B. D. Julien not out 26, D. L. Murray c&b Gilmour 14, V. A. Holder not out 6
Extras lb 6, nb 11
Total (60 overs) 291 for eight
Fall of wickets 12, 27, 50, 199, 206, 209, 261, 285
Did not bat: A. M. E. Roberts
Bowling
Lillee 12-1-55-1, , Gilmour 12-2-48-5, Thomson 12-1-44-2, Walker 12-1-71-1, G. Chappell 7-0-33-0, Walters 5-0-23-0

AUSTRALIA

R. B. McCosker c Kallicharran b Boyce 7, A. Turner run out 40, I. M. Chappell run out 62, G. S. Chappell run out 15, K. D. Walters b Lloyd 35, R. W. Marsh b Boyce 11, R. Edwards c Fredericks b Boyce 28, G. J. Gilmour c Kanhai b Boyce 14, M. H. N. Walker run out 7, J. R. Thomson run out 21, D. K. Lillee not out 16

Extras b 2, lb 9, nb 7

Total (58.4 overs) 274

Fall of wickets 25, 81, 115, 162, 170, 195, 221, 231, 233

Bowling

Julien 12-0-58-0, Roberts 11-1-45-0, Boyce 12-0-50-4, Holder 11.4-1-56-0, Lloyd 12-1-38-1

Umpires: H. D. Bird and T. W. Spencer

EAST AFRICA AND HONG KONG
BREAK NEW GROUND

A combined East African team played at Lord's for the first time in the summer of 1972. Their captain, the Kenyan Jawahir Shah, was part of the East African team that returned three years later to compete in the first World Cup, so for him at least, this was valuable preparation.

The entire programme of twenty-one matches had been arranged by MCC. For most of the team of sixteen, drawn from Kenya, Uganda and Tanzania, playing on natural grass wickets was something new. 'They had certainly never played cricket under such extremely cold and damp conditions as were experienced,' said team manager Maj. Hugh Collins.

The weather did relent for their visit to Lord's where MCC president Freddie Brown was on hand to welcome the tourists.

Charanjive Sharma top scored with 44. He was a consistent performer throughout the tour and also returned to England. His trip came in 1979 to play in the ICC Trophy. Harihal Shah proved the best all-rounder and he scored 22, but East Africa were bowled out for 163.

'There is no doubt that they returned as much better cricketers than when they left,' said Collins.

17 June 1972
MCC won by 86 runs

MCC
G. Dawson c Mehta b Zulfiqar 41, A. R. Day run out 67, E. A. Clark lbw b Lakhani 8, M. P. Murray b Lakhani 12, D. L. Hays not out 64, C.M. H. Greetham not out 40
Extras b 12, lb 4, nb 1
Total 249 for four declared
Fall of wickets 81, 105, 127, 151
Did not bat: R. C. Kerslake, D. Bennett, D. Piachaud, R. Jefferson, W. G. Jones
Bowling
Tapu 9-3-23-0, Upendra Patel 14-0-62-0, Lakhani 19-1-44-2, Zulfiqar Ahmed 18-2-56-1, Fernandes 4.1-0-29-0, Vasani 3-0-18-0

EAST AFRICA
A. Lakhani b Kerslake 37, P. Mehta b Jefferson 1, Mehmood lbw b Piachaud 8, Jawahir Shah b Jefferson 11, C. Sharma c Hays b Day 44, Harilal Shah c Greetham b Kerslake 22, Upendra Patel b Jefferson 5, L. Fernandes b Piachaud 11, Zuquifar Ahmed b Day 8, V. Tapu st Hays b Kerslake 8, K. Vasani not out 7
Extras nb 1
Total 163

Fall of wickets 15, 45, 57, 61, 94, 99, 139, 139, 148
Bowling
Jefferson 14-4-32-3, Jones 7-3-17-0, Greetham 4-1-5-0, Clark 6-2-9-0, Piachaud 13-6-31-2, Kerslake 17-6-43-3, Day 8-2-25-2

Cricket had been played in Hong Kong for over a century by the time they visited Lord's for the first time in 1976. It was their fifth game of an eleven-match tour.

The previous year, they had entertained an MCC side that was to all intents the England Test eleven. Their opposition at Lord's was of an older generation.

Former Middlesex and England batsman Eric Russell opened the batting and made 47. Five of the MCC team had played Test cricket and three had captained England. M. J. K. Smith and Colin Cowdrey had only retired from first-class cricket the previous season and were evidently in good touch as both scored half-centuries.

When Hong Kong batted, Laurie Champniss, a stalwart of minor county cricket with Buckinghamshire, returned figures of 5 for 72. Hong Kong were 22 runs short of victory when stumps were drawn.

'I was proud that our best performance came at Lord's,' said Hong Kong Cricket Association president Ted Wilson. 'This tour has long been my dream and although the results may have been disappointing we have made many friends wherever we have played.' They presented MCC with an unusual souvenir – a crafted silver dragon.

12 July 1976
Match drawn

MCC
W. E. Russell b Myatt 47, A. Stewart b Lalchandani 4, M. J. K. Smith c&b Myatt 56, M. C. Cowdrey not out 66, E. R. Dexter c&b Myatt 0, B. Taylor c Hughes b Myatt 19, J. K. Fawcett not out 21
Extras b 3, lb 3, w 2
Total 220 for five declared
Fall of wickets 5, 107, 118, 118, 156
Did not bat: A. C. Smith, N. J. Evans, D. W. Henry, L. J. Champniss

HONG KONG
J. A. Bygate lbw b A. Smith 31, B. J. Willson c M. Smith b Champniss 30, D. L. Budge lbw b Champniss 1, R. W. Mulready b Champniss 0, D. Clinton lbw b Champniss 17, P. W. Anderson b Cowdrey 39, G. Lalchandani c Evans b Champniss 13, R. J. Starling c&b Dexter J. Hughes not out 26, M.R. Bullfield not out 18
Extras b 7, lb 8, nb 1
Total 199 for eight
Did not bat: P. C. Myatt`

Umpires: C. Mitchell and H. E. Robinson

WOMEN AT LORD'S

Shortly before eleven o'clock on a glorious August day in 1976, Rachael Heyhoe-Flint led her England team down the pavilion steps; they were first women to play a cricket match at Lord's.

Blue skies greeted this special day in the history of the sport and roses had even been placed in the dressing room. It had been a long time coming.

As early as 1803, the Duke of Dorset had written in *The Sporting Magazine*, 'The ladies have lately given us a specimen that they know how to handle the ball and the bat with the best of us.'

In 1929, three years after the foundation of the Women's Cricket Association (WCA), they had written to the committee asking for a match at Lord's. The response was a cool 'regret'.

During the Second World War, Fay Ashmore (née Speed) kept the score for some matches played on the ground, but that was as close as women got to the playing area. Diana Rait Kerr did become the curator of the new Cricket Museum when it opened in 1953, but then again she was daughter of the club secretary.

In 1970 came a further breakthrough when two Cheltenham Ladies players, Sian Davies and Sally Slowe, took part in the MCC Easter coaching classes. According to James Dunbar of the National Cricket Association, it was

a scene that a few years ago might well have raised a few eyebrows … As one presumes that future test talent will come from the male of the species, they must take priority at these coaching classes, but not to the exclusion of young ladies.

In 1973, six Bedfordshire schoolgirls were among a group of young players who were chosen to take part in the NCA Personal Performance Award Scheme. These six became the first female players to play the game officially on the main Lord's ground. It was also the year of the first Women's Cricket World Cup. A request to have at least one match at Lord's was turned down because the square was being relaid. The teams did at least get the chance to practice in the nets at the Nursery End, but the final was played at Edgbaston. MCC president Aidan Crawley attended the match and was impressed by what he saw. It seemed that a date at headquarters was no longer a pipe dream.

The following year, the first noises were made about a match at Lord's to mark the Golden Jubilee of the WCA, to be celebrated in 1976, but once again the response was not promising. When the fixture list first came out, it indicated that the second one-day international against Australia on 4 August was to be played at Sunbury. Some writers drew attention to the new government legislation that introduced the Equal Opportunities Commission (EOC). It clearly touched a nerve at Lord's and at their meeting on 18 February

1976, attended by former England Test captains Freddie Brown, George Mann and Peter May, MCC considered their next move.

Item 5B began, 'The secretary has made enquiries as to the possible position of MCC vis-à-vis the Equal Opportunities Commission should the club agree to stage a WCA fixture at Lord's.'

Solicitors suggested there would be no 'insurmountable problems'.

It was 'Tagg' Webster, then chairman of the grounds and fixtures subcommittee who made the historic recommendatio, 'that the WCA be advised that Lord's could be available to them on Wednesday Aug 4th next, subject to the Gillette Cup quarter final not being completed on that day at Lord's'.

The decision was eventually made public in May.

'We kept plugging away with gentle persuasion and this is the result. I am thrilled and delighted about the news,' said England captain Rachael Heyhoe-Flint.

'Suddenly we are all being rather cruel in secretly hoping that Middlesex either lose their second round tie on July 14 or should they win they will not be drawn at home,' she confided to the readers of *The Cricketer* in her monthly column.

Flint and her teammates need not have worried. Middlesex lost their second-round tie to eventual finalists Lancashire.

On 4 August, coincidentally the seventy-sixth birthday of the Queen Mother, the weather was set fair when the teams arrived at Lord's, although newspaper reporters revealed that some less enlightened members had been praying for rain. 'There was a good crowd which swelled during the day, many spectators coming from a distance to be present at this unique event on a flawless summer day,' said *Wisden*.

The Australians were led by thirty-three-year-old Anne Gordon, described as a 'housewife from Victoria' in the official tour brochure. Each member of the touring party had paid around £1,500 towards the cost of the tour.

The players, but not spectators, were permitted into the long room.

England captain Rachael Heyhoe-Flint won the toss and put the Australians in. It was a sensible move, as there was bound to be nervous tension on such a symbolic occasion. Jan Stephenson bowled the first over from the Pavilion End. Australia's star bat, left-hander Lorraine Hill, was caught down the leg side second ball by wicketkeeper Shirley Hodges, before some spectators had even so much as taken their seats. Hill was not normally one to be overawed. On this tour alone she had scored five hundreds, so to see her depart so early was a blow to Australian morale. Her dismissal set the tone for their entire innings.

Swing bowler Glynis Hullah, a physical education teacher, took a wicket in the sixth over. Shortly afterwards, swimming teacher Enid Bakewell removed two more Australians in the same over to leave them all at sea.

Had it not been for Victoria's Sharon Tredrea, matters might have been completed in time for lunch. As it was, she etched a small footnote in the history of Lord's as the first woman to score a half-century. A sixth-wicket stand made the score more respectable but after Wendy Hills was run out, the Australian batting collapsed, though the last wicket pair added 34.

England's victory target was a modest one. They boasted the experienced opening pair of Enid Bakewell and Lynne Thomas. Both had played in the 1973 World Cup. Bakewell, who played for the East Midlands, was one of the outstanding players of the era. She reached her half-century and hit six boundaries. Thomas, from Llanelli, was the first Welsh woman to play at Lord's. Together they posted 92 for the first wicket, but by modern one-day standards, their progress seems pedestrian. Lynne Thomas, was caught at mid-on in the thirty-ninth over. The innings briefly faltered when Bakewell was run out two overs later.

Chris Watmough, a Lancastrian who now played for Kent, kept her nerve. She had once scored an even time century playing against the men, and here she joined Heyhoe-Flint to guide the team home. After Heyhoe-Flint's tireless work in ensuring that Lord's took notice of women's cricket, it was appropriate that the skipper was at the wicket when the winning runs came.

The victory was not sufficient for England to claim the series. Australia won the St Ivel Trophy. The sponsors presented blue cricket balls to the players as a souvenir of the occasion, recalling that balls of the same colour had been manufactured for women cricketers in the late nineteenth century. A barrier had come down but the struggle for equality would continue for more than twenty years.

4 August 1976
England beat Australia by eight wickets

AUSTRALIA
L. Hill c Hodges b Stephenson 0, M. J. Jennings lbw b Bakewell 18, J. Tredrea b Hullah 9, J. K. Lumsden run out 8, D. A. Gordon c Hodges b Bakewell 3, S. A. Tredrea c Flint b Allen 54, W. J. Hills run out 27, K. Price c Hullah b Allen 4, P. May lbw b Thomas 1, M. A. Lutschini run out 27, W. A. Blundsden not out 7
Extras lb 3
Total (59.4 overs) 161
Fall of wickets 0, 15, 34, 38, 41, 112, 118, 127, 127
Bowling
Stephenson 10.4-3-27-1, Hullah 11-0-23-1, Bakewell 12-3-30-2, Court 12-3-34-0, Allen 9-2-28-2, Thomas 5-1-16-1

ENGLAND
L. Thomas c Price b May 30, E. Bakewell run out 50, C. Watmough not out 50, R. Heyhoe-Flint not out 17
Extras b1, lb 13, nb 1
Total (56.2 overs) 162 for 2
Fall of wickets 85, 93
Did not bat: M. Lear, J. Court, J. Allen, J. Cruwys, J. Stephenson, G. Hullah, S. Hodges
Bowling
S Tredrea 12-4-23-0, Price 10-2-26-0, Gordon 12-3-37-0, May 12-1-24-0, Blundsden 10.2-1-37-0

Umpires: M. Bragger and I. Nowell-Smith

ENGLAND AT THE DOUBLE

By the time Sir Ian Botham played his first Lord's Test, he had already made his mark on international cricket. The ground was also familiar to him for he had spent time there as an MCC Young Cricketer and, in 1978, he had taken a hat-trick in the opening fixture of the season.

These were turbulent times in world cricket. The launch of Kerry Packer's World Series Super Tests in Australia had caused shockwaves throughout the game. Erstwhile England captain Tony Greig had played a key role in recruitment for a series that did not have ICC sanction.

This Lord's Test was the first to be sponsored. It was part of a £1 million deal with Cornhill Insurance and in an official brochure produced by the sponsors, Botham was described as 'one of the most promising all-rounders England has produced in years. Many good judges reckon that he is coming through so fast that he would beat Tony Greig for the England all-rounder berth even if Greig were still a contender.'

England had won the first of the three-match series against Pakistan by an innings, so they were in confident mood as they headed for Lord's. Even though rain washed out the first day, it was still a memorable one for the two sides, as they were both presented to the Queen.

Before this Test, there had been a meeting between captains Mike Brearley and Wasim Bari to determine which of the tail-enders on each side should be considered 'non recognised batsmen' and therefore immune from bouncers.

The Pakistanis were without their senior strike bowler Sarfraz Nawaz, but they started what was now effectively a four-day match in impressive fashion.

England batted and Brearley became the first batsman to wear a full helmet with grill in a Test match at Lord's. He lasted only 4 overs before he was dismissed. His Middlesex teammate Clive Radley followed him for 19. Though Graham Gooch and David Gower, playing only his second Test match, shored up the innings, a flurry of wickets left England struggling. When Geoff Miller was out for a duck, England were 134 for five. This was the cue for Botham to take the stage for his first Test innings at Lord's. His second scoring stroke was a six off Iqbal Qasim into the mound stand, and he never looked back. He brought up his 50 with a huge lofted drive into what is now the Allen Stand. With Graham Roope, he added 118 for the sixth wicket in 105 minutes.

In the last over of the day, Botham slashed aggressively on the off side and his eleventh four took him to a first Test century at Lord's. His runs had come in 2 hours 40 minutes as England closed 309 for eight.

Most of the 20,000 Saturday crowd were disappointed to see him depart early on, but they did see a straight drive into the pavilion for six by Phil Edmonds in a last wicket partnership of 40 with Bob Willis. Botham was given little opportunity to make an impact with the ball in the Pakistan first innings as Willis took five for 47 in 13 overs, and Edmonds was almost as devastating. His four wickets cost only 6 runs in an eight-over spell.

When the tourists followed on, Willis had the experienced opener Sadiq Mohammed caught at the wicket for a duck before Botham claimed his first victim of the match.

After a rest day, Pakistan resumed at 95 for two on Monday morning. Botham came on at the Nursery End, ostensibly to allow Willis to change ends. His first over was so impressive that he stayed on for the remainder of the match. The ball had been replaced late on Saturday night and now, on a hot, sunny morning, he swung it prodigiously. His magnificent spell of 13 overs and 5 balls decided the match. He took seven of the last eight wickets to fall for 14 runs, and the match was all over five minutes before lunch. Botham had eight wickets in the innings to go with his century, the first time this had been achieved in any Test match, let alone at Lord's.

15 (no play), 16–19 June 1978
England beat Pakistan by an innings

ENGLAND First Innings
J. M. Brearley lbw b Liaqat 2, G. A. Gooch lbw b Wasim Raja 54, C. T. Radley c Mohsin b Liaqat 8, D. I. Gower b Qasim 56, G. R. J. Roope c Mohsin b Qasim 69, G. Miller c Miandad b Qasim 0, I. T. Botham b Liaqat 108, R. W. Taylor c Mudassar b Sikander 10, C. M. Old c Mohsin b Sikander 0, P. H. Edmonds not out 36, R. G. D. Willis b Mudassar 18
Extras lb 2, nb 1
Total 364
Fall of wickets 5, 19, 120, 120, 134, 252, 290, 290, 324, 364
Bowling
Sikander 27-3-115-2, Liaqat 18-1-80-3, Mudassar 4.2-0-16-1, Iqbal Qasim 30-5-101-3, Wasim Raja 12-3-49-1

PAKISTAN First Innings
Mudassar Nazar c Edmonds b Willis 1, Sadiq Mohammed c Botham b Willis 11, Mohsin Khan c Willis b Edmonds 11, Haroon Rashid b Old 15, Javed Miandad c Taylor b Old 0, Wasim Raja b Edmonds 28, Talat Ali c Radley b Edmonds 2, Wasim Bari c Brearley b Willis 0, Iqbal Qasim b Willis 0, Sikander Bakht c Brearley b Edmonds 0, Liaqat Ali not out 4
Extras nb 9
Total 105
Fall of wickets 11, 22, 40, 41, 84, 96, 97, 97, 97
Bowling
Willis 13-1-47-5, Old 10-3-26-1, Botham 5-2-17-0, Edmonds 8-6-6-4

PAKISTAN Second Innings
Mudassar Nazar c Taylor b Botham 10, Sadiq Mohammed c Taylor b Willis 0, Mohsin Khan c Roope b Willis 45, Talat Ali c Roope b Botham 40, Haroon Rashid b Botham 4, Javed Miandad c Gooch b Botham 22, Wasim Raja c&b Botham 1, Wasim Bari c Taylor b Botham 2, Sikander Bakht c Roope b Botham 1, Iqbal Qasim b Botham 0, Liaqat Ali not out 0
Extras b 1, lb 3, nb 4, w 5

Total 139
Fall of wickets 1, 45, 100, 108, 114, 119, 121, 130, 130
Bowling
Willis 10-2-26-2, Old 15-4-36-0, Botham 20.5-6-34-8, Edmonds 12-4-21-0, Miller 9-3-9-0

Umpires: W. L. Budd and D. J. Constant

Two months after Botham had swept Pakistan aside, he joined forces with Bob Willis to do the same to New Zealand.

It was the first time that England had won two Test matches at Lord's in a single summer. (The twin tour programme that made the feat possible had been introduced in 1965.)

On the first day, New Zealand batted well to reach 280 for five. Openers John Wright and Bruce Edgar gave them a good start but both departed within 5 runs of one another. Edgar was caught by Phil Edmonds to give his Middlesex spin partner John Emburey a first Test wicket with only his fourth ball. Geoff Howarth battled not only the English bowlers but also a bout of influenza to score a century. He put on 130 for the fourth wicket with Mark Burgess and reached his century five minutes before the end of the day. Botham took six wickets in the innings. When England batted, they recovered from the early loss of Graham Gooch, who was caught second ball at short leg. This was thanks mainly to Clive Radley and David Gower whose third-wicket stand was the most substantial of the innings. They added 109 in 1 hour 50 minutes on the second evening, 75 of which came in the last 75 minutes. On the third day, England had designs on a first innings' lead until Richard Hadlee took three wickets for 8 runs in his first 45 balls. Shortly after five o'clock on Saturday evening, New Zealand were 10 without loss in their second innings. Then it happened: Botham struck the first blow, removing Bruce Edgar. By the close of play, Bob Willis and Botham had left them reeling at 37 for seven. The last three wickets had fallen for only 4 runs. New Zealand added a further 30 on Monday, but Botham took the remaining wickets to fall and ran Richard Hadlee out for good measure. England needed only 118 to win. It was their second Test victory at Lord's and five out of six in home tests in 1978.

24–26, 28/29 August 1978
England beat New Zealand by seven wickets

NEW ZEALAND First Innings
J. G. Wright c Edmonds b Botham 17, B. A. Edgar c Edmonds b Emburey 39, G. P. Howarth c Taylor b Botham 123, J. M. Parker lbw b Hendrick 14, M. G. Burgess lbw b Botham 68, B. E. Congdon c Emburey b Botham 2, R. W. Anderson b Botham 16, R. J. Hadlee c Brearley b Botham 0, R. O. Collinge c Emburey b Willis 19, S. L. Boock not out 4, B. P. Bracewell st Taylor b Emburey 4
Extras b 4, lb 18, nb 7, w 4
Total 339
Fall of wickets 65, 70, 117, 247, 253, 290, 290, 321, 333
Bowling
Willis 29-9-79-1, Hendrick 28-14-39-1, Botham 38-13-101-6, Edmonds 12-3-19-0, Emburey 26.1-12-39-2, Gooch 10-0-29-0

ENGLAND First Innings

G. A. Gooch c Boock b Hadlee 2, G. Boycott c Hadlee b Bracewell 24, C. T. Radley c Congdon b Hadlee 77, D. I. Gower c Wright b Boock 71, J. M. Brearley c Edgar b Hadlee 33, I. T. Botham c Edgar b Collinge 21, R. W. Taylor lbw b Hadlee 1, P. H. Edmonds c Edgar b Hadlee 5, J. E. Emburey b Collinge 2, M. Hendrick b Bracewell 12, R. G. D. Willis not out 7

Extras b 7, lb 5, nb 22
Total 289
Fall of wickets 2, 66, 180, 211, 249, 255, 258, 263, 274
Bowling
Hadlee 32-9-84-5, Collinge 30-9-58-2, Bracewell 19.3-1-68-2, Boock 25-10-33-1, Congdon 8-1-12-0

NEW ZEALAND Second Innings

J. G. Wright b Botham 12, B. A. Edgar b Botham 4, R. W. Anderson c Taylor b Willis 1, J. M. Parker c Taylor b Botham 3, M. G. Burgess c Hendrick b Botham 14, B. E. Congdon c Taylor b Willis 3, S. L. Boock c Radley b Willis 0, B. P. Bracewell c Hendrick b Willis 0, G. P. Howarth not out 14, R. J. Hadlee run out 5, R. O. Collinge b Botham 0

Extras lb 3, nb 8
Total 67
Fall of wickets 10, 14, 20, 29, 33, 37, 37, 43, 57
Bowling
Willis 16-8-16-4, Botham 18.1-4-39-5, Emburey 3-2-1-0

ENGLAND Second Innings

G. A. Gooch not out 42, G. Boycott b Hadlee 4, C. T. Radley b Hadlee 0, D. I. Gower c Congdon b Bracewell 46, J. M. Brearley not out 8

Extras lb 3, nb 11, w 4
Fall of wickets 14, 14, 84
Bowling
Hadlee 13.5-2-31-2, Collinge 6-1-26-0, Boock 5-1-11-0, Bracewell 6-0-32-1

Umpires: H. D. Bird and B. J. Meyer.

SRI LANKA AND ZIMBABWE
FLEX THEIR MUSCLES

Sri Lanka's first Test match at Lord's came at the end of an exhausting and dispiriting summer for England, who had lost heavily to the West Indies. Most backed England to win easily against the newcomers. Some even uncharitably compared the Sri Lankan side to a university team.

Skipper David Gower put the tourists in and Jonathan Agnew opened the bowling with Ian Botham. Botham struck early to trap Amal Silva and Richard Ellison bowled Ranjan Madugalle. But Sri Lanka recovered from a position of 43 for two to end the first day on 226 for three, thanks to opener Sidath Wettimuny, who was 116 not out by the close. In all, he occupied the crease for a mammoth 10 hours 42 minutes for his 190.

Duleep Mendis became the first Sri Lankan captain to score a Test hundred at Lord's. He was eventually dismissed by Pat Pocock, who had been recalled to the England team eight years after his last appearance.

England did not begin their innings until the third day and progress was initially slow. Openers Chris Broad and Chris Tavare added only 49 in 27 overs between lunch and tea. Broad occupied the crease for 5 hours 41 minutes for his 86 and Allan Lamb's century took over 4½ hours. The highlight of Sri Lanka's second innings on the final day was a century from wicketkeeper Amal Silva. Mendis missed out by 6 runs on a hundred in each innings. His runs had come off only 97 balls. *Wisden* called it 'a splendid performance which won them a host of new admirers', and in only their twelfth match at this level, they left few in any doubt about their right to Test status.

The draw meant England had endured twelve Test matches without a win.

23–25, 27/28 August 1984
Match drawn

SRI LANKA First Innings
S. Wettimuny c Downton b Allott 190, S. A. R. Silva lbw b Botham 8, R. S. Madugalle b Ellison 5, R. L. Dias c Lamb b Pocock 32, A. Ranatunga b Agnew 84, L. R. D. Mendis c Fowler b Pocock 111, P. A. de Silva c Downton b Agnew 16, A. L. F. de Mel not out 20, J. R. Ratnayake not out 5
Extras b 2, lb 8, nb 8, w 2
Total 491 for seven declared
Fall of wickets 17, 43, 144, 292, 442, 456, 464
Did not bat: D. S. de Silva and V. B. John
Bowling
Agnew 32-3-123-2, Botham 29-6-114-1, Ellison 28-6-70-1, Pocock 41-17-75-2, Allott 36-7-89-1

ENGLAND First Innings

G. Fowler c Madugalle b John 25, B. C. Broad c de Silva b de Mel 86 , C. J. Tavare c Ranatunga b D. S. de Silva 14, D. I. Gower c Silva b de Mel 55, A. J. Lamb c Dias b John 107, I. T. Botham c sub (Vonhagt) b John 6, R. M. Ellison c Ratnayake b de Silva 41, P. R. Downton c Dias b de Mel 10, P. J. W. Allott b de Mel 0, P. I. Pocock c Silva b John 2, J. P. Agnew not out 1

Extras b 5, lb 7, nb 6, w 5

Total 370

Fall of wickets 49, 105, 190, 210, 218, 305, 354, 354, 369, 370

Bowling

De Mel 37-10-110-4, John 39.1-12-98-4, Ratnayake 22-5-50-0, D. S. de Silva 45-16-85-2, Ranatunga 1-1-0-0, Madugalle 3-0-4-0

SRI LANKA Second Innings

S. Wettimuny c Gower b Botham 13, S. A. R. de Silva not out 102, R. S. Madugalle b Botham 3, R. L. Dias lbw b Botham 38, A. Ranatunga lbw b Botham 0, L. R. D. Mendis c Fowler b Botham 94, P. A. de Silva c Downton b Botham 3, A. L. F. de Mel c Ellison b Botham 14, J. R. Ratnayake not out 7

Extras b 5, lb 4, nb 11,

Total 294 for seven declared

Fall of wickets 19, 27, 111, 111, 118, 216, 276

Bowling

Agnew 11-3-54-0, Botham 27-6-90-6, Ellison 7-0-36-0, Pocock 29-10-78-1, Allott 1-0-2-0, Lamb 1-0-6-0, Tavare 3-3-0-0, Fowler 1-0-8-0

Umpires: H. D. Bird and D. G. L. Evans.

When Zimbabwe finally became independent in 1979, they rejoined the international cricketing fraternity. Their first appearance at Lord's came in 1986 in the final of the ICC Trophy. This tournament for associate nations served as the qualifying tournament for the 1987 World Cup. It was the first time that the final had been held at Lord's.

Led by wicketkeeper batsman David Houghton, it was no surprise that they reached the final, for they had dominated cricket among the associate nations. Their opponents from the Netherlands had qualified for the final for the first time and brought over a thousand enthusiastic supporters with them. One part of the ground was decorated by a 20-foot Dutch flag.

The Dutch could boast P. J. Bakker and Roland Lefebvre, both to play county cricket. Over half of the Zimbabwe XI would go on to play Test cricket. One of them already had. Veteran bowler John Traicos, now aged thirty-nine, had appeared in three Tests for South Africa before they were expelled from international cricket in the apartheid era.

The Zimbabwe innings was founded on 60 from Robin Brown, a tobacco farmer from Mashonaland. Batting somewhat incongruously in a broad-brimmed sun hat on a rain-interrupted day, he stayed for 51 overs for his 60 runs.Andy Pycroft tried to move things along and was twice dropped before he was finally caught for 30.

It had been slow progress. Leg spinner Steve Lubbers took a wicket with his first ball at Lord's and Zimbabwe were 101 for four in the 37th over. Andy Waller then put on 69 with Robin Brown in 14.1 overs. He went to his own half-century in 51 balls. The Zimbabwe tail raised an additional 73 in the last nine overs to reach 243 for nine.

A reserve day had been set aside in the event of bad weather, which was just as well. The Dutch resumed at 11 for no loss. Traicos had Durham-born Steve Atkinson, now a teacher in the Netherlands, caught by Pycroft as they lost four quick wickets. They took lunch at 131 for five off 44 overs. The odds were against the Dutch, who were further hampered when Steve Lubbers fell awkwardly on his ankle and was carried from the field. His partner, Ron Elfernick, was already batting with a runner. He'd twisted his knee on the damp outfield on the first day. They needed 70 to win from the last ten, but although Elfernick continued to strike the ball well, he was out in the 57th over. Lubbers hobbled back to the middle to try and force the victory, but wickets fell around him and Zimbabwe had retained the ICC Trophy.

7/8 July 1986
Zimbabwe beat Netherlands by 25 runs

ZIMBABWE
R. D. Brown c Van Weelde b Lubbers 60, G. A. Paterson c Vissee b Van Weelde 11, A. H. Shah c Litman b Van Weelde 12, A. J. Pycroft c Schoonheim b Lubbers 30, D. L. Houghton b Lubbers 3, A. C. Waller run out 59, G. C. Wallace c Schoonheim b Lefebvre 28, P. W. E. Rawson run out 1, I. P. Butchart not out 13, E. A. Branders b Bakker 6 , A. J. Traicos not out 0
Extras lb 8, nb 2, w 12
Total 243 for nine
Fall of wickets 18, 41, 93, 101, 170, 204, 205, 229, 238
Bowling
Bakker 12-0-58-1, Van Weelde 12-1-46-2, Elferink 9-2-31-0, Lefebvre 12-2-34-1, Lubbers 11-0-44-3, Visee 4-1-22-0

NETHERLANDS
S. R. Atkinson c Pyecroft b Traicos 31, R. Littmann lbw b Shah 41, R. Gomes c Rawson b Butchart 27, S. Lubbers not out 35, R. Lefebvre b Brandes 8, R. Entrop b Shah 0, D. Vissee b Brandes 5, R. Elferink b Butchart 31, P. J. Bakker b Rawson 11, R. Schoonheim b Butchart 2, R. Van Weelde b Butchart 0
Extras b 1, lb 19, nb 1, w 6
Total (58.4 overs) 218
Fall of wickets 50, 109, 109, 129, 130, 139, 206, 216, 218
Bowling
Rawson 11-3-27-1, Butchart 11.4-1-33-4, Traicos 12-2-31-1, Brandes 12-1-52-2, Shah 12-0-55-2

Umpires: P. Ogden and A. Inman

THE G-FORCE HITS LORD'S

On a steamy day in 1990, Graham Gooch became the first man to score a Test triple century at Lord's. His mammoth innings came after Indian captain Mohammad Azharuddin won the toss but invited England to bat.

'Graham Gooch spent the entire day demonstrating to his Indian counterpart the error of his ways,' wrote Alan Lee in *The Times*.

Kapil Dev had struck to remove Mike Atherton bowled off the pads and Gooch himself was dropped at 36 by wicketkeeper Kiran More. 'We should have had Gooch out cheaply and if that wicket had gone down it could have turned into a very good start,' claimed Azharuddin at the end of the day.

Christopher Martin Jenkins said in *The Cricketer*,

> He [Gooch] was in prime form and once he had made up his mind that the Indian bowling on such a pitch was no more threatening than a county attack, he seized the stage and bestrode it with a magnificent unyielding command.

By tea, Gooch had reached his century from 172 balls. He thus became the first man to score four Test match hundreds at Lord's in an international career.

He had made 177 two days before to guide Essex to victory over Lancashire and this was his fourth consecutive century in first-class matches.

Allan Lamb's own ton came up with the fiftieth boundary of the day. This was also his fourth in a Lord's Test match.

At the end of the opening day, England were 359 for two, of which Gooch had made 194.

Gooch soon brought up his double century with an on drive for three off Prabhakar. The partnership continued without remorse. When he reached 255, Gooch surpassed Don Bradman who had made the highest Test score on the ground sixty years before. His runs had come in 381 balls, only five more than the total amount faced by The Don himself.

Gooch and Lamb were eventually parted when their stand had realised 308 for the third wicket.

In the last over before tea, Gooch took a single, which lost him the strike. However, from the first ball afterwards, Gooch glanced off Shastri to bring up his triple century. It had taken 594 minutes and came in 454 balls. He hit four and then six into the scaffolding at the Nursery End of the ground where construction of the new Compton and Edrich stands was underway. A Test triple was a milestone even Denis Compton had not achieved. Gooch was eventually dismissed for a symmetrical 333 made out of 653 for four.

'My arms were a bit tired by the end,' said Gooch with typical understatement. 'Lord's has always been my lucky ground.' Gooch also revealed that he had been suffering from an ear infection.

GA GOOCH RECORD INNINGS AT LORD'S (0 denotes dot ball)
Minutes 628, balls 485, fours 43, sixes 3
FIRST DAY 0000011000000400000044041000200002010000000010000000001
1000100004000400000000200001000100010010100 (43 at lunch) 0000004064
410000010000100100010000041410100000040010010011204400001000000 00
44010000000010400040010001000001 (117 at tea) 0043000000101-11441100 14
40001000000014000001404040121021000601111110011100210110000 1 (194
at close)
SECOND DAY 00000000000000040300000440040000001001000020000 00
(217 rain stopped play) 010000000000400404140000041110110001 (245 at lunch)
110104002001100004010010110010201011140111001000010001041020010
20011110020000000011 (299 at tea) 12210100041010146 01 (324 rain stopped
play) 010141010100W (333)

India responded positively. Ravi Shastri and Azharuddin both scored hundreds and Kapil
Dev's unbeaten 77 saved the follow-on in heroic fashion. He struck four successive sixes
off Eddie Hemmings. They were hit with such certainty that it never seemed in doubt.

In England's second innings, Atherton also partook of the feast in an opening stand
of 204, but there was no overshadowing Gooch. His 123 came off only 113 balls and
included thirteen fours and four sixes. Before him, no one had followed up a Test triple
century with another hundred in the same game. Even though he was only seventeen,
Sachin Tendulkar had already played seven Test matches and announced himself to the
Lord's crowd with a stunning catch at the Nursery End to dismiss Allan Lamb.

England twice declared with only four wickets down and, despite spirited resistance,
India were dismissed for 224. Sharma was the last man to go, run out by a direct hit from
who else? Gooch had the final say.

26–28, 30/31 July
England beat India by 247 runs

ENGLAND First Innings
G. A. Gooch b Prabakhar 333, M. A. Atherton b Kapil Dev 8, D. I. Gower c
Manjrekar b Hirwani 40, A. J. Lamb c Manjrekar b Sharma 139, R. A. Smith not out
100, J. E. Morris not out 4
Extras b 2, lb 21, nb 4, w 2
Total 653 for four declared
Fall of wickets 14, 141, 449, 641
Did not bat: R. C. Russell, C. C. Lewis, E. E. Hemmings, A. R. C. Fraser, D. E. Malcolm
Bowling
Kapil Dev 34-5-120-1, Prabakhar 43-6-187-1, Sharma 33-5-122-1, Shastri 22-0-99-0,
Hirwani 30-1-102-1

INDIA First Innings
R. J. Shastri c Gooch b Hemmings 100, N. S. Sidhu c Morris b Fraser 30, S. V. Manjrekar
c Russell b Gooch 18, D. B. Vengsarkar c Russell b Fraser 52, M. Azharuddin b
Hemmings 121, S. R. Tendulkar b Lewis 10, M. Prabakhar c Lewis b Malcolm 25,
Kapil Dev not out 77, K. S. More c Morris b Fraser 8, S. K. Sharma c Russell b Fraser
0, N. D. Hirwani lbw b Fraser 0

Extras lb 1, nb 8, w 4
Total 454
Fall of wickets 63, 102, 191, 241, 288, 348, 393, 430, 430
Bowling
Malcolm 25-1-106-1, Fraser 39.1-9-104-5, Lewis 24-3-108-1, Gooch 6-3-26-1,
Hemmings 20-3-109-2

ENGLAND Second Innings
G. A. Gooch c Azharuddin b Sharma 123, M. A. Atherton c Vengsarkar b Sharma
72, D. I. Gower not out 32, A. J. Lamb c Tendulkar b Hirwani 19, R. A. Smith b
Prabakhar 15
Extras b 11
Total 272 for four declared
Fall of wickets 204, 207, 250, 272
Bowling
Kapil Dev 10-0-53-0, Prabakhar 11.2-2-45-1, Shastri 7-0-38-0, Sharma 15-0-75-2,
Hirwani 11-0-50-1

INDIA Second Innings
R. J. Shastri c Russell b Malcolm 12, N. S. Sidhu c Morris b Fraser 1, S. V. Manjrekar
c Russell b Malcolm 33, D. B. Vengsarkar c Russell b Hemmings 35, M. Azharuddin
c Atherton b Lewis 37, S. R. Tendulkar c Gooch b Fraser 27, M. Prabakhar lbw b
Lewis 8, Kapil Dev c Lewis b Hemmings 7, K. S. More lbw b Fraser 16, S. K. Sharma
run out (Gooch) 38, N. D Hirwani not out 0
Extras b 3, lb 1, nb 6
Total 224
Fall of wickets 9, 23, 63, 114, 127, 140, 158, 181, 206
Bowling
Fraser 22-7-39-3, Malcolm 10-0-65-2, Hemmings 21-2-79-2, Atherton 1-0-11-0,
Lewis 8-1-26-2

Umpires: H. D. Bird and N. T. Plews

AN AFTERNOON WITH GARY LINEKER AND THE GERMANS

In 1992, a German cricket team played a match at Lord's for the first time. Teams from East and West Germany had played hockey there in 1967.

Much of the interest in the match centred on the number five batsman for MCC, listed as G. W. Lineker of Cross Arrows. Better known as Gary Lineker (the 'W' stands for 'Winston'), lately captain of the England football team and the second highest goalscorer in the country's history, he made it clear that playing at Lord's meant everything.

'It is a great a thrill for a cricket lover like me to play at the home of cricket. It as a big a buzz as captaining England at Wembley,' he said.

Lineker had done just that against Germany in 1991. Now he found himself in opposition to Germany's cricketers as they made their first appearance at Lord's. Cricket had long been established in Germany, albeit played mostly by expatriates who lived there. Seventy-five years before, the Berlin Cricket Club had written to MCC to ask for a fixture but the committee minutes of 25 April 1927 reveal that they answered 'regret no dates'.

This time, they found the club much more welcoming. With a little poetic licence, 1992 could be claimed as the only year Germany's cricketers did better than their footballers. The German cricket team beat France by three wickets in final of the European Cricketer Cup, a competition designed to boost the sport on the continent.

The German team was skippered by an Australian molecular biologist, Francis Stewart. 'Winning the competition gives enormous credibility to the Deutscher Cricketbund,' he said.

It had been arranged that the winners of the tournament would play MCC at Lord's, so the red, black and gold German tricolour fluttered for the first time alongside the red and gold MCC banner. Three weeks earlier, Germany's football team had reached the European Championship final but suffered a shock defeat at the hands of Denmark.

Lineker's own memories of that tournament were even unhappier. Exactly a month before, he had left the field grim-faced when substituted against Sweden amid tales of a rift with manager Graham Taylor. England went on to lose 2-1 and it proved to be Lineker's final international cap. His had been a stellar career. He had scored forty-eight goals, one behind the record held by Sir Bobby Charlton. His next appearance was in front of a rather smaller crowd. MCC were put into bat, so a morning with Gary Lineker was spent on the balcony waiting for his turn in the middle. New Zealand Test player Ken Rutherford opened with former Essex player Bob Cooke in a strong batting line-up. They put on 138 for the first wicket in little more than an hour.

Lineker's turn came in early afternoon. He had borrowed a bat from David Gower, another favourite son of Leicestershire and England. With MCC's score at a healthy 246 for three, he walked out, shirt buttoned to the wrist, to face his first ball on the main ground. 'I felt more nervous walking through the long room than I was in the World Cup semi final against West Germany two years ago,' he admitted later.

He played the first four balls confidently before taking a quick single on the fifth to retain the strike. Five balls later he was out, hitting uppishly to cover where Gary Stevens, an advertising executive who worked in Frankfurt, took the catch. Curiously, Lineker had played in the same England football team as two men named Gary Stevens during the 1980s.

'I always score one against the Germans,' joked Lineker, a reference to his goal in the 1990 World Cup semi-final. He was followed out by Roger Knight, MCC captain. In his capacity as Headmaster of Worksop School, he had played a key role in hosting the tournament. When Knight was out for a brisk 20, he brought the MCC innings to close at 289.

The target was a stiff one for the German team.

Lineker put one catch down at square leg early in the German innings. South African Finley Brooker, a batsman with Griqualand West had taken the wicketkeeping gloves, but halfway through he handed over the gloves to Lineker, who then took a catch to dismiss Sanjeev Taneja.

Amir Bin Jung had scored a match-winning 99 in Germany's victory over France in the European final. Undaunted by his impressive surroundings, he scored 52. Few should have been surprised at his prowess, he was a nephew of the Nawab of Pataudi.

MCC could not quite complete the job and the match was left drawn. Appropriately, the principal speaker at the banquet was Sir Leon Brittan, then a vice president of the European Community Commission.

17 July 1992
Match drawn

MCC

K. R. Rutherford c Newton b Taneja 87, R. M. O. Cooke b Taneja 53, R. O. Butcher c Stewart b Taneja 68, F. Brooker c Stevens b Taneja 34, G. W. Lineker c Stevens b Zaidi 1, R. D. V. Knight c Newton b Bhatti 20, G. J. Toogood not out 11
Extras b 2, lb 3, nb 5
Total 289 for six
Fall of wickets 138, 161, 246, 247, 271, 289
Did not bat: A. C. Reeves, A. P. Jones, K. J. Crossley, C. F. Brown
Bowling
Zaidi 13-0-71-1, H Bhatti 6.1-0-28-1, Sahi 4-0-32-0, Newton 3-0-21-0, Stewart 6-0-33-0, Taneja 14-0-84-4, Rathor 1-0-15-0

GERMANY

G. Stevens b Jones 5, A. Jung c Knight b Crossley 52, A. Bhatti b Brown 29, S. Taneja c Lineker b Brown 7, S. Fernando C Reeves b Crossley 0, T. Rathor lbw b Cooke 16, H. Bhatti c&b Cooke 57, P. Zaidi c Butcher b Jones 9, F. Stewart lbw b Cooke 0, G. Newton not out 0, P. Sahi not out 0
Extras b 2, lb 3
Total 180 for nine
Fall of wickets 16, 56, 84, 87, 98, 161, 180, 180, 180

Umpires: M. J. Harris and G. Sharp

THE NEW RAINBOW

Transvaal's first visit to Lord's was much more important than a simple cricket match. They were the first South African team to be seen on the ground since the dismantling of Apartheid. The year was 1992 and South Africa had reached the semi-final of the ICC World Cup, made their return to Test cricket and the Olympic team had taken part in the Barcelona Olympic Games.

MCC's South African-born skipper, Ian Greig, won the toss and asked the tourists to bat. He had a powerful attack at his disposal. Joel Garner opened with a no-ball, but at 6 foot 7 his angle of delivery made it difficult for batsmen, especially at Lord's. He had Transvaal's captain Jimmy Cook superbly caught by Phil Edmonds. Darryl Cullinan made 18 and Clive Exteen hit an unbeaten 18. The trio would all go on to play Test cricket.

The Transvaal side also included a name from a famous family – nineteen-year-old Anthony Pollock, a left-hander just like his father, Graeme. The young player made only 8 before he was bowled by Eugene Antoine. Transvaal were all out in 42 overs.

19 July 1992
MCC beat Transvaal by seven wickets

TRANSVAAL
S. J. Cook c Edmonds b Garner 12, B. M. White c Greatbatch b Garner 5, R. F. Pienaar c Hegg b Benjamin 1, D. J. Cullinan lbw b Greig 18, G. A. Pollock b Antoine 8, V. B. N. Vermeulen b Greig 9, S. Jacobs c Hegg b Greig 4, B. McBride c Richardson b Benjamin 6, C. E. Eksteen not out 18, S. D. Jack c Greig b Benjamin 8, G. C. Yates c Hegg b Edmonds 17
Extras lb 4, nb 4, w 1
Total (42 overs) 115
Fall of wickets 16, 21, 21, 42, 52, 62, 65, 75, 87
Bowling
Garner 8-1-17-2, Benjamin 11-1-40-3, Antoine 8-4-18-1, Greig 8-1-17-3, Edmonds 7-1-19-1

MCC
M. J. Greatbatch c Vermeulen b Yates 47, M. A. Atherton c&b Yates 6, R. B. Richardson c McBride b White 20, K. R. Rutherford not out 32, I. A. Greig not out 4
Extras b 5, lb 1, w 1
Total (23.2 overs) 116 for three
Did not bat: C. G. Greenidge, W. K. Hegg, K. C. G. Benjamin, J. Garner, P. H. Edmonds, E. C. Antoine

Fall of wickets 57, 57, 108
Bowling
Jack 4-0-28-0, Yates 7-2-28-2, Jacobs 5-0-34-0, Eksteen 4.2-0-11-0, White 3-0-9-1

Umpires: H. D. Bird and B. Dudleston

South Africa's reintegration into international sport was completed in 1994 with their re-appearance at Lord's. On the eve of the match, MCC announced it had granted life membership to Barry Richards and Graeme Pollock. South Africa's long absence had shortened the Test career of both, and Richards never did play a Test innings at Lord's. South Africa were managed by another great player from that era, Mike Procter. The flag of the new Rainbow Nation fluttered above the pavilion for the first time. 'South Africa's cricket is at last shedding its unwanted burden of politics,' said an editorial in *The Times*. The South African Vice President Thabo M'beki was present for the first of three Test series, and his nation rose to the occasion magnificently. Skipper Kepler Wessels won the toss and openers Gary Kirsten and Andrew Hudson received a standing ovation as they walked through the pavilion gates, but it was Wessels who galavanised the innings with a century. South Africa's first innings of 357 left them firmly in control. Peter and Gary Kirsten became the first half-brothers to play together in a Lord's Test match. Alan Donald and Fanie de Villiers blasted through the England batting and when South Africa batted again, they set England 456 to win. The innings was most notable for an incident on the Saturday of the match – Mike Atherton was caught by the television cameras apparently applying dirt from his pocket to the ball. Although he was found not guilty of an infringement of rule 42.5, which concerns 'action to alter the condition of the ball', Atherton was fined £2,000. He did not resign the captaincy after the episode.

He was the first man to go in England's second innings. Gooch and Stewart added 39 for the fourth wicket in England's best partnership of the match. In the process, Gooch became the first man to pass 2,000 runs in Test matches at Lord's, but England lost their last six wickets for 25 runs. To bowl England out for 99 was beyond expectation for Wessels.

The whole of England's second innings took less than four hours. Atherton called it, 'the most disappointing performance since I became captain'.

21–25 July
South Africa beat England by 356 runs

SOUTH AFRICA First Innings
A. C. Hudson c Gough b Gooch 8, G. Kirsten c De Freitas b Hick 72, W. J. Cronje c Crawley b Fraser 7, K. C. Wessels c Rhodes b Gough 105, P. N. Kirsten c Rhodes b Gough 8, J. N. Rhodes b White 32, B. M. McMillan c Rhodes b Fraser 29, D. J. Richardson lbw b Gough 26, C. R. Matthews b White 41, P. S. De Villiers c Rhodes b Fraser 8, A. A. Donald not out 5
Extras lb 9, nb 9
Total 357
Fall of wickets 18, 35, 141, 164, 239, 241, 281, 334, 348
Bowling
De Freitas 18-5-67-0, Gough 28-6-76-4, Salisbury 25-2-68-0, Fraser 24.5-7-72-3, Hick 10-5-22-1, White 13-2-43-2

ENGLAND First Innings

M. A. Atherton c Wessels b Donald 20, A. J. Stewart b Donald 12, J. P. Crawley c Hudson b De Villiers 8, G. A. Hick c Richardson b De Villiers 38, G. A. Gooch lbw b De Villiers 20, C. White c Richardson b Donald 10, S. J. Rhodes b Mcmillan 15, I. D. K. Salisbury not out 6, P. A. J. De Freitas c Wessels b Donald 20, D. Gough c&b Donald 12, A. R. C. Fraser run out 3

Extras b 2, lb 5, nb 8

Total 180

Fall of wickets 19, 41, 68, 107, 119, 136, 141, 161, 176

Bowling

Donald 19.3-5-74-5, De Villiers 16-5-28-3, Matthews 16-6-46-0, McMillan 16-1-25-1

SOUTH AFRICA Second Innings

A. C. Hudson lbw b Fraser 3, G. Kirsten st Rhodes b Hick 44, W. J. Cronje c Fraser b Gough 32, K. C. Wessels c Crawley b Salisbury 28 , P. N. Kirsten b Gough 42, J. N. Rhodes b Gough 32, B. M. McMillan not out 39, D. J. Richardson c Rhodes b Fraser 3, C. R. Matthews b Gough 25

Extras b 8, lb 10, nb 12

Total 278 for eight declared

Fall of wickets 14, 73, 101, 141, 208, 209, 220, 278

Bowling

Fraser 23-5-62-2, Gough 19.3-5-46-4, De Freitas 14-3-43-0, Hick 24-14-38-1, Salisbury 19-4-53-1, White 3-0-18-0

ENGLAND Second Innings

M. A. Atherton c Mcmillan b De Villiers 8, A. J. Stewart c Richardson b Matthews 27, J. P. Crawley c Hudson b Mcmillan 7, G. A. Hick lbw b McMillan 11, G. A. Gooch lbw b Donald 28, C. White c Wessels b Matthew 0, S. J. Rhodes not out 14, P. A. J. De Freitas c Kirsten b Matthews 1, D. Gough retired hurt 0, I. D. K. Salisbury lbw d Donald 0, A. R. C. Fraser lbw b McMillan 1

Extras b 1, lb 1

Total 99

Fall of wickets 16, 29, 45, 74, 82, 86, 88, 99

Bowling

Donald 12-5-29-2, De Villiers 12-4-26-1, Matthews 14-6-25-3, McMillan 6.5-2-16-3, Cronje 1-0-1-0

Umpires: H. D. Bird and S. G. Randell
Television umpire: M. J. Kitchen
Match referee: P. J. Burge

A DECADE OF STRUGGLE

In 1993, the Women's World Cup returned to England and, for the first time, their showpiece final was permitted at Lord's. It was a competition that caught the imagination and there were letters to *The Times* complaining about the way the women cricketers were portrayed. On the eve of the showpiece at Lord's, it was announced that Rachael Heyhoe-Flint intended to lobby MCC again about the question of women members. She did so with the support of musician Tim Rice, who was now on the committee.

In the meantime, England faced New Zealand.

Former Test star Sarah Potter identified England's opening bat, Janette Brittin, as the key to the outcome: 'She has the grace and flair to command centre stage.'

Brittin did indeed seize the moment in front of a crowd approaching 5,000. Her 48 took her past a thousand runs in World Cup cricket. It gave her side just the start they needed before she was caught at midwicket in the last quarter of an hour before lunch. England lost their way a little after that, but enter Jo Chamberlain, a delivery driver when not playing cricket for Leicestershire. She hit 38 off 33 balls to restore England's momentum, and added 57 in 9 overs with Barbara Daniels. When Chamberlain was out, Daniels and captain Karen Smithies kept up the pressure, 81 came in their last 12 overs to set a victory target of 196. It was 100 more than New Zealand had been asked to chase in the entire tournament.

Chamberlain's turn with the ball was also decisive but although the fastest of the England bowlers, she was held back to first change. It was a smart move. New Zealand had been 7 to 4 favourites to lift the trophy and they were making ominous progress at 51 for one when Chamberlain had Kirsty Bond caught brilliantly at second slip. The coup de grace came when she also ran out New Zealand opener Debbie Hockey from cover.

England were soon celebrating in front of the pavilion.

1 August 1993
England beat New Zealand by 67 runs

ENGLAND
J. Brittin c Gunn b McLauchlan 48, W. A. Watson b McLauchlan 5, C. A. Hodges st Illingworth b Campbell 45, H. C. Plimmer run out 11, J. M. Chamberlain b Harris 38, B. A. Daniel not out 21, K. Smithies not out 10
Extras b 8, lb 7, w 2
Total (60 overs) 195 for five
Fall of wickets 11, 96, 114, 118, 175.
Did not bat: J. Cassar, C. E. Taylor, G. A. Smith, S. J. Kitson

Bowling
Turner 8-1-32-0, Harris 12-3-31-1, McLauchlan 10-2-25-2, Campbell 12-2-45-1, Gunn 12-5-33-0, Drumm 6-1-14-0

NEW ZEALAND
P. D. Kinsella c Cassar b Taylor 15, D. A. Hockley run out 24, K. E. Bond c Kitson b Chamberlain 12, M. A. M. Lewis lbw b Taylor 28, S. L. Illingworth c&b Smithies 4, E. C. Drumm c Chamberlain b Smith 0, K. V. Gunn b Smith 19, S. McLauchlan c Brittin b Kitson 0, J. A. Turner c Taylor b Smith 2, J. E. Harris not out 5, C. A. Campbell c Brittin b Kitson 6
Extras lb 8, w 5
Total (55.1 overs) 128
Fall of wickets 25, 51, 60, 70, 71, 110, 112, 114, 120
Bowling
Taylor 12-3-27-2, Hodges 5-2-11-0, Chamberlain 9-2-28-1, Smithies 12-4-14-1, Smith 12-1-29-3, Kitson 5.1-1-11-2

Umpires: V. Gibbens and J. A. West

Although women's matches were a regular sight at Lord's, women could still not become members. But, in 1998, they found a new champion in MCC president Colin Ingleby-Mackenzie. A vote in that year did not get the required majority, but he was undeterred.

'We will continue to nudge members in the right direction but change will be gradual acceptable and civilised,' said Ingleby-MacKenzie.

MORI (Market & Opinion Research International) were commissioned to poll members on the issue and a glossy brochure set out the arguments:

Commercial sponsors have already indicated that they are concerned about MCC's all male status. Two major companies have declined sponsorship opportunities with MCC purely on these grounds.

In the meantime, there had been other significant developments. On 20 July 1998, a short ceremony took place in the Harris Gardens at Lord's. With more than a passing nod to the creation of the original urn, the Women's Ashes were created. A miniature bat signed by the Australian and England teams was burned, along with a book detailing the constitution of the Women's Cricket Association, which had governed the women's game since 1926. Henceforth, women's cricket in England would be part of the England and Wales Cricket Board (ECB).

The following day, England played Australia in the last match in a series of five one-day internationals. Australia had already won the first four and were set to dominate this match too. Skipper Belinda Clark won the toss and opened the batting herself. With Balmain clubmate Lisa Keightley, they posted a century stand for the first wicket. Both were dropped, but it was not until the score had reached 173 that Clark top edged a pull to square leg. It was the only success for the English bowlers in the 50 overs. Keightley went to her century with an on drive, the first woman to do so at Lord's. She remained unaware of the milestone until it was announced over the public address.

The victory target was always beyond England, although captain Karen Smithies hit an unbeaten 62. Australian fast bowler Cathryn Fitzpatrick's five for 47 included a wicket with her last two balls.

21 July 1998
Australia beat England by 114 runs

AUSTRALIA
B. J. Clark c Winks b Reynard 89, L. M. Keightley not out 113, J. Broadbent not
out 42
Extras lb 21, nb 2, w 9
Total (50 overs) 256 for one
Fall of wickets 171
Did not bat: K. L. Rolton, M. Jones, B. L. Calver, O. J. Magno, J. C. Price,
C. L. Fitzpatrick, C. L. Mason, A. J. Fahey
Bowling
Taylor 7-0-37-0, Collyer 10-2-42-0, Smithies 10-0-46-0, Connor 6-0-31-0, Winks
6-0-41-0, Leng 6-0-30-0, Reynard 5-1-28-1

ENGLAND
C. M. Edwards c Fahey b Fitzpatrick 28, K. M. Leng c Magno b Mason 0, B. A.
Daniels b Fitzpatrick 17, K. Smithies not out 62, C. J. Connor b Fitzpatrick 17,
J. Cassar st Price b Rolton 8, S. J. Metcalfe lbw b Fitzpatrick 5, M. A. Reynard b
Fitzpatrick 0, C. E. Taylor not out 0
Extras b 1, w 4
Total (50 overs) 142 for seven
Fall of wickets 2, 41, 48, 74, 94, 140, 140
Did not bat: S. V. Collyer, K. V. Winks
Bowling
Mason 10-1-24-1, Magno 6-3-15-0, Calver 10-0-30-1, Fitzpatrick 10-1-47-5, Fahey
7-2-16-0, Rolton 7-2-9-1

Umpires: L. E. Elgar and J. West

The drama then switched away from the playing area. On 28 September, at a special
general meeting, MCC members were once again asked to vote on the amendment to rule
2.2 that 'men and women shall be eligible for membership'.

Objectors included one who feared that 'the membership of MCC will be taken over by
the fancy hat brigade so that Lord's will become just another Ascot'.

When the votes were counted, 9,394 were in favour. This represented 69.8 per cent of
the 13,482 members. The meeting was described as 'acrimonious' by Ingleby-Mackenzie.
'At times it was quite nerve wracking before the result was finally announced.'

The decision was taken to nominate a maximum of ten honorary members. Trials were
to begin the following spring for a pool of around sixty playing members.

'It is a triumph for both Colin Ingleby-Mackenzie, the outgoing president who batted
so tenaciously for it during his two-year innings and for common sense. MCC is taking
down the sign and can now truly move onto the front foot,' said Sarah Potter.

On 16 March 1999, the new MCC president Tony Lewis welcomed the ten newest
members of the club. These were Betty Archdale, who had captained the first England
touring team in 1934/35; Surrey and South of England captain Edna Barker; former WCA
president Audrey Collins; Carol Cornthwaite, who skippered England in the eighties;
Jackie Court, a member of the England team that lifted the 1973 World Cup; Rachael

Heyhoe-Flint, who had captained England in the first match played at Lord's; Sheila Hill, umpire in the 1973 World Cup final; Norma Izard, a former WCA president and long-serving England team manager; MCC Museum curator Diana Rait Kerr; and 1948/49 England player-manager Netta Rheinberg, who also served as WCA secretary and co-wrote the jubilee history of the women's game.

'The unanimous thinking of the committee was simply this – we could not claim to be a great cricket club unless we had a women's team and women members,' said the new MCC president Tony Lewis.

A Cold Welcome for Zimbabwe and Bangladesh

Zimbabwe's first Test at Lord's was also the first played on the ground in the new millennium. It was also the first to begin in May. In fact, it was held the same week as the FA Cup final.

Andy Flower led a Zimbabwe side that included his brother, Grant. Both men had gained experience of English conditions in county cricket.

England captain Nasser Hussain won the toss and had no hesitation in asking the tourists to bat. Within half an hour, they were 8 for three after a fine spell of bowling from Andy Caddick. With 7 overs before lunch, Ed Giddins came on and with his fourth ball he had Andy Flower caught at first slip.

By the time he had taken his sweater, Giddins had five wickets and Zimbabwe had been hustled out for 83.

Henry Olonga was the outstanding Zimbabwean bowler at the time, but he was injured, and without him their attack was seriously weakened. Even so, England lost Mark Ramprakash early and closed the first day on 29 for one. On the second day, the weather closed in again. England were 113 for three at one stage before Hick and Stewart came together.

The following day, their partnership flourished even though Hick spent 22 minutes on 99 before at last pushing to midwicket to bring up his century against the country of his birth. Stewart also made a hundred and England eventually totalled 415. When Stewart returned to the pavilion, he had a second reason to be cheerful – his team Chelsea had won the FA Cup.

Yorkshire's Darren Gough tore into the Zimbabwe innings a second time round. He took three wickets in his first 4 overs and though they held on to the close of play, they were 39 for five and defeat was a matter of time.

The following morning, Heath Streak and Guy Whittall offered some late resistance but England completed their victory by lunchtime.

18–21 May 2000
England beat Zimbabwe by an innings and 209 runs

ZIMBABWE First Innings
G. Flower b Caddick 4, T. R. Gripper c Stewart b Caddick 1, M. W. Goodwin c Knight b Gough 18, A. D. R. Campbell c Stewart b Caddick 0, A. Flower c Atherton b Giddins 24, N. C. Johnson c Gough b Giddins 14, G. J. Whittall b Giddins 14, H. H. Streak c Atherton b Giddins 4, B. C. Strang c Ramprakash b Giddins 0, B. A. Murphy c Stewart b Gough 0, M. Mbangwa not out 1

Extras lb 2
Total 83
Fall of wickets 5, 8, 8, 46, 48, 67, 77, 79, 82
Bowling
Gough 12.3-1-36-2, Caddick 8-3-28-3, Flintoff 3-2-2-0, Giddins 7-2-15-5

ENGLAND First Innings
M. A. Atherton lbw b Streak 55, M. A. Ramprakash lbw b Streak 15, N. Hussain c
Murphy b Streak 10, G. A. Hick lbw b Streak 101, A. J. Stewart not out 124, N. V.
Knight c Johnson b Whittall 44, A. Flintoff c Streak b Whittall 1, C. P. Schofield c
Johnson b Whittall 0, A. R. Caddick c A. Flower b Streak 13, D. Gough c Campbell
b Murphy 5, E. S. H. Giddins c Strang b Streak 7
Extras b 5, lb 29, w 1, nb 5
Total 415
Fall of wickets 29, 49, 113, 262, 376, 378, 378, 398, 407
Bowling
Streak 35.5-12-87-6, Strang 27-4-86-0, Mbangwa 21-5-69-0, Johnson 20-5-55-0,
Whittall 7-0-27-3, Murphy 25-6-57-1

ZIMBABWE Second Innings
G. Flower lbw b Gough 2, T. R. Gripper c Knight b Gough 5, M. W. Goodwin lbw
b Caddick 11, A. D. R. Campbell lbw b Gough 4, B. A. Murphy lbw b Giddins 14,
A. Flower lbw b b Gough 2, N. C. Johnson c Hick b Caddick 9, G. J. Whittall c
Hick b Caddick 23, H. H. Streak c Knight b Giddins 0, B. C. Strang not out 37,
M. Mbangwa b Caddick 8
Extras lb 1, nb 7
Total 123
Fall of wickets 2, 7, 18, 33, 36, 49, 74, 74, 92
Bowling
Gough 15-3-57-4, Gough 16.2-5-38-4, Giddins 7-3-27-2

Umpires: D. L. Orchard (South Africa) and P. Willey (England)

The first Test appearance by Bangladesh at Lord's in 2005 was a brief and not altogether
happy experience. England captain Michael Vaughan won the toss and invited the visitors
to bat first. They were hustled out for 108 in 39 overs and the entire innings was over in
under three hours. A watching Alec Bedser was not impressed. 'And to think, every one of
those wickets is worth the same as Bradman's in the record books,' he said.

Marcus Trescothick and Vaughan both made centuries as England tightened their grip.

When the two centurions were finally dismissed, Ian Bell, who was making his second
Test appearance, shared an unbroken stand of 113 with Graham Thorpe, playing his
ninety-ninth.

England declared with only three wickets down at 528.

Bangladesh had less than two hours to bat but they were 90 for five by the close off
22 overs – they were staring defeat in the face. Khaled Mashud and Anwar Hossain put
on 57 for the ninth wicket, but it was all over by noon on the third day.

26–28 May 2005
England won by an innings and 261 runs

BANGLADESH First Innings
Javed Omar c Trescothick b S. Jones 22, Nafees Iqbal c Trescothick b Harmison 8, Habibul Bashar c G. Jones b Hoggard 3, Aftab Ahmed c Strauss b Flintoff 20, Mohammed Ashraful lbw b Flintoff 6, Mushfiqur Rahim b Hoggard 19, Khalid Mashud lbw b Hoggard 6, Mohammed Rafique run out (Vaughan Hoggard) 1, Mashrafe Mortaza b Harmison 0, Anwar Hossein Monir not out 5, Shahadat Hossain c G Jones b Hoggard 4
Extras b 1, lb 1 nb 12
Total 108
Fall of wickets 31, 34, 65, 65, 71, 89, 94, 98, 98
Bowling
Hoggard 13.2-5-42-4, Harmison 14-3-38-2, Flintoff 5-0-22-2, Jones 6-4-4-1

ENGLAND First Innings
M. E. Trescothick c Khaled Mashud b Mohammed Rafique 194, A. J. Strauss lbw b Mashrafe Mortaza 69, M. P. Vaughan c Khaled Mashud b Mashrafe Mortaza 120, I. R. Bell not out 65, G. P. Thorpe not out 42
Extras b 4, lb 11, nb 20, w 3
Total 528 for three declared
Fall of wickets 148, 403, 418
Did not bat: A. Flintoff, G. O. Jones, G. J. Batty, M. J. Hoggard, S. P. Harmison, S. P. Jones
Bowling
Mashrafe Mortaza 29-6-107-2, Shahadat Hossain 12-0-101-0, Anwar Hossain Monir 22-0-110-0, Mohammed Rafique 41-3-150-1, Aftab Abib 8-1-45-0

BANGLADESH Second Innings
Javed Omar c Thorpe b S Jones 25, Nafees Iqbal c Flintoff b Hoggard 3, Habibul Bashar c Hoggard b S. Jones 16, Aftab Ahmed lbw b Hoggard 32, Mohammed Ashraful c Harmison b Flintoff 2, Mushfiqur Rahim c Jones b Flintoff 3, Khalid Mashud c Thorpe b Flintoff 44, Mohammed Rafique c G. Jones b Harmison 0, Mashrafe Mortaza b Harmison 0, Anwar Hossein Monir c Trescothick b S. Jones 13, Shahadat Hossain not out 2
Extras b 1, lb 4, nb 14
Total 159
Fall of wickets 15, 47, 57, 60, 65, 96, 97, 97, 155
Bowling
Hoggard 9-1-42-2, Harmison 10-0-39-2, Flintoff 9.5-0-44-3, S. Jones 11-3-29-3

Umpires: K. Hariharan (India) and D. J. Harper (Australia)

MCC *v.* MCC

Two famous cricket clubs share the initials MCC, but until 1993 they had never met on the cricket field. The Melbourne Cricket Club was founded in 1838, a year after its counterpart in Marylebone had celebrated a golden jubilee. It was in Melbourne that the first Test match was played in 1877, and a representative of the host club had concentrated the minds of Marylebone on taking responsibility for English touring teams. Travelling to England or Australia remained a major undertaking until air travel became affordable. The idea for the match was first suggested in 1989 when Melbourne CC president Donald Cordner had helped organise a dinner for members of the two clubs during The Ashes series in England. This was held at the Clothworkers Hall and was a great success, but Cordner wanted to extend relations between the sides. He suggested a match between the two clubs. This idea was warmly received by Lord Bramall, then president of MCC, and secretary John Stephenson. With MCC treasurer Michael Melluish also on board, a match was arranged for 1993, timed to coincide with the Lord's Test match, a time when many Australian visitors were at Lord's in any case.

In the early 1990s, Allan Border's Australian Test team were in their pomp and won the Lord's Test by an innings. Two days later, Marylebone captain Jack Simmons lost the toss to Melbourne captain John Lill, formerly of South Australia.

From the outset, Chris Broad, a member of England's victorious team in 1986/7, set about the Melbourne attack and struck a superb century in an opening stand of 156. MCC eventually closed their innings on 251.

Surrey's Jonathan Robinson and Lancashire's Jimmy Cumbes got among the early wickets, but Melbourne's Steven McCooke scored a century. He called it 'an engulfing experience'. It was his first hundred in nearly three years, but it was not sufficient to bring the Australians victory.

The winners received a salver, presented by the Melbourne club. Crafted by Flynn's silversmiths in Kyneton it was to be a perpetual trophy. A tradition had been born.

'It is proposed that the matches be played every two years with Lord's and the MCG the venues,' said Melbourne president John Mitchell. 'Two clubs maintain high standards a point that is inclined to be overlooked in modern society.'

There is one thing that will bind us and keep us together and that is this wonderful game of cricket. The ambition of Australian cricketers will remain first to play on the turf of the Melbourne cricket club and beyond that on the ground that gave birth to the game, Lord's.

23 June 1993
Marylebone beat Melbourne by 6 runs

MARYLEBONE CRICKET CLUB

B. C. Broad c Edwards b McCooke 116, A. F. D. Ellison c McCooke b Phillips 41, J. C. Henderson lbw b Anderson 18, J. D. Robinson c Templeton b Anderson 0, G. J. Toogood not out 25, N. J. L. Trestrail c Templeton b Anderson 30, J. Simmons not out 0
Extras 21
Total 251 for five
Fall of wickets 156, 173, 181, 196, 248
Did not bat: A. C. Reeves, R. J. Maru, T. Hodson, J. Cumbes
Bowling
Phillips 8-1-37-1, Edwards 11-2-58-0, Fildes 11-4-36-0, McInnes 5-0-30-0, McCooke 11-2-38-1, Anderson 9-0-38-3

MELBOURNE CRICKET CLUB

B. J. Matters c Hodson b Cumbes 4, J. C. Lill c&b Reeves 22, M. W. D. Sholly st Hodson b Maru 41, S. McCooke b Robinson 104, M. S. Anderson b Simmons 4, R. I. Templeton b Cumbes 44, R. G. Lloyd lbw b Robinson 0, R. McInnes run out 8, I. Edwards run out 1, C. Fildes not out 5, N. Phillips not out 3
Extras 9
Total 245 for nine
Fall of wickets 4, 61, 80, 93, 198, 199, 230, 233, 239
Bowling
Cumbes 10-1-47-2, Robinson 10-0-41-2, Maru 11-0-32-1, Reeves 11-0-42-1, Simmons 9-0-50-1, Trestrail 4-0-29-0

Lighting up Lord's
and a Twenty20 Vision

When the newest format of the game was launched in 2003, ECB chief executive Tim Lamb called it 'the most ambitious and revolutionary step county cricket has taken since 1963'.

Twenty20 (T20) was launched with mascot races, pop concerts and even, on one ground, a hot tub, but it was not until the second season that a T20 match was played at Lord's for the first time.

The competition was designed to attract those who did not want to or were unable to spend an entire day at the cricket. A total of 21,000 tickets were snapped up in advance and organisers confidently predicted the highest attendance for a county match in the regular season since 1953. By the time the MCC and Middlesex members were taken into account, this had swelled to a sell-out crowd of 27,509.

For the first time, music jingles accompanied the arrival of the umpires and players, though the volume was carefully controlled. Environmental engineers from Westminster city Council were in attendance to ensure the sound barrier was not breached, and even went to the trouble of taking sound recordings around the ground.

'We want to show that we can keep the noise at a reasonable level,' said MCC chief executive Roger Knight.

Instead of the football-style plastic dugouts used for T20 at other venues, the players were seated on traditional Lord's benches in front of the pavilion.

Andrew Strauss won the toss and sent Surrey in to bat. After 7 overs, they were 66 for two before Paul Weekes came on and then only 19 runs came from the next five. The tide turned in Surrey's favour when Adam Hollioake was dropped by Ben Hutton. He went on to top score with 65 off 41 balls. His innings included five fours and two sixes as Surrey accelerated in the prescribed manner – 98 came from the last 8 overs.

When Middlesex began their pursuit of 184, Strauss found runs hard to come by. His eleven came off 16 balls, too slow for this format of the game. Although Lance Klusener scored a half-century in 32 balls, Middlesex fell behind the asking rate and Surrey won by 35 runs.

15 July 2004
Surrey beat Middlesex by 37 runs

SURREY
A. D. Brown b S. J. Cook 13, J. E. G. Benning c Compton b Klusener 30, M. R. Ramprakash run out 38, N. Shahid lbw b Weekes 1, A. J. Hollioake not out 65, Azar Mahmood c Hutton b Weekes 9, J. N. Batty not out 16
Extras b 7, w 4
Total (20 overs) 183 for five

Fall of wickets 30, 46, 68, 129, 146
Did not bat: T. J. Murtagh, J. Ormond, P. J. Sampson, N. D. Doshi
Bowling
Cook 3-0-29-1, Betts 2-0-28-0, Klusener 4-0-36-1, Hayward 3-0-33-0, Weekes 4-0-20-2, Dalrymple 4-0-33-0

MIDDLESEX
P. N. Weekes b Doshi 33, A. J. Strauss c Ormond b Sampson 11, O. A. Shah c Hollioake b Doshi 16, L. R. Klusener c Sampson b Hollioake 53, J. M. W. Dalrymple b Ormond 14, B. L. Hutton c Benning b Doshi 5, N. R. D. Compton c Doshi b Hollioake 5, S. J. Cook not out 0, B. J. M. Scott not out 0
Extras lb 2, nb 2, w 5
Total (20 overs) 146 for seven
Fall of wickets 29, 64, 64, 95, 104, 146, 146
Did not bat: M. M. Betts, M Hayward
Bowling
Azar Mahmood 3-0-18-0, Sampson 4-0-26-1, Murtagh 3-0-21-0, Doshi 4-0-26-3, Ormond 4-0-26-1, Hollioake 2-0-27-2

Umpires: M. J. Harris and R. Palmer.

A second division match in the Pro40 League was a very low-key way to usher in the most dramatic change in almost two centuries of watching cricket at St John's Wood. It was the first match seen at Lord's under lights, but it arrived almost by accident.

Day/night cricket had become the norm in Australia and at other grounds in England, but MCC chief executive Keith Bradshaw, a Tasmanian, was planning for its introduction to Lord's in 2008.

The Middlesex v Derbyshire match had originally been scheduled for Southgate. Middlesex secretary Vinny Codrington had been concerned that the match might not be viable, but his MCC counterpart suggested that the game should be switched to Lord's.

'A match under temporary floodlights will not only end the season at Lord's on a high note, but will provide us with very useful information with regards the staging of such matches here,' said Bradshaw.

Temporary lights were installed and when they were tested a few days before the match, they were an immediate hit with local residents. This was always a sensitive area to overcome.

'Some rang to say how marvellous the illumination was,' said Bradshaw, who had become the first overseas chief executive of MCC. Appropriately, two of his fellow Tasmanians were the first to shine in the match itself. Michael Dighton and Travis Birt put on 71 for the second wicket as Derbyshire batted. Jamie Dalrymple broke the stand and removed the dangerous Australian test player Simon Katich for five, before Smith and Adnan added brisk runs. Then Tim Murtagh took three wickets in five balls as Derbyshire crumbled from 179 for four to 181 for seven.

The lights came on for the Middlesex reply as they set about chasing a victory target of 196. Ed Joyce led the way with 68 in only 53 balls to give his side a superb start. Ed Smith shared in an opening stand of 93 and maintained pace in partnership with Andrew Strauss, who scored his 43 in 40 balls.

Murtagh and Dalrymple, the two bowlers who had done much to make the victory possible, saw Middlesex home with twelve balls to spare.

10 **September 2007**
Middlesex beat Derbyshire by four wickets

DERBYSHIRE
W. P. C. Weston c Scott b Finn 7, M. G. Dighton c Murtagh b Dalrymple 67,
T. R. Birt c Strauss b Dalrymple 47, S. M. Katich c&b Dalrymple 5, G. M. Smith lbw
b Murtagh 31, Hassan Adnan b Murtagh 21, D. J. Pipe b Murtagh 0, J. Needham
lbw b Kartik 4, J. L. Clare c Compton b Finn 0, T. Lungley not out 6, K. J. Dean not
out 0
Extras lb 2, nb 3, w 3
Total (40 overs) 196 for nine
Fall of wickets 43, 114, 127, 128, 179, 180, 184, 190.
Bowling
Murtagh 8-1-26-3, Williams 6-1-49-0, Finn 6-0-26-2, Kartik 8-0-32-1, Dalrymple
8-0-36-3, Compton 4-0-25-0

MIDDLESEX
E. C. Joyce c&b Clare 68, E. T. Smith c Dighton b Smith 32, A. J. Strauss b Dean
43, E. J. G. Morgan b Clare 14, J. M. W. Dalrymple not out 21, N. R. D. Compton b
Clare 1, B. J. M. Scott b Lungley 9, T. J. Murtagh not out 4
Extras lb 6, w 1
Total (38 overs) 199 for six
Fall of wickets 91, 132, 152, 167, 175, 194
Did not bat: M. Kartik, R. E. M. Williams, S. T. Finn
Bowling
Dean 8-0-37-0, Lungley 6-1-34-1, Dighton 6-0-35-0, Clare 8-0-44-3, Needham
3-0-17-0, Smith 7-1-26-1

Umpires: R. J. Bailey, B. Leadbetter
Television umpire: N. L. Bainton

The experiment was considered a success, so plans were made to install permanent lights
that rose above the Tavern, behind the Warner Stand and at the back of Compton and
Edrich stands. Built at a cost of £2.7 million, at full height they were 48 metres and could
be retracted to 29 metres when not in use. These were installed ready for the 2009 ICC
T20 World Cup, although usage was restricted to twelve days and ten nights every season,
and the club was forced to seek permission from Westminster City Council.

It was the first time international T20 cricket had been played at Lord's, twenty-four
years almost to the day that the first World Cup over 60 overs had begun.

To capitalise on the growing interest in women's cricket, their competition was held in
parallel with the men's and the final would be a double-header at Lord's, another first.

England's first opponents in this new brand of cricket was a team from the Netherlands.
Dutch amateur sides had been visitors to the ground in the nineteenth and early twentieth
century. The current crop included young all-rounder Daan Van Bunge, for whom these
were familiar surroundings. He had been an MCC Young Cricketer under the tutelage of
Clive Radley in 2003. Four other players in the side had experience of county cricket.

They made an immediate impression as they took to the field, dressed head to toe in
bright orange. Perhaps that was what gave them the confidence to ask England to bat on a

murky evening when the new lights were put to the test. It looked as though the plan had backfired when Ravi Bopara and Luke Wright posted a century stand for the first wicket in only 71 balls, but England lost their way after that. In the circumstances, 162 off their twenty represented a disappointing return.

Jimmy Anderson struck in the first over to remove Alexei Kervezee. The experience of Sussex player Bas Zuiderent told. New Zealand-born Darron Reekers and Peter Borren, who hit a huge six off Paul Collingwood, helped the Netherlands reach a hundred three balls faster than England had done. This meant they were always ahead of Duckworth-Lewis. The methods employed by Tom de Groot, a player centrally contracted to the Dutch Board, incorporated improvisation learnt on the hockey field. He top scored with 49, an innings that earned him the man of the match award.

By the time it came to the last over, the Dutchmen needed seven runs to win. Stuart Broad came on and was unable to take a chance of a run out off the first and second balls. Off the third, Essex batsman Ryan ten Doeschate gave a sharp return chance to Broad who put it down. The batsmen scampered three singles and a bye, and off the last ball, the Dutchmen needed two to win. Most experts agreed there wasn't even a single as Broad, fielded in his follow through. He went for the run out and to the astonishment of all, he missed the target. *Wisden* called it 'a wretched nadir in the painful saga of England's one-day humiliations'.

5 June 2009
Netherlands beat England by four wickets

ENGLAND
R. S. Bopara c Seelar b ten Doeschate 46, L. J Wright c Borren b ten Doeschate 71, O. A. Shah c de Grooth b Schiferli 5, E. J. G. Morgan c Zuiderent b Borren 6, P. D. Collingwood c Schiferli b Seelar 11, R. W. T. Key not out 10, J. S. Foster not out 3
Extras w 10
Total (20 overs) 162 for five
Fall of wickets 102, 113, 127, 144, 153
Did not bat: A. U. Rashid, S. C. J. Broad, J. M. Anderson, A. Sidebottom
Bowling
Nannes 4-0-30-0, Schiferli 4-0-33-1, ten Doeschate 4-0-35-2, Seelar 4-0-33-1, Borren 4-0-31-1.

NETHERLANDS
A. N. Kervezee c Broad b Anderson 1, D. J. Reekers c Shah b Broad 20, B. Zuiderent st Foster b Rashid 12, T. N. De Grooth c Key b Collingwood 49, P. W. Borren c Shah b Anderson 30, R. N. ten Doeschate not out 22, D. L. S. Van Bunge c Wright b Anderson 8, E. Schiferli not out 5
Extras b 1, lb 13, w 1
Total 163 for five
Fall of wickets 2, 23, 66, 116, 133, 146
Did not bat: P. M. Seelar, D. P. Nannes
Bowling
Anderson 4-0-23-3, Sidebottom 4-0-23-0, Broad 4-0-32-1, Rashid 4-0-36-1, Wright 2-0-18-0, Collingwood 2-0-17-1

Umpires: S. J. Davis (Australia), E. A. De Silva (Sri Lanka), A. L. Hill (third umpire; New Zealand)

This was the year Lord's staged two World Cup finals on the same day. England's men had gone out of the tournament at the Super 8 stage, but the women were in superb form. They had won the 50-over World Cup earlier in March. Captain Clare Taylor had been named one of Wisden's five cricketers of the year, the first woman ever accorded the honour. She struck an unbeaten 76 as England beat Australia to reach the final with three balls to spare. New Zealand were waiting for them. England opened their bowling with spinner Laura Marsh, and the innovative tactical move paid immediate dividends. Suzi Bates was stumped off the fifth ball of the innings. Katherine Brunt had received a black eye in an accident during fielding practice, but her aim was true as she took a career-best 3 for six. New Zealand were bowled out for 85. By now, some 10,000 were in the ground, the largest crowd ever to watch a women's match in England to see Taylor guide England home to with 3 overs to spare.

21 June 2009
England beat New Zealand by six wickets

NEW ZEALAND
S. W. Bates st S. J. Taylor b Marsh 1, L. R. Doolan st Taylor b Brunt 14, A. L. Watkins b Brunt 2, A. Satterthwaite c S. C. Taylor b Shaw 19, R. H. Priest c&b Brunt 0, N. J. Browne b Shaw 1, S. J. McGlashan c Greenway b Gunn 9, S. J. Tsukigawa c S. J. Taylor b Gunn 5, K. L. Pulford c S. C. Taylor b Edwards 14, S. E. A. Ruck not out 0
Extras b 1, lb 4, nb 1, w 4
Total 20 overs 85
Fall of wickets 2, 10, 23, 23, 31, 48, 58, 62, 84
Bowling
Marsh 4-0-16-1, Brunt 4-2-6-3, Shaw 4-0-17-2, Colvin 4-0-16-0, Gunn 3-0-19-2, Edwards 1-0-6-1

ENGLAND
S. J. Taylor c Priest b Pulford 23, C. M. Edwards b Ruck 9, S. C. Taylor not out 39, B. L. Morgan c McGlashan b Browne 6, L. S. Greenway b Devine 3, J. L. Gunn not out 2
Extras lb 1, w 3
Total (17 overs) 86 for four
Fall of wickets 19, 39, 70, 74
Did not bat: C. M. G. Atkins, N. J. Shaw, K. H. Brunt, H. L. Colvin, L. A. Marsh
Bowling
Devine 3-0-12-1, Ruck 4-0-17-1, Pulford 4-0-20-1, Bates 2-0-8-0, Browne 3-0-18-1, Doolan 1-0-10-0

Umpires: Aleem Dar (Pakistan), R. D. Koertzen (South Africa)

There was scarcely a seat to be had for the men's final. Three days before, Pakistan had edged home by seven runs against the in-form South Africans, who many had considered likely to lift the trophy. Sri Lanka were rather more convincing winners in their semi-final against the West Indies at the Oval.

Despite an unbeaten 64 from Kumar Sangakarra, Sir Lanka posted only 138 in their 20 overs. In their previous Lord's final in 1999, Pakistan has scored six fewer runs in almost twice as many overs, but this time the total they had been set held no terrors.

Shahid Afridi lived up to his fearsome reputation in this form of the game. He hit two big sixes in his unbeaten 54 from 40 balls. Pakistan coasted to victory with eight balls to spare.

21 June 2009
Pakistan beat Sri Lanka by eight wickets

SRI LANKA
T. M. Dilshan c Shahzaib Hassan b Mohammad Asir 0, S. Jayasuriya b Abdul Razzaq 17, J. Mubarak c Shahzaib Hassan b Abdul Razzaq 0, K. Sangakarra not out 64, D. P. M. D. Jayawardene c Misbah ul Haq b Abdul Razzaq 1, L. P. C. Silva c Saeed Ajmal b Umar Gul 14, I. Udana b Shahid Afridi 1, A. D. Matthews not out 35
Extras lb 3, w 2, nb 1
Total (20 overs) 138 for six
Fall of wickets 0, 2, 26, 32, 67, 70
Did not bat: S. L. Malinga, M. Muralitharan, B. A. W. Mendis
Bowling
Mohammad Amir 4-1-30-1, Abdul Razzaq 3-0-20-3, Shahid Afridi 4-0-20-1, Saeed Amjal 4-0-28-0, Shoaib Malik 1-0-8-0, Umar Gul 4-0-29-1

PAKISTAN
Kamran Akmsal st Sangakarra b Jayasuriya 37, Shahzaib Hassan c Jayasuriya b Muralitharan 19, Shahid Afridi not out 54, Shoaib Malik not out 24
Extras lb 2, nb 1, w 2
Total (18.4 overs) 139 for two
Fall of wickets 48, 63
Did not bat: Abul Razzaq, Younis Khan, Misbah U. L. Haq, Fawad Alam, Umar Gul, Saaed Amjal, Mohammad Amir
Bowling
Matthews 2-0-17-0, Udana 4-0-44-0, Malinga 3.4-0-14-0, Muralitharan 3-0-20-1, Mendis 4-0-34-0, Jayasuriya 2-0-8-1

Umpires: D. J. Harper (Australia), S. J. A. Taufel (Australia), S. Davis (third umpire; Australia).

After 125 years, artificial light was used to illuminate the playing area in a Lord's Test match for the first time during the 2009 Ashes Test. ICC playing regulations had been altered to make this possible.

If in the opinion of the umpires, natural light is deteriorating to an unfit level, they shall authorise the ground authorities to use the available artificial lighting so that the match can continue in acceptable conditions.

There had been no problems with the light when England batted. They had scored 22 boundaries in the first session. Captain Andrew Strauss made 161. The aim was to score rapidly in the first innings and then allow 'scoreboard pressure' to intimidate the opposition.

On day two, the regulation was invoked for the first time. Australia were 31 for 2 in their first innings and as the clouds rolled in, the lights flickered into life to illuminate a Test match at Lord's for the first time. The traditional visit by the Queen at lunchtime was conducted under natural light.

By the end of second day, England had seized control. Australia were in trouble at 158 for eight. England had certainly profited from the somewhat disjointed day. The frequent breaks enabled the bowlers to recuperate. For the batsmen, each new beginning was awkward. The following day, the tail did well to lift the score to 215.

With so much time left, England chose not to enforce the follow-on, but it wasn't until Paul Collingwood and Matt Prior increased the scoring tempo that runs flowed to maximum effect. Australia were asked to chase a victory target of 522. They were reduced to 128 for five when Michael Clarke and Brad Haddin came together to add 185. Clarke finally departed for 136 but Australian resistance was not completely over as Mitchell Johnson lifted Australia to 406 – the highest score in the fourth innings of a Test match at Lord's. It was the first time England had experienced a Lord's Test victory against Australia since 1934, a statistic that led *Wisden* to draw unflattering comparisons with the frequency of Halley's Comet.

16–20 July 2009
England beat Australia by 115 runs

ENGLAND First Innings
A. J. Strauss b Hilfenhaus 161, A. N. Cook lbw b M. Johnson 95, R. J. Bopara lbw b Hilfenhaus 18, K. P. Pietersen c Haddin b Siddle 32, P. D. Collingwood c Siddle b M. Clarke 16, M. J. Prior b M. Johnson 8, A. Flintoff c Ponting b Hilfenhaus 4, S. C. J. Broad b Hilfenhaus 16, G. P. Swann c Ponting b Siddle 4, J. M. Anderson c M. Hussey b Johnson 29, G. Onions not out 17
Extras lb 2, b 15 ,nb 8
Total 425
Fall of wickets 196, 222, 267, 302, 317, 333, 364, 370, 378
Bowling
Hilfenhaus 31-0-103-4, Johnson 21.4-2-132-3, Siddle 20-1-76-2, Hauritz 8.3-1-26-0, North 16.3-2-59-0, Clarke 4-1-12-0

AUSTRALIA First Innings
P. J. Hughes c Prior b Anderson 4, S. M. Katich c Broad b Onions 48, R. T. Ponting c Strauss b Onions 2, M. E. K. Hussey b Flintoff 51, M. J. Clarke c Cook b Anderson 1, M. J. North b Anderson 0, B. J. Haddin c Cook b Broad 28, M. G. Johnson c Cook b Broad 4, N. M. Hauritz c Collingwood b Onions 24, P. M. Siddle c Strauss b Onions 35, B. W. Hilfenhaus not out 6
Extras b 4, lb 6, nb 2
Total 215
Fall of wickets 4, 10, 103, 111, 111, 139, 148, 152, 196
Bowling
Anderson 21-5-55-4, Flintoff 12-4-27-1, Broad 18-1-78-2, Onions 11-1-41-3, Swann 1-0-4-0

ENGLAND Second Innings

A. J. Strauss c Clarke b Hauritz 32, A. N. Cook lbw b Hauritz 32, R. S. Bopara c Katich b Hauritz 27, K. P. Pietersen c Haddin b Siddle 44, P. D. Collingwood c Haddin b Siddle 54, M. J. Prior run out North 61, A. Flintoff not out 30, S. C. J. Broad not out 0
Extras b 16, lb 9, nb 5, w 1
Total 311 for six declared
Fall of wickets 67, 74, 147, 175, 260, 311
Bowling
Hilfenhaus 19-5-59-0, Johnson 17-2-68-0, Siddle 15.2-4-64-2, Hauritz 16-1-80-3, Clarke 4-0-15-0

AUSTRALIA Second Innings

P. J. Hughes c Strauss b Flintoff 17, S. M. Katich c Pietersen b Flintoff 6, R. T. Ponting b Broad 38, M. E. K. Hussey c Collingwood b Swann 27, M. J. Clarke b Swann 136, M. J. North b Swann 6, B. J. Haddin c Collingwood b Flintoff 80, M. G. Johnson b Swann 63, N. M. Hauritz b Flintoff 1, P. M. Siddle b Flintoff 7, B. M. Hilfenhaus not out 4
Extras b 5, lb 8, nb 8
Total 406
Fall of wickets 17, 34, 78, 120, 128, 313, 356, 363, 388
Bowling
Anderson 21-4-86-0, Flintoff 27-4-92-5, Onions 9-0-50-0, Broad 16-3-49-1, Swann 28-3-87-4, Collingwood 6-1-29-0

Umpires: B. R. Doctrove (West Indies), R. D. Koertzen (South Africa)
Television umpire: N. J. Llong

TARGETING A SUMMER LIKE NO OTHER

When it became clear that London was to bid for the 2012 Olympic Games, MCC president Lord Alexander and secretary Roger Knight were both keen to give 'every practicable assistance in bringing the Olympics to the capital for the first time since 1948'.

When the bid was tabled, Lord's was included as the proposed venue for the archery.

To help promote the bid, a demonstration of the sport was held during the 2005 Test match against Bangladesh, and on 6 July, at the IOC session in Singapore, London was duly confirmed as the host city of the Games of the 30th Olympiad.

The first formal international archery competition took place on the ground in August 2007. China and India joined host nation Great Britain in a three-team invitational tournament for the MCC Cup. A smattering of curious spectators watched proceedings on a sunny morning and the club offered some helpful hints: 'MCC strongly recommends that spectators bring binoculars with them.'

The archers released their arrows from in front of the Tavern Stand towards targets set below the Warner Stand. In perfect weather, the trophies were won by the Indian women and Great Britain's men, and the Chinese team made a presentation of their team shirt to the museum – their national colours are the same as MCC.

The competition had an impact on the Olympic planning. Organisers realised that the backdrop of the pavilion would be better seen if the targets were positioned at the Nursery End. The new configuration was introduced for a test event in October 2011, the first full-scale international competition held on the ground. The victorious teams received miniature cricket bats and two MCC presidents, incumbent Philip Hodson and his immediate predecessor Christopher Martin-Jenkins, were both part of the presentation party.

The following July, London was buzzing, and on the morning of 27 July, the hallowed turf at Lord's became Olympic soil. The ranking round of the archery competitions on the Nursery Ground was the first competition of the 2012 Games to actually take place in London.

Organisers had faced a race against time to get the ground ready for its Olympic role. There had been two one-day internationals at the beginning of July, as soon as these had been completed, the Olympic workers moved in. Temporary stands were built on the main ground either side of the pavilion gate. The media centre was emblazoned with giant Olympic rings and the ground was decorated with the 'heritage' purple colour scheme, known as 'the look of the Games'.

In the ranking round, all sixty-four archers shot simultaneously. Their scores formed the basis for seeding for the competition proper, which was held on the main ground. On the first morning, there was a world-record score – 699 of a possible 700 set by Korea's Im Dong-Hyun, who is almost blind in one eye.

For the main competition, the archers shot towards targets positioned below the media centre. In the pavilion, members of the IOC, arguably the most powerful club in world sport, watched proceedings from the long room. The flag of five Olympic rings flew from the balcony of the visitors' dressing room.

The BBC even despatched *Test Match Special* commentator Jonathan Agnew to cover proceedings, who described archery as a 'gripping' and 'ruthless' sport.

In the first title to be decided, Italy won the men's team competition, thanks to an inner gold finish from Michele Frangili, which gave his team victory over the USA by one point.

Competition lasted for the first week of the Games, but no sooner had the last arrow had been fired, the race was on to make ready for the third Test against South Africa. Groundsman Mick Hunt and his team restored the ground to its cricketing self in less than three weeks, using replacement turf that had been grown in Scunthorpe.

For the first time, the number one in the ICC World Test Ranking was to be decided at a Lord's Test. England had been top since 2011, but anything less than victory would allow South Africa to claim the ceremonial mace. The tourists won the toss and batted but were reduced to 54 for four. Jacques Rudolph and J. P. Duminy rescued matters and a maiden half-century from Vernon Philander took them to 309.

On the second day, England found themselves in an identical position after the departure of Strauss, Trott, Cook and Taylor, but Ian Bell was joined by Jonny Bairstow. Together they put on 124. Bairstow reached 95 but thereafter did not score off 14 balls and was out driving to the next. When South Africa went in again, the prodigious Hashim Amla escaped when Prior was unable to hold a catch behind. He completed his second century of the series as South Africa set England a victory target of 346.

England's prospects seemed as unpromising as the weather on the final morning when they began at 16 for two. Overnight batsman Ian Bell did not add a run before he was caught at slip and when James Taylor was run out after a mix up, England were 45 for four. Jonathan Trott and Jonny Bairstow took play into the afternoon, and Bairstow's half-century had come from only 41 balls. Trott's more patient vigil ended in mid-afternoon, but Stuart Broad helped add 74 with Matt Prior and the crowd grew increasingly expectant.

At tea, England needed 125 from 33 overs with three wickets in hand. Matt Prior and Graeme Swann played with conviction to add 62 in 8.4 overs. The match turned one final decisive time when Imran Tahir returned sharply to run out Swann. The return of fast bowler Vernon Philander proved decisive. Prior had a number of escapes but was eventually caught by Graeme Smith, as Philander completed a five-wicket hall to give South Africa the series, the Basil D'Oliveira Trophy and that cherished number one status.

16–20 August 2012
South Africa beat England by 51 runs

SOUTH AFRICA First Innings
G. C. Smith c Prior b Anderson 14, A. N. Petersen c Prior b Finn 22, H. M. Amla b Finn 13, J. H. Kallis c Prior b Finn 3, A. B. De Villiers c Cook b Anderson 27, J. A. Rudolph b Swann 42, J. P. Duminy c Prior b Anderson 61, V. D. Philander st Prior b Swann 61, D. W. Steyn c Swann b Broad 26, M. Morkel c Prior b Finn 25, Imran Tahir not out 2
Extras b 7, lb 5, w 1
Total 309
Fall of wickets 22, 49, 50, 54, 105, 163, 235, 270, 307
Bowling
Anderson 29-5-76-3, Broad 29-4-69-1, Finn 18-2-75-4, Swann 24.2-6-63-2, Trott 6-1-14-0

ENGLAND First Innings
A. J. Strauss b Morkel 20, A. N. Cook c Kallis b Steyn 7, I. J. L. Trott lbw b Steyn 8,
I. R. Bell c Petersen b Philander 58, J. W. A. Taylor c Smith b Morkel 10, J. M.
Bairstow b Morkel 95, M. J. Prior c Kallis b Philander 27, S. C. J. Broad c Amla b
Steyn 16, G. P. Swann not out 37, J. M. Anderson c Rudolph b Steyn 12, S. T. Finn c
Duminy b Morkel 10
Extras lb 10, nb 4, w 1
Total 315
Fall of wickets 29, 38, 39, 54, 178, 221, 252, 264, 283
Bowling
Morkel 28.3-6-80-4, Philander 24-9-48-2, Steyn 29-4-94-4, Kallis 12-3-29-0, Imran
Tahir 14-3-54-0

SOUTH AFRICA Second Innings
A. N. Petersen lbw b Broad 24, G. C. Smith lbw b Swann 23, H. M. Amla b Finn 121,
J. H. Kallis lbw b Finn 31, D. W. Steyn c Taylor b Broad 9, A. B. De Villiers c Strauss
b Finn 43, J. A. Rudolph c Prior b Finn 11, J. P. Duminy not out 26, V. D. Philander c
Bairstow b Anderson 35, M. Morkel st Prior b Swann 9, Imran Tahir b Anderson 1
Extras b 6, lb 8, nb 2, w 2
Total 351
Fall of wickets 46, 50, 131, 164, 259, 268, 282, 336, 348
Bowling
Anderson 25.2-4-73-4, Broad 21-2-85-2, Swann 47-14-94-2, Finn 27-5-74-4, Trott
4-0-11-0

ENGLAND Second Innings
A. J. Strauss lbw b Philander 1, A. N. Cook lbw b Philander 3, I. J. L. Trott c Kallis
b Steyn 63, I. R. Bell c Smith b Philander 4, J. W. A. Taylor run out (Amla/Steyn/De
Villiers) 4, J. M. Bairstow b Imran Tahir 54, M. J. Prior c Smith b Philander 73,
S. C. J. Broad c Amla b Kallis 37, G. P. Swann run out (Rudolph/Imran Tahir) 41,
J. M. Anderson not out 4, S. T. Finn c Kallis b Philander 0
Extras b 7, nb 1, w 2
Total 294
Fall of wickets 5, 6, 34, 45, 134, 146, 208, 282, 294
Bowling
Morkel 17-3-58-0, Philander 14.5-4-30-5, Steyn 16-4-61-1 , Kallis 11-2-50-1, Imran
Tahir 24-3-88-1

Umpires: H. D. P. K. Dharmasena (Sri Lanka) and S. J. A. Taufel (Australia)
Television umpire: R. J. Tucker (Australia)

JAPANESE FIRST

In 2013, the first international tourists to visit Lord's were from Japan.

Their debut came on the Nursery Ground on a chilly April day. Most of the Japanese team only had experience of matting wickets prior to this tour, so a grass pitch was something new. They also had never before needed to wear sweaters to play cricket.

'England is the home of classical cricket. The problem Japan has is that very few people know about the game but for me cricket is the greatest team game. It is an amazing experience for us to enjoy,' said fast bowler Kazuyuki Ogawa.

The visit was in commemoration of the 150th anniversary of the first match played on Japanese soil, but Lord's was better known to most Japanese television viewers as an archery venue. Takaharu Furukawa won Olympic silver in the men's competition at London 2012.

MCC won the toss and batted first in a match played on the Nursery Ground. Former Kent and Sussex player Will House and Rob Turner, once of Somerset, gave the club a sound start. Turner's century came at a run a ball and included five sixes as he made the most of the shorter boundaries.

The major stand of the match came with Tom Webley. They put on 160 as MCC declared their innings on 250. It was a stiff target for the tourists.

Many of the Japanese players had used the internet to develop their techniques. Wicketkeeper and captain Tatsuro Chino logged on to the web find footage of legendary Australian 'keepers Ian Healy and Adam Gilchrist. The team even had an Australian coach.

'We don't get much television coverage so we have to use the internet as our source,' said Japan Cricket Association chief executive Naoki Alex Miyaji.

The match helped raise funds for 'Cricket for Smiles', which aimed to help victims of the Japanese Tsunami. Cricket is being used as a way of rehabilitating youngsters caught up in the disaster. 'Cricket for Smiles is Cricket's way of making a difference and bringing people together', said organisers of the scheme which received a spirit of cricket award from the ICC.

The Japanese women's team toured in tandem with the men but on this occasion they had the unusual role of explaining the intricacies of the game. The crowd had been swelled by many from the Japanese community in London but few had seen cricket before.

Despite a fighting 45 from Tuyoshi Takada, the Japanese were never up with the asking rate and were eventually bowled out for 144.

The team signed off in courteous fashion as Chino invited his teammates to bow in unison. It was a stylish way to take their leave.

28 April 2013
MCC beat Japan by 106 runs

MCC

W. House c S. Ogawa b Hagihara 25, R. J. Turner c Miyaji b Taniyama 111, M. R. Tipping lbw b Taniyama 1, T. Webley c Hagihara b Miyaji 72, J. R. Irvine-Fortescue c Miyaji b Hagihara 9, C. D. Grange c Chino b Hagihara 19, I. C. Hampshire not out 1

Extras b5, lb 1, nb 2, w 4
Total 46.1 overs 250 for six declared
Fall of wickets 39, 45, 205, 207, 244, 250
Did not bat: M. J. Dennington, C. E. H. Hopkins, A. D. Clarke, N. E. D. Brand
Bowling
Hagihara 8.1-0-41-3 (nb2), Takada 8-1-27-0 (w 3), Taniyama 10-0-70-1 (w 1), Miyaji 10-0-33-2, Nakano 5-0-42-0

JAPAN

M. Kobayashi c Turner b Hopkins 18, N. Miyaji c Gange b Dennington 12, S. Sugiaru b Hopkins 9, T. Chino b Brand 24 , K. Ogawa c Clarke b Brand 0, T. Hagihara c Irvine-Fortescue b Clarke 3, M. Taniyama b Clarke 8, T. Takada c Irvine Fortescue b Hampshire 45, S. Nakano b Hampshire 5, Y. Uehara b Clarke 13, S. Ogawa not out 3

Extras nb 1, w 3
Total (37.3 overs) 144
Fall of wickets 15, 39, 44 59, 68, 78, 78, 91, 124
Bowling
Dennington 7-1-29-1, Hopkins 6-2-19-2 (w 1), Brand 8-1-20-2 (2 w, 1 nb), Clarke 12-2-52-3, Hampshire 4.3-0-24-2

Umpires: D. Burden and J. R. Milton

THE TIME AND THE PLACE

The first Lord's Test match took place in June, but from 1896 it became a June occasion more often than not.

When twin tour were introduced in 1965, the second Lord's Test of the summer was typically in June. The final day of the 1967 match against Pakistan was scheduled for the first day of August. In 1973, Lord's had five August days of Test cricket against West Indies – they scored 652 for eight. This included 150 from Garry Sobers by way of farewell. Play was interrupted on the third day after a bomb hoax and England lost by an innings and 226 runs. The sun shone throughout. The Centenary Test in 1980 was not as fortunate, much of the showpiece Saturday was washed out. The last two days of the match were in September. Perversely, the weather was at its best.

In the new millennium, the touring schedule was altered again. The first visitors arrived earlier than ever before and in 2000, the Test match against Zimbabwe became the first at Lord's to begin in May.

Unreliable weather has made it difficult to have a showpiece opening match to the season at Lord's. From 1934 through to the late sixties, MCC v Yorkshire was the opening match. In 1970, Champion county Glamorgan faced MCC, and variations of this fixture were held until it was switched to Dubai in 2010.

Although the ground was named after Lord and the pavilion incorporated the likenesses of Lord Harris and Sir Spencer Ponsonby-Fane, no part of the ground bore the name of any cricketer.

When W. G. Grace died, however, the club was determined that there should be a fitting memorial and decided that the man they wanted to design it was Herbert Baker, soon also to mastermind the construction of a new grandstand. Matters were delayed because Baker was in India and it was decided to wait until he returned before proceeding.

When Baker did return, he set to work. A report of significant progress in the project was reported at a meeting held on 18 July 1921, an appropriate time to do so. It was the anniversary of W. G.'s birth.

The minutes reveal 'it had been decided that the gates at the entrance should be the Grace Memorial'. According to Sir Pelham Warner, it was Stanley Jackson who suggested the simple epitaph to be inscribed 'The Great Cricketer'. The idea was accepted.

'There the inscription stands, governed by the all important word *the,* there like the image to Horatius, it stands plain for all folks to see,' said Warner.

The club minutes in 1922 announced that the memorial gates were now complete. It was decided there should be no opening ceremony and the reason was soon clear. MCC minutes show that 'Mrs Grace was asked to open it formally but did not feel able to accept the invitation.' Even without fanfare, they have become the most famous thoroughfare onto the ground.

Lord Harris was another England captain who dedicated his life to cricket. MCC created the Harris garden in his honour, which was highly appropriate for a man from Kent.

On 2 May 1934, after play in the MCC v Surrey match, both teams joined Viscount Hailsham for a short ceremony to inaugurate the garden. Kent captain Percy Chapman sent a telegram message:

> The Kent team playing at Cardiff today would very much appreciate being associated with the unveiling of the memorial at Lord's. At the same time appreciating his great work for English and cricket.

The memorial stone was faced with flints from the Harris estate at Belmont. Wrought-iron gates were positioned at the entrance to the gardens. The final result of the match would surely not have pleased His Lordship. Surrey beat MCC by an innings and 173 runs.

Pelham Warner had taken up the administrative baton from Lord Harris. His own connections had lasted almost three-quarters of a century, during which time he had filled almost every role. Warner made his debut there as a cricketer in 1889, when he played for Rugby School against Marlborough. He had represented Oxford there in the Varsity Match and went on to play for and lead England. He had been chosen to lead the first touring team to wear MCC colours and successfully came back with The Ashes.

He skippered Middlesex to the 1920 championship and managed the infamous 'Bodyline' tour to Australia in 1932/33. He was also assistant MCC secretary during the Second World War.

On his eightieth birthday in 1953, the club lit up the Baker's famous Grandstand score box and staged a celebration banquet in his honour, which was rare. Five years later came the ultimate accolade – the MCC committee had decided to name the new stand next to the pavilion in his honour, the first time any stand on the ground had been named after a player.

On 7 May 1958, during the tea interval of a County Championship match between his old county Middlesex and Nottinghamshire, the eighty-five-year-old Sir Pelham Warner was shown to his seat by Bernard, Duke of Norfolk and then MCC president. 'No cricketer deserved the honour more,' said the Duke.

He had founded *The Cricketer* magazine, written extensively about the game and made the first BBC radio broadcast from Lord's. So perhaps it was appropriate that the stand that bore his name also incorporated the press box.

The only players to have been honoured since are Compton and Edrich, whose names appropriately adorn twin stands at the Nursery End, and Sir George 'Gubby' Allen, after whom the Q stand was renamed.

Yet the most famous monument at Lord's is to a mythical figure. It was the gift of Sir Herbert Baker, the designer of the Grandstand, in 1926. It was a distinctive weather vane that depicted Father Time stooping over the stumps. It was placed above the Grandstand scoreboard for the first time. It remained in the same place for almost seventy years but during the war cables from a stray barrage balloon dragged it from the roof.

When the new Grandstand was built, the weather vane was carefully winched down and repositioned on the opposite side of the ground. Its new location was on the top of a clock tower between the Mound and Tavern stands.

Father Time has become such a symbol of Lord's that it was featured on the illuminated scroll when the club was accorded a royal charter in 2013.

ACKNOWLEDGEMENTS

The author would like to thank Neil Robinson and Robert Curphey at the MCC Library for their assistance and encouragement. Thanks also to Andrew Hignell at Glamorgan; Neil Leitch from Cricket Scotland; Ger Siggins at Cricket Ireland; cricket statistician John Bryant; Dil Bhara at the National Hockey Museum; Terry Carter at Troon Cricket Club; John Goulstone; Elaine Cracknell at Eton College Archives; and Angharad Meredith at Harrow School Archives.

SELECT BIBLIOGRAPHY

NEWSPAPERS AND MAGAZINES
Bell's Life in London, and Sporting Chronicle; Cricket a Weekly Record of the Game; Etoniana (Eton College magazine); *Melbourne Cricket Club News; Playfair Cricket Monthly; Revue Olympique; Sporting Gazette; Sports Quarterly; The Cricketer; The Guardian; The Observer; The Sporting Life; The Times; The Wisden Cricketer; Wisden Cricket Monthly*

BOOKS
Bentley, Henry, *A Correct Account of All the Cricket Matches Which Have Been Played by the Marylebone Cricket Club* (T. Traveller, 1823)
Chesterton, George, Doggart, Hubert, *Oxford & Cambridge Cricket* (Collins Willow, 1989)
Epps, William, *William Epps's Cricket: A Collection of All the Grand Matches Played in England from 1771 to 1791* (Troy Town, Rochester, 1799)
Frith, David, *England Versus Australia* (Penguin Viking, 2006)
Gaby, Dick, *Cross Arrows: Cricket Club 1880–1980* (Cross Arrows Cricket Club, 1980)
Gavaskar, Sunil, *Sunny Days* (Rupa & Co., 1980)
Green, Stephen, *Lord's: The Cathedral of Cricket* (Tempus, 2003)
Haygarth, Arthur, *Scores and Biographies*, Volumes 1–16
Lewis, Tony, *Double Century* (Hodder and Stoughton, 1987)
Mallett, Ashley, *Lord's Dreaming* (Souvenir Press, 2002)
Marshall, Julian, *Annals of Tennis* (The Field Office, 1878)
Matthews, Peter; Brooke, Robert, *Guinness Cricket Firsts* (Guinness Publishing Ltd, 1988)
Mote, Ashley, *The Glory Days of Cricket* (Robson Books, 1997)
Noel, E. B., Clarke, J. O. M., *A History of Tennis* (1924)
Nyren, John, *Cricketers of My Time* (1833)
Pycroft, James, *The Cricket Field* (Guild Publishing London, 1859)
Rice, Jonathan, Bradman, Sir Donald (foreword), *About One Hundred Lord's Tests* (Methuen Publishing Ltd, 2001)
Ross, Gordon, *The Gillette Cup: 1963 to 1980* (Queen Anne Press, 1981)
Slatter, W. H., *Recollections of Lord's and the MCC* (privately published, 1914)
Swanton, E. W. G. Plumptre (eds), *Barclays World of Cricket* (1987)
Wynne-Thomas, Peter, *The Complete History of Cricket Tours* (1986)
The Times MCC 1787–1937
Warner, Sir Pelham, *Lord's 1787–1945* (George G. Harrap & Co. Ltd, 1946)
Warner, Sir Pelham, *Gentlemen v Players* (1860–1949)
Wisden, John, *Wisden Cricketers' Almanack*

INDEX